The Archaeological Process

To Kyle and Nicky

The Archaeological Process

An Introduction

Ian Hodder

Blackwell
Publishing

BLACKWELL PUBLISHING
350 Main Street, Malden, MA 02148-5020, USA
108 Cowley Road, Oxford OX4 1JF, UK
550 Swanston Street, Carlton, Victoria 3053, Australia

First published 1999
Reprinted 1999, 2000, 2002, 2003, 2004

Library of Congress Cataloging-in-Publication Data

Hodder, Ian.
    The archaeological process: an introduction / Ian Hodder.
        p. cm.
    Includes bibliographical references (p.) and index.
    ISBN 0–631–19884–9 (hb: alk. paper).— ISBN 0–631–19885–7 (pbk. : alk. paper)
    1. Archaeology—Methodology.   2. Archaeology—Philosophy.
    I. Title.
    CC75.H56 1999
    930.1'028—dc21   98–24008
                                                              CIP

A catalogue record for this title is available from the British Library.

Set in 11 on 13 pt Baskerville
by PureTech India Ltd, Pondicherry

The publisher's policy is to use permanent paper from mills that operate a sustainable forestry policy, and which has been manufactured from pulp processed using acid-free and elementary chlorine-free practices. Furthermore, the publisher ensures that the text paper and cover board used have met acceptable environmental accreditation standards.

For further information on
Blackwell Publishing, visit our website:
www.blackwellpublishing.com

Contents

Illustrations

Figures

Table

Preface: *Digging Outside the Shelter*

Archaeological fieldwork remains relatively untheorized. By this I mean that the practice of archaeology in the field has not, despite a few articles to be discussed in this volume, been subjected to the reflexive scrutiny experienced in recent decades in ethnography.

Archaeologists sometimes dig in caves and shelters. But many of us have come to dig 'sheltered' from outside criticism and untroubled by reflexive analysis. In our shelters we use techniques that appear to us to be self-evident and unquestionable. We take them for granted. The commercial pressures of contract archaeology have further forced a standardization and a routine.

Reflexivity in ethnography has in part been forced by engagement with 'other' voices and by the processes of postcolonialism. Archaeological data, on the other hand, can be thought of as objects which cannot 'talk back' (see chapter 3). However, in many parts of the world, contemporary communities have increasingly made claims for, and spoken on behalf of, archaeological data. As archaeology becomes ever more disseminated through global information networks, new communities form with varied interests in the archaeological past.

In the world of heritage and museums there has for some time been a critical discussion of how the past is presented, how reflexivity can be incorporated into displays, how multiple voices can be engaged in dialogue. Merriman (1991) has discussed the need for museum curators to move 'beyond the glass case'.

So, increasingly, it becomes difficult for archaeologists to resist moving 'beyond their shelters'. It becomes necessary to deal with plurality and interaction with diverse constituencies. In the process, reflexive (by which I mean self-critical) thought is engendered. Reflexivity needs to extend down into the trench, to the trowel's edge, and down onto the laboratory bench, if it is to respond adequately to the world outside the shelter.

This engagement with other voices forces a reconsideration of the way in which archaeologists 'collect data'. It forces a critical analysis of the degree to which archaeologists in the western academy have constructed the past within their specific historical perspectives. Indeed, it could be argued that the archaeological case forces a more thorough reappraisal than in ethnography. In the latter case, the focus has been on the 'textualization' of 'the other' – that is on the strategies by which other groups are 'written into' a western discourse (Clifford and Marcus 1986). But in the emphasis on writing, perhaps less attention has been paid to what happens before pen hits paper. Ethnographic 'data collection' is perhaps too readily seen as dialogical since it involves dealing with people. But in archaeology, before or alongside writing, there is the need to handle large amounts of 'objective' data, and to deal with the problems of 'data construction', leading to reflexive critique of even the most mundane and direct processes of observation. The methodological challenges are perhaps greater and more severe in archaeology. Perhaps this is why archaeological fieldwork has resisted and largely avoided the critical re-evaluation seen in other areas of the discipline and in ethnography.

This book then, is an attempt, from a particular perspective, to encourage debate about archaeological field method, 'data collection', and archaeological reasoning in general. I am painfully aware that it makes only an initial foray and that it is an inadequate response to the overall task of theorizing method in archaeology. It results from many years of thought and trial, but the more progress is made the more appears that needs to be done. This book describes a problem and a project; it is an account of progress made so far, and a statement of intent about future directions.

In this faltering and tentative process I wish to thank all those who have with such good will and patient humour entered into these debates within the Çatalhöyük team. There are too many to name individually, but I hope they sense the deep gratitude I feel. I also wish to thank Randy McGuire and Matthew Johnson for their comments on an earlier draft, Carol McDavid for introducing me to the reading used in chapter 10, and Julia Shaw, Lynn Meskell and Ayfer Bartu for other references and ideas. A version of chapter 11 appeared in Spanish in *Trabajos de Prehistoria* (1998).

Acknowledgements

The author and publisher gratefully acknowledge the following for permission to reproduce copyright material:

Fig. 1.1 from D. Clark, *Analytical Archaeology*, 1968, by permission of Methuen & Co.;

figs 3.1–3.3 from I. Hodder, *Theory and Practice in Archaeology*, 1992, by permission of Routledge;

fig. 5.6 from A. C. Renfrew and P. Bahn, *Archaeology*, 1991 (second edition 1996), by permission of Thames and Hudson;

fig. 6.1 from E. C. Harris, *Principles of Archaeological Stratigraphy*, second edition 1989, by permission of Academic Press;

fig. 6.2 from A. J. Barham, Methodological approaches to archaeological context recording: X-radiography as an example of a supportive assessment and interpretive technique. In A. J. Barham and R. L. Macphail (eds), *Archaeological Sediments and Soils*, 1995, 145–82, by permission of the Institute of Archaeology, University College, London;

fig. 8.2 from A. Sherratt, Plough and Pastoralism. In I. Hodder, G. Isaac and N. Hammond (eds), *Pattern of the Past*, 1981, by permission of Cambridge University Press; and A. Sherratt, What would a Bronze

Age world system look like? *Journal of European Archaeology*, 1993, 1.2, 1–58; and I. Hodder, *The Domestication of Europe*, 1990, by permission of Blackwell Publishers;

fig. 9.1 from M. Adams and C. Brooke, Managing the past: truth, data and the human being, *Norwegian Archaeological Review*, 1995, 28, 93–104;

table 6.1 from W. Matthews, C. French, T. Lawrence and D. Cutler, Multiple surfaces: the Micromorphology. In I. Hodder (ed.), *On the Surface*, 1996, pp. 301–42, by permission of the McDonald Archaeological Institute and the British Institute of Archaeology at Ankara.

The publisher apologizes for any errors or omissions in the above list and would be grateful to be notified of any corrections that should be incorporated in the next edition or reprint of this book.

1 Crises in Global Archaeology

One Archaeology or Many?

Perhaps it never was straightforward. But in retrospect it seems to have been. Traditionally, the object of archaeology was to obtain better scientific knowledge of human activities in the past, on the basis of material remains. The aim was to get closer to the truth. In its infancy, archaeology opposed itself to myth and folklore and to antiquarianism. In the eighteenth century it developed a clear identity for itself by opposing science to non-science. The beginning of the first volume of *Archaeologia*, published by the Society of Antiquaries of London in 1770, opposed a historical science dealing with truth and evidence to an unscientific archaeology trading falsehoods, tradition and the vanity of inventors and propagators. 'The arrangement and proper use of facts is history; – not a mere narrative taken up at random and embellished with a poetic diction, but a regular and elaborate inquiry into every ancient record and proof' (*Archaeologia* 1 (1770), 2). The primary underlying theme here was empiricism – the separation of facts and theories. In order to be scientific it was assumed that beliefs and ideas needed to be separated from data. One had to stay as close as possible to the facts themselves, and distinguish well-grounded statements from flights of imagination. As Pitt-Rivers (1894) enjoined, to be a scientist the archaeologist had to record meticulously and publish facts from which conclusions could then be drawn.

There was also a social identity to archaeology, within the upper and the upper middle classes. The association between archaeology and these social milieux in the nineteenth and early-twentieth centuries has been demonstrated for Scandinavia by Kristiansen (1981), for Britain by Hudson (1981), and for North America by Patterson (1995).

Belief in the possibilities of science, when allied with a limited western social focus, often led to a unified and global perspective. As Wheeler claimed in *Archaeology from the Earth* (1956, 36), 'there is no method proper to the excavation of a British site which is not applicable – nay, must be applied – to a site in Africa or Asia'. But the colonial context did not always lead to such views. Seton Lloyd (1963, 30) suggested that British and Near Eastern sites were so different that different methods of excavation should be used. In the United States, Hole and Heizer (1973, 187) argued that 'there are no rules for digging a particular site'. Variation in method was linked to the type of site being excavated and to the archaeologist. Use of a bulldozer differs substantially from the use of a fine dental pick. But such variation was encompassed within an empiricist position – appropriate methods were to be used at specific sites, but the overall method of objective recording of layers, artifacts and their superimposition was seen as general.

The height of this confidence in universal methods was perhaps reached by David Clarke when he declared in 1968 that 'archaeology is archaeology is archaeology'. The New Archaeology generally exuded confidence. Binford (1962) argued that all aspects of past sociocultural systems are available to us. This optimism remained based on a belief in science and objective methods. It was also based, in USA at least, on a supreme conviction that the object of archaeology was to be anthropological. But the positivist separation of facts from theories underpinned the scientific claims for a general methodology. There was only one way to do science (Schiffer 1976). Other factors played a role in the development of this new confident science. For example, the expansion of Cultural Resource Management led to the need for systematic control and monitoring on a far greater scale of archaeological enquiry. The result, allied with the widespread use of computers, was a strong emphasis on codification and rigorous management systems (Adams and Brooke 1995). Standardized and repeatable procedures were espoused both because of the commitment to positivism and because of the need to cope with and publically account for an expanding but limited archaeological resource.

It is widely recognized that early processual archaeology embraced the notion of universals and global theory. But it is important to recognize that in parallel with this stance towards theory, method too was seen as universal. Gradually (e.g. Binford 1977; Schiffer 1976) a general Middle Range Theory was espoused dealing with the formation of the archaeological record. Processual archaeology coupled with the rise of contract archaeology also had an impact on field methods. The following changes can be discerned: the development of field projects with well-defined research objectives; the development of a regional (ecological) approach to sites in their settlement systems and environments; new techniques of intensive survey, sampling and screening (sieving). In an introductory textbook, Renfrew and Bahn (1996) have recently argued that the widespread application of these points 'has begun to create for the first time a true world discipline: an archaeology that reaches geographically right round the globe, and an archaeology that reaches back in time to the beginnings of human existence and right up to the modern period' (pp. 39–40).

Many people since the 1970s have written about the philosophy of archaeology. These authors often commented on the discipline from a position at least partially external to it (Salmon 1982; Bell 1994; Watson 1991). While they held different positions they all talked about *the* reasoning process in archaeology, *the* philosophy of archaeology. Perhaps because they came in from the outside, they saw archaeology as an entity, an object for their study which had coherence. This is also true of those like Courbin (1988) and Gardin (1980) who tried to analyse archaeological procedures from the inside. Clarke (1968) developed a systems view of the archaeological process (figure 1.1). In all cases there is an overall description for archaeology as a whole.

Processual, postprocessual and post-postprocessual archaeologies

By *processual archaeology* I mean a belief in objective science in the form expounded in the 1960s to the 1980s, especially in the United States by Binford (1962; 1989). This view held that there was one right way to do archaeological science, involving the testing of propositions against data. Universalizing anthropological and (at least initially) evolutionary assumptions were made.

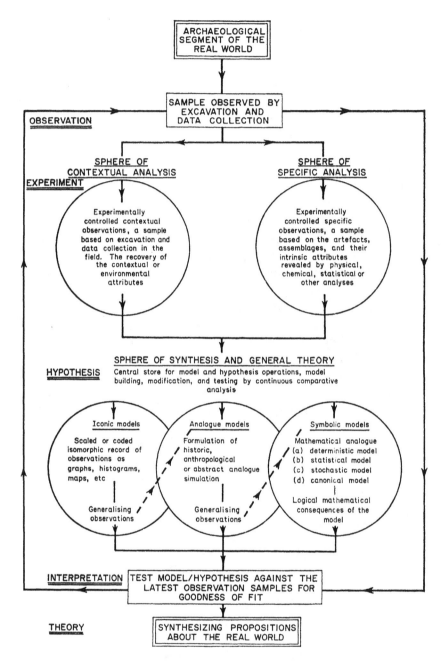

Figure 1.1 David Clarke's (1968) general model for archaeological procedure, described as 'for the organisation and relation of archaeological activities within a disciplined procedure' (ibid., 36).

By *postprocessual archaeology* I mean a group of views based on a critique of processual archaeology (Hodder 1982b; Shanks and Tilley 1987). These views could crudely be described as interpretive and self-reflexive as opposed to processual archaeology's emphasis on science and the objective. Emphasis was often placed on the individual, agency, historical contexts and meaning. However, a wide range of very different perspectives could be described as postprocessual. These include Marxist and dialectical Marxist positions (Leone 1984; McGuire 1992), feminist perspectives (e.g. Gero and Conkey 1991), interpretive positions (Tilley 1993), structurationist theories (Barrett 1994) and phenomenological approaches (Thomas 1996; Gosden 1994). I will try to use the term in this volume to refer to a limited set of authors in the 1980s for whom the view that 'material culture is meaningfully and historically constituted' is key (Hodder 1982a; Shanks and Tilley 1987).

What is *post postprocessual archaeology?* One of the main reasons for using the term 'post' in postprocessual archaeology was that a diversity of views was to be espoused, with no singular and unified perspective imposed on the discipline. This emphasis on diversity has continued on into the 1990s. Even processual archaeology has seen its splits, as in the emergence of cognitive processual archaeology (Renfrew and Zubrow 1994) and neo-Darwinian archaeology (e.g. Dunnell 1989). The end of grand narratives, regionalism and the embrace of multivocality are characteristics of archaeology in this period. There is greater personal choice and eclecticism in the putting together of theoretical positions.

The theories of postprocessual archaeologists such as Shanks and Tilley (1987) and Hodder (1986) claimed to be open to a wider set of influences (Hodder 1992) and yet they undoubtedly assumed some coherence and universality when they argued, for instance, for archaeology as a social practice (Shanks and Tilley 1987). It has also been objected that the theories espoused were those of an intellectual elite and that they failed to be inclusive in both the areas of heritage (Smith 1994) and feminist archaeology (Engelstad 1991). Certainly there has been a limited impact of postprocessual archaeology outside the centres of western academe.

On the other hand, postprocessual archaeology was much less unified than processual archaeology (Trigger 1995). In questioning the separation between observer and observed it opened up doubt and uncertainty. It undermined the notion of a universal science and a universal methodology. Adams and Brooke (1995, 94) argue that 'it is essential to ask why the rise of postprocessualism has not given rise to an archaeological methodology'. Certainly, apart from a few studies such as Tilley (1989a; see also Carver 1989; 1990; Shanks and McGuire 1996; Chadwick 1998; Bender et al. 1997) there has been little attempt to discuss field methods. This was partly because of the focus on textuality in some types of postprocessual work (e.g. Tilley 1990). But there has been little argument for a unified analytical methodology in any area of postprocessual research. This is because the separation of a general method from interpretation, or description from explanation, was suspect within any approach which links the observer to the observed. It might be expected that each archaeologist would approach each site with an appropriate, rather than with a universal, methodology.

I shall argue in chapters 9 and 11 that the embrace of theoretical and methodological diversity by many archaeologists is parallel to a wider introduction of multivocality and pluralism in the area of heritage. This concern to open up the past to 'other' voices has been seen as threatening to many western archaeologists (e.g. Renfrew 1989; Binford 1989; Kohl and Fawcett 1995; Kohl 1993; Yoffee and Sherratt 1993; Bintliff 1993; Trigger 1998).

Policing the boundaries of the discipline has become a major preoccupation for many. Because the past, and specifically the material past, plays such an important role in forming the identities of groups and individuals, archaeology has a large public 'margin' which extends well beyond the disciplinary core. And yet groups in the margin do not see themselves as marginal. They often wish to appropriate some of the terrain of archaeological science itself. Over the past 20 to 30 years, establishment archaeologists have had running battles with metal detector users (*Treasure Hunting* 1982), ley line hunters (Williamson and Bellamy 1983), believers in von Daniken, Mother Goddess cults (Meskell 1995; Conkey and Tringham 1996), Druids (Chippindale 1990), Creationists (see http://www.geocities.com/Athens/Delphi/4881/frameset.html), readers of Jean Auel (1980) and so on (for a broad ranging view of 'popular archaeology' see http://www.unm.edu/rleonard/230.html). In all such cases, the problem has been to establish a disciplinary authority. It might be thought that the end result of this process is greater coherence about the discipline itself, a clarification of its boundaries. But I suspect that in fact the opposite has also happened. The discipline has had to open up and accept greater diversity. After all, the debate with metal detector users ended up favouring closer integration and mutual understanding.

Examples of the new openness to alternative perspectives is provided in the now numerous cases of archaeologists and Native American groups working together in the United States and Canada. As one such instance, in 1994 the Arizona Archaeological Council held a workshop in order to bring together a diverse group of archaeologists and Native Americans so that they could share in a dialogue dealing with three issues: consultation between Native Americans and federal agencies; Native Americans' role in archaeology; oral tradition and archaeology. In the last of these areas, it was noted that cultural anthropologists and archaeologists had long discounted the historical value of Native American oral traditions (Anyon et al. 1996). Yet recently there has been a renewal of interest in linking Native American oral traditions and archaeological evidence. This working together has produced statements as radical as any from the post-processual theorists. 'Scientific knowledge does not constitute a privileged view of the past that in and of itself makes it better than oral traditions. It is simply another way of knowing the past' (ibid., 15). There has been accommodation and transformation on both sides of the reburial debate in North America and Australia.

Of course, the internal critique of western culture and western science as seen in the above comments of Anyon et al. is a more general characteristic of high- or postmodern society. I shall return in chapter 9 to the links between modernity and processual archaeology and between postmodernism and postprocessual archaeology. For the moment it is possible to recognize a number of ways in which western academia is being confronted by alternative perspectives. One of the distinctive characteristics of the postmodern trend is the blurring of 'high' and 'popular' culture. Archaeology is inevitably involved in this process where heritage is commercialized into 'theme parks' and where popularization erodes 'serious' in-depth coverage of debates in prehistory. 'The postmodernization of culture is of course a profound challenge to the monopolistic hold over high culture and elite values which has traditionally been enjoyed by the intellectual within the Academy' (Turner 1994, 18).

Clarke's claim that 'archaeology is archaeology is archaeology' seems increasingly anachronistic in the 1990s; there is too much diversity and dissent for a global view on theory and method to be sustained. Schiffer

(1988, 479) has argued that archaeological theory appears to have fragmented into 'a thousand archaeologies'. For example, feminists often argue in the following terms: 'we see an increasing recognition that knowledge-making is a pluralistic enterprise with, for example, more recognition and institutional rewards for collaborative multiperspective research, teaching and writing, and increased recruitment of the still-silenced (ethnic, gender, racial) voices that should be integral to archaeological discourse' (Conkey and Gero 1997, 430). Another perspective on diversity is the following: 'archaeology has lost its former hegemonic identity as a discipline, which has been replaced by a conglomerate of different, sometimes separate, sometimes overlapping functions and identities' (Kristiansen, personal communication). I suspect now that both the object (aim) and objective method of archaeology are under threat – this constitutes the double crisis of archaeology.

The example of 'prehistory'

Many archaeologists are content, even proud, to call themselves prehistorians. In Europe the term creates links to the great tradition of writers such as Montelius and Childe and to all the knowledge that has been amassed of European prehistory. The term is a good description of the interests of many European archaeologists. But there are now difficulties in using the term. In a global context the term, taken for granted for so long in Europe, becomes politically incorrect. For example, when used in Australia the term implies that aboriginal groups had no history (see Wolf 1982). This is because 'history' in the word 'prehistory' means written history. But of course, non-western and non-literate peoples did have a vibrant history, even without written records of it. There is no such thing as a time before history unless we privilege the written over the unwritten, the western over the non-western, which is clearly unacceptable.

Archaeologists in the West who are sensitive to such issues may no longer call themselves prehistorians but they may be uncertain as to which label to use instead. Even the term 'archaeologist' can be seen as problematic in its logocentric assumptions of an origin, an 'arche' which can be reached through analytical procedures (Bapty and Yates 1990). The game of origins is always contested (Conkey with Williams 1991) and the search for the arche always excludes.

Perhaps to be without a label is part of the openness and fluidity of high-or postmodern society. Perhaps any label would make global and universal claims. Perhaps we can only define ourselves locally.

What is the 'Object' of Archaeology?

The aims and methods of archaeology have now diversified within the discipline and been challenged from without. Internal diversification is linked to the expansion and specialization of the discipline. The term 'archaeology' now provides a broad umbrella for an enormous variety of activities, goals and interests. It encompasses the collection and study of modern refuse in landfills in the USA (Rathje and Murphy 1992; Rathje and Thompson 1981) and the collection and study of industrial machinery ('industrial archaeology', see Jones 1996). It incorporates experiments with ancient farming tools (Coles 1979) and the study of modern beer cans (Shanks and Tilley 1987). It involves studying contemporary peoples from Africa to Scandinavia (Orme 1981; Yates 1989). The term 'archaeology' can be used to refer to modern material culture studies which have no reference to the past (Miller 1997) or to the study of the earliest hominid traces.

The different specialisms within the discipline have increasingly developed their own perspectives and methods – their own ways of talking about things; that is their own discourses. For example, in much classical archaeology in Britain or the Mediterranean, excavation methods have been developed which include limited wet or dry screening (sieving), which only record 3D proveniences for 'special' or 'small' finds, and which focus on architectural reconstruction. In many Palaeolithic cave excavations, on the other hand, excavation proceeds at the micro-level, all deposits are carefully screened, all finds are 'small' finds, and the emphasis is placed on understanding the sedimentary and site formation processes.

There are also important regional traditions in methods and aims. The distinctive Japanese approach has been described by Barnes (1990). In Europe and the Near East, it is widely recognized that German archaeologists dig with a different method. Such regional differences are often brought out most acutely when international field projects are undertaken. At one such project recently in Turkey, British and Greek teams found themselves working side by side on a prehistoric tell excavation (Hodder 1996). Both sides were surprised at the extent of the differences.

The Greek prehistorians identified an important aim as the recording of their own excavation process. Thus they would dig in trenches, they kept a detailed day book and changed recording units every day, they were willing to dig several phases at the same time, and they made plans of whole horizons of activity. The British, on the other hand, used a 'single context recording' technique which involved digging strictly in phase, planning one context or unit at a time, and placing sections or 'trenches' only where a specific question had to be answered. These radical differences are based on different histories and contexts of research – in Greece, some prehistoric archaeologists have reacted against the techniques used in Classical archaeology and they work within a largely state-funded framework. In Britain, on the other hand, the system widely used today came about as a reaction to the Wheeler (1956) box method of trench excavation and in the context of developer-funded archaeology.

If the differences between Palaeolithic archaeologist and Classical archaeologist have increased, and if the contrasts between regional traditions have deepened, so too have the special expertises proliferated and diverged. Lithic analysts have increasingly developed a discourse and a body of knowledge which is entirely their own – and which is itself subdivided into sub-areas such as use-wear, or replication studies, production versus typology, and so on. They have their own conferences, meetings, books and journals. The same can be said for ceramic study groups, faunal specialists, micro-faunal specialists, archaeobotanists. The list of specialists today is endless. There are those who provide special services in ground stone, residue analysis, phosphate analysis, geophysical survey, magnetic susceptibility, phytolith analysis, pollen analysis, diatom analysis, the study of human remains, taphonomy, bead analysis, DNA analysis, optically stimulated thermoluminescence dating, micromorphology, dendrochronology, and so on.

Diversity in archaeological reasoning – examples from the field

He handed me a trowel and said 'what do you *think*'. The social anthropologist working with us on the dig was amazed at this. It did not seem so remarkable to me. After all, I knew that often the only way to understand which layer is under which is to use the trowel. But the anthropologist saw it as thinking by feeling. The reasoning process was a physical one. It is true that this archaeologist often said 'you can feel that...'. His reasoning seemed diametrically opposed to the more cerebral laboratory specialists. Indeed emphasis on feel was one of the reasons he preferred to dig in plan rather than in section – he could 'feel' which layer he was on and trusted this knowledge more than what he could 'see' in the sections (profiles). He did not trust sections.

The micromorphologist on site, however, spent much of her life 'looking'. She could not 'feel' the layers in her glass slides. Her training was very visual. She observed what she could see. Partly as a result, she argued that we should dig in section rather than in plan. She did not trust digging in plan. After all, you could not see what you had dug through.

But there were differences too in the way the laboratory specialists worked. I watched the animal bone specialist working at her desk. Her head was up. She would take a bone and start flipping through books that lay open in front of her. She was comparing the archaeological bones with drawings of the bones of sheep, cattle and so on. She had little need for anything else at this identification stage. Of course, she said, you have to learn what sheep look like at this particular site. But the basic biology and anatomy of sheep were the main things. Her identification work seemed comparative and universal and relatively secure. She was working from the outside in, deductively, perhaps in a positivist mode.

I looked over at the ceramics specialist. Even his body position looked different. He had his head down. He was having a hard time. There were no reference books he could flip through. No one had developed a proper type series for this region, and even if they had, he would have had to convince himself first that the site fitted into a regional sequence. He had to get absorbed in this particular set of pottery, to get to know it well. He sought for internal patterns and covariations in order to work out what attributes of the pots were significant in determining chronological and social variation. He was working from the inside out in a more inductive, even hermeneutic procedure.

I thought, 'These are all archaeologists but I'm not sure they are all doing the same thing'. Evans (1998) discusses a related point in the history of archaeology, noting that Bersu in his excavation in Britain in the 1930s and 1940s thought in terms primarily of a visual record rather than a textual record.

One of the clearest examples of specialism and fragmentation within the discipline is the growth of 'archaeological theory'. Archaeologists have always discussed the theoretical aspects of their work, such as theories of stratigraphy, typology, inference (e.g. Pitt Rivers 1896; Childe 1949; Collingwood 1946). In the period of the New Archaeology in USA and UK, theory came to be foregrounded. The objective scientific process required a transparency in the construction and testing of theories. This reflexivity was described by Clarke (1973) as a 'loss of innocence'. One product in Britain was the emergence of a series of conferences organized by the Theoretical Archaeology Group ('TAG'). One effect of this emphasis on theory was that it allowed young archaeologists to specialize in theory. Quite understandably, such specialization led to the opening up of the domain to include radical alternatives, Continental Philosophy and current social theory (Shanks and Tilley 1987). Indeed, the level of knowledge needed to understand the debates quickly surpassed the resources, time or interest of most archaeologists. In recent reviews, Thomas (1995) and Champion (1991) noted that only a small proportion of archaeologists in Britain were likely to list 'theory' as within their area of interest. Archaeological theory, which could and perhaps should be a central component of all archaeological work has become so specialized that few can participate. Theory could provide a central coherence and definition of objects and objectives of study. In fact, theoretical debate has become factional and divisive and exclusionary.

It could be argued that the different theoretical perspectives in archaeology are not contradictory but complementary. For example, the overall division between processual and postprocessual archaeologies can be interpreted in terms of different objects of study. Postprocessual approaches (Shanks and Tilley 1987; Hodder 1986) focus on interpretation, multivocality, meaning, agency, history. It can be argued that such themes are best followed in areas of heritage and in areas of archaeology dealing with complex historical societies about which there is a considerable amount of fine-grained information. It is indeed in such areas that postprocessual archaeology has had most impact. Processual archaeology (Binford 1989) might appear more appropriate in the study of long-term constraints and large-scale structures. It has been most widely applied in relation to hunter-gatherers and their settlement systems, economies and technologies. Much the same point can be made for the social sciences generally. Individual agency and thick description of particular events are central to those approaches such as phenomenology, symbolic interactionism and eth-nomethodology which eschew a positivist stance. On the other hand, large scale trends in economies and societies lend themselves more easily to a distanced and quantified analysis.

We are, however, very far from being able to write a 'grand nar-rative' or 'grand unified theory' which incorporates all perspectives. While it may be true that different theories are appropriate for different objects of study, there are many examples of attempts to break out of any rigid categorization that might be made. Thus processual archae-ology has made a foray into the study of cognition (as in Renfrew's (1989) 'cognitive processual' archaeology), and into the study of indi-vidual agency and mind (Mithen 1996). There is little consensus that the different theories are relevant at different scales. Specialists in the realm of archaeological theory tend to want their perspectives to be generalized rather than localized.

These few examples indicate the burgeoning of the specialisms in archaeology. On the one hand the specialisms are central to the expansion of the discipline and they offer an enormous potential today for gaining new information about past activities from material remains. Never before has there been so much opportunity to get a handle on some of the major mysteries which still confront us, whether these be the origins of our species, the development of human culture, the origins of agriculture or the formation of complex or modern ways of life. No one can deny the great achievements of modern archae-ology, from the understanding of the antiquity of European cultures (Renfrew 1973) to debates about the behaviour and cognitive capacities of our earliest ancestors (Binford 1989; Foley 1987), from the discovery of early agricultural systems in Papua New Guinea (Golson and Gard-ner 1990) to the detailed reconstruction of the last moments alive of the Alpine 'Ice Man' (Spindler 1993). All archaeologists will have their own list of the most important advances that the discipline has made. And few would argue that the gradual development of an archaeological science cannot claim great successes.

On the other hand, the growth of specialisms and diversity of approach have resulted in a loss of confidence about the objectives of the discipline (Watson 1986). Despite the diversity of their specific aims and methods, it might be thought that most archaeologists would argue that their prime focus is to recover information about the past, espe-cially where survival of that information is being threatened by devel-opment, looting, erosion or whatever. The aim should be to use modern scientific techniques in order to obtain information about, and to protect, the archaeological resource.

It might at least be argued that there was a consensus on this overall aim of archaeology. Surely the overall aim is to understand what happened in the past and to preserve that information wherever possible. But this is no longer the case. Some modern material culture studies are concerned more with contributing to an understanding of the present. Indeed, this focus on the present is now widely found. Many archaeologists would now say that we study the past in order better to understand ourselves. Thus the aim of archaeology for Leone et al. (1987) might be seen as to expose taken-for-granteds in the present. For Shanks and Tilley (1987) it might be to be active and relevant and to transform contemporary inequalities.

I have noticed a subtle shift in conferences and written papers in the UK over the past 20 years. Whereas the primary aim used to be to say something about the past which was 'true', the emphasis has shifted towards saying something interesting or meaningful. What I mean by this is that authors used to gauge the success of their work in terms of its contribution to knowledge. More recently, the central issue has become whether the work resonates with contemporary concerns and issues, particularly with reference to understanding of the self. Certainly archaeologists have always related their work to current issues. Grahame Clark in 1934 was concerned about the relationship between archaeology and the state; he also wrote (1939) about 'archaeology and society'. Childe, too, wrote books intended for a general audience (e.g. 1936) and was concerned, from a Marxist position, about the relationship between archaeology and society (1949). Social relevance was also a theme of the early New Archaeology; the aim of building general laws was to find a way of using the past that would contribute to planning the present and predicting the future (Watson, Leblanc and Redman 1971). But in all these examples the social contribution was always to be achieved through the construction of secure knowledge about the past. More recently, there has been an explosion of interest in the 'past as self discovery'. For example, many New Age groups use the past in this way (Meskell 1995). Spector (1993) and Tringham (1991) have, with other feminists, made calls for a more 'peopled' past. Shanks (1992) has written about 'experiencing' the past. More generally, many writers today (Gosden 1994; Thomas 1996; Tilley 1994) focus on being, phenomenology and ontology. They are concerned with how people in the present and the past experience monuments and landscapes through their bodily movements. Ultimately the justification of such work seems to be less about constructing secure knowledge and more about whether it opens up new understanding of the self. Such concerns resonate with the aims of heritage organizations to reach a wider and more popular audience, to provide virtual experiences for a wide range of people, to involve and engage. Generally the objects and aims of archaeology have shifted or at least diversified.

Even the consensus on preservation is under threat. Conservation and preservation can come into conflict with the goals of development corporations (which in some countries like the USA and UK now increasingly fund archaeology). The aim of preservation also runs into difficulties when it is asked 'preservation for and by whom?' It is often the nation state that legislates and defines conservation and preservation goals. National museums and central institutions regulate the survival of the past. But increasingly, across the globe and at various scales and levels, marginal, subordinate or disadvantaged groups are claiming an interpretation of the past which is their own.

Rather than preserving or protecting the past behind iron fences or glass cases, these social movements are concerned with engaging the past in the activities of daily life. A living past is opposed to a dead past. Interpretive centre is opposed to museum. Knowledge about self is opposed to intellectual knowledge about the past.

What is the Archaeological 'Object'?

All this diversity not only undermines the sense of a coherent aim or objective for archaeology. It also undermines any sense of unanimity about what it is we are studying. Surely, you might argue, 'it is obvious that archaeologists dig up material objects. At least that is a sure ground on which to base the discipline'.

But it is not as simple as that. In the sixteenth century in Europe, people thought that Neolithic axes were thunderbolts (Daniel 1962). The objects could not be seen as archaeological until they had been thought about and constructed in a certain way. A similar point can be made today. Objects only exist within traditions of inquiry. For example, whether small bones or lithics exist within an archaeological domain depends entirely on the methods used. Thus, at a site where there is wet sieving and then sorting of heavy residues down to 1 mm, a wide range of small artifacts will exist which will not occur at all in the universe of a site which does not sieve, or which sieves selectively, or which sieves down to a different mesh size. So, whether an object in the ground has any chance of becoming an 'archaeological object' depends on the perspectives and methods of the recovery process.

Well, you might counter, 'surely archaeological entities such as "layers" are examples of archaeological units of study which have great clarity'. To some degree perhaps. But note that at many sites there are layers which are natural rather than human products. This is especially true in early sites and cave sites. Here the layer is a sedimentological or geological rather than an archaeological object of study. Even with layers deposited by human actions there are difficulties in definition. The identification of a layer depends very much on the scale or resolution of observation. Anyone who has tried to dig the fine lenses of a midden will know the 'lumping versus splitting' problem. It becomes impossible to excavate separately each lens, and so interpretive judgements have to be made in the field about what constitutes a 'layer'. How can very small lenses be lumped to produce layers? The problem is exacerbated when soil deposition is subjected to micromorphological analysis (e.g. Matthews et al. 1996). Here the focus is on the deposition of particles and their treatment (such as trampling) after deposition. At the microscopic level there are only minerals and organic particles being deposited and transformed in a sequence. The 'layers' are summary interpretations of these micro-actions. Their self-evident nature as objects of study is questioned.

Similar effects are found in other examples of 'going micro'. For example, at less than 2 mm few lithic flakes, ceramic or bone fragments can be identified typologically. Few specialists will include such fragments in their data base. The 'objects' such as lithics, ceramics or animal bone thus only 'exist' at a certain scale. At smaller scales, the fragments still have a use – for example, in the study of formation processes or activity areas – but they become different 'objects'. Indeed, at this small scale the objects might change their nature. For example, very small lithic flakes may get incorporated into the fabric of pottery as filler or temper. The lithics have become ceramics. Another example is the archaeological object 'ground stone'. When it becomes very small it becomes a bead (which may not be studied by the ground stone specialist). There are many such examples which demonstrate that as artifacts come to be studied at the micro-scale, new definitions of these artifacts become necessary. The effect is perhaps parallel to physics where, in microphysics, uncertainty increases as scale decreases (Lyotard 1984, 56).

Increasingly there are calls in archaeology for detailed sampling at the micro level. For example, study of ceramic residues involves sampling soil from around the sherds (Evershed et al. 1992). Phosphate analysis increasingly involves detailed micro-sampling in order to evaluate post-depositional processes (Jenkins 1994). The study of microdebitage in order to reconstruct activity areas on prehistoric floors is increasingly a routine part of archaeological enquiry (e.g. Hull 1987; Metcalfe and Heath 1990), and chemical analysis of house floor samples also has proved successful in differentiating activities (e.g. Barba 1985; Middleton and Price 1997). Certainly more information is obtained but in a research excavation context so much detailed sampling may be required that excavation is impeded.

Indeed the pressures from specialist sampling may be so great that one is sometimes led to ask whether modern archaeology is possible. The costs of laboratory analysis and specialist equipment are themselves very high. And the time and resources needed to undertake the sampling in the field may not be supported by the available funding agencies. Indeed, archaeology is increasingly supported by public bodies (commercial sponsors, development corporations etc.) which may have limited interest in the detailed results of micro-sampling and may be more interested in fulfilling legal obligations or in spectacular headline stories.

Conclusion

The objects and aims of archaeology are thus becoming very diverse (Shanks and McGuire 1996). It is no longer even clear that consensus exists on what an archaeological object (artifact) is. This diversity undermines any attempt to specify a unified description of archaeology itself.

It will be objected that I am focusing on and celebrating diversity at the expense of the obvious unity that exists. 'Surely', it might be said, 'when push comes to shove, archaeologists know the limits which define the discipline. Surely, for example, all archaeologists will agree on the absolute necessity to record artifacts from different layers separately. Surely they will all accept that lower layers are earlier than layers superimposed on them. Surely they will all come out in unified protest when sites are wantonly dug up and destroyed'.

In fact, none of these rules are held to without exception, even within the canonical discipline. The law of superposition holds in general terms, but it does not uniquely define the discipline since the same law occurs in geology. In any case, a theoretical emphasis on stratigraphy does not produce a unity of approach to layering during excavation. For example, digging by arbitrary level or 'spit' may contradict the aim of separating artifacts from different layers. Some archaeological traditions, as we have seen above, involve digging strictly 'in phase' (stratigraphically) whereas others involve digging 'out of phase'. Post-depositional micro-partical movement can disturb the relationship between artifacts and depositional units (Schiffer 1987). As regards the destruction of sites, archaeologists frequently sit on opposite sides of the court when it comes to legal action on development and planning proposals.

'Surely', the objection comes again, 'at least there is one distinctive thing which makes archaeology archaeology. Archaeologists dig; whatever the variation in methodology, at least archaeology involves digging'. The trouble here is that historically there have been many people who have dug in order to find out about the past; and we do not necessarily call all these archaeologists. In a ground-breaking volume, Schnapp (1993) has written a new type of history of archaeology. He shows that we cannot assume that archaeological excavation began in the Enlightenment era. He argues that even Sumerians and Egyptians dug – in order to destroy, or alternatively to gain power from, artifacts in the tombs of ancestors or powerful leaders. Schnapp also shows a sixteenth century European painting of the excavation in 181 BC of the tomb of Numa, a seventh-century BC philosopher. The aim here was to gain access to the philosopher's books. Schnapp provides accounts of the excavation of the bones of saints, such as those of St Etienne in the eleventh century. These historical examples disturb the notion that the discipline can be defined in terms of excavation. Much the same can be said of the modern era in which archaeological excavation might be defined by a particular type of rigorous methodology. However, detailed and scientific digging may take place as part of forensic police work – such excavation may or may not include self-styled archaeologists.

In any case, many 'archaeologists' do not dig. Indeed, in Britain the recent government advice has often been towards conservation and non-destructive 'landscape archaeology' (Hunter and Ralston 1993), indicating a clear move away from the centrality of digging within archaeological practice. Once one moves out of the arena of excavation it becomes even more difficult to identify unifying themes. After all, what does an archaeologist reconstructing the climate at 40,000 BC have in common with an archaeologist studying gravestones in nineteenth-century AD New York State? I suspect very little.

The apparent 'discipline' of archaeology thus appears very undisciplined (Clarke 1973). It would seem that any apparent unity results from a contingent negotiation between a great variety of interests. Any resulting coherence is provisional, contested and temporary. The aims and goals and boundaries of the discipline are in a continual state of flux.

Rather than celebrating this diversity, many archaeologists decry the lack of authority and control (Renfrew 1989; Binford 1989). Many feel threatened by the loss of scientific unity (Bintliff 1993; Kohl and Fawcett 1995). However, in this book I will argue that the diversity is appropriate in an increasingly fragmented and multiple world. In the practices of our lives as archaeologists we increasingly have to work with this diversity. Anyone who has directed the excavation of a site will know of the need to write different reports for different audiences (funders, developers, government agencies, academic colleagues, the general public, schoolchildren and so on). Conclusions are always being reinterpreted for different constituencies. Archaeology begins to look less like a well-defined discipline with clear boundaries and more like a fluid set of negotiated interactions. Less a thing than a process.

It is necessary in the following chapters to explore and understand the diversity more fully, and to place it within a wider context. I have emphasized the diversity of current archaeology in this chapter because it is diversity which creates the need for the reflexivity which is the theme of this volume. After all, within a diverse and multivocal arena, it becomes difficult to justify the imposition of unified perspectives without a consideration of their impact on different communities. We need to move towards the recognition that there is not only *one* right way to do archaeology. There are many right ways. This statement does not deny that there are also many wrong ways. It is the focus on singularity which is dangerous. In the next chapter I wish to consider the claims that have been made for a unified epistemological position within archaeology.

2 Archaeology – Bridging Humanity and Science

It is remarkable that there is almost no literature available on how archaeologists come to their conclusions (but see Courbin 1988 and Gardin 1980). Of course, much has been written on method – how archaeologists dig, label, analyse. But little has been published on how archaeologists decide that they have reached a satisfactory interpretation.

Certainly archaeologists have written a lot about the testing of theories, and on the need to ask testable questions rather than imaginative reconstruction. But what is it that makes a test satisfactory? I intend to explore this question in chapter 4. For the moment, it is worth pointing out that several of the classic examples of testing in archaeology proved to be unsuccessful. A good example is the matrilocal residence hypothesis, which was used early in the New Archaeology as a prime indicator of the way forward (Binford and Binford 1968). Later, it was recognized that residence patterns could not be read from ceramic style distributions on archaeological sites (e.g. Stanislawski 1978; Lathrap 1983) and that the processes of sherd fragmentation, deposition and dispersal needed to be taken into account. In another classic example, the use of rigorous testing procedures did not seem immediately to resolve the controversy of whether pits excavated in the Mississippi valley were used for smoking hides (Binford 1967) or smudging pottery (Munsen 1969). Courbin (1988), perhaps overly mischievously, argues that it is difficult to identify any examples of successful testing in processual archaeology. Certainly some pessimism emerged. Binford and Sabloff (1982) admitted that, properly, it was only possible to test propositions in the present, rather than in the past. Given all this, Watson (1986) was led to comment on the general pessimism and scepticism apparent in various archaeologies of the 1980s and 1990s – she called this the period of 'Terminal Skeptical Crisis' (ibid., 450).

During excavation, unexpected lines of enquiry are opened up and any rigid adherence to the testing of initial hypotheses (as in some of the work of the Cambridge Palaeoeconomy School – Higgs 1972; Higgs and Jarman 1975) would involve ignoring evidence that may be relevant to the question in hand or that might be of interest to other archaeologists. In fieldwork, the questions are always changing and new lines of argument become available. In both rescue and research contexts a good excavator is not a rigid hypothesis-tester (see Barker 1982).

It does not seem that 'testing' can provide a unity and coherence to archaeological epistemology. The underlying reason for this is that testing and the experimental approach seem more successful in non-cultural domains – for example, with taphonomy and use-wear. They seem less useful in regard to cultural areas – for example, the social and symbolic reasons involved in depositing artifacts in burials or on house floors. This difference between n- and c-transforms (Schiffer 1987) is the underlying reason behind the 'ladder of inference' identified by Hawkes (1954). As one moves up the ladder from technology and economy to society and religion, there are fewer non-cultural universals on which testing can be based. Universal understanding of matter-matter interactions may allow testing of theories about how pots were made and metal artifacts used, but theories about social behaviour cannot be so easily supported by theories about matter-culture interactions. It has been less easy to develop universals in this latter area. Any emphasis on testing thus tends to exacerbate the conflict between the science and humanism sides of the discipline and does not create unity (Shanks and McGuire 1996).

To what extent can the archaeological record be seen as independent and objective, a testing ground for archaeological theory (Patrik 1985)? Carver (1990) argues that two different approaches to the archaeological record can be discerned since the inception of rigorous archaeological excavation. On the one hand, there stands perhaps the first truly scientific field archaeologist, General Pitt-Rivers. 'Excavators, as a rule, record only those things which appear to them important at the time, but fresh problems in archaeology and anthropology are constantly arising, and it can hardly have failed to escape the notice that on turning back to old accounts in search of evidence, the points that would have been most valuable have been passed over from being thought uninteresting at the time. Every detail should therefore be recorded in the manner most conducive to facility of reference, and it ought at all times to be the chief object of an excavator to reduce his own personal equation to a minimum' (Pitt-Rivers 1887). Flinders Petrie, on the other hand, starting from similar observations, reached different conclusions. He was less convinced of the data as independent arbiters of hypotheses. 'The old saying that a man finds what he is looking for in a subject is too true; or, if he has not enough insight to ensure finding what he looks for, it is at least sadly true that he does not find anything he does not look for' (Petrie 1904, 49). Carver (1990) notes that these two attitudes to the past are present in archaeology today. 'In the State Archaeological Services we find mainly empiricists, protecting a national archive of buried data for the future or organizing its 'preservation by record' before destruction. But in the Universities lurk the heirs of Petrie and Wheeler, for whom data are all in the mind' (ibid., 257).

The Contribution of Philosophy

Given these basic and long-held disagreements about how archaeologists work, from where did the impetus come for a unity of reasoning process in the discipline? Apart from the functional needs already described, an important influence has been the type of philosophy which was, through various mechanisms, attracted to the discipline during the 1970s and 1980s. Archaeologists became very dependent on philosophy-led accounts which prescribed what archaeologists should do. In practice, archaeologists found it difficult to follow these schemes (some of the failures have been described above). In theory too, problems emerged since many of the philosophy-led accounts assumed that all the sciences used the same set of logical procedures, a position which is now largely discredited. Minimally, the philosophers who have commented on archaeology (e.g. Salmon 1982; Bell 1994 and Watson 1991) have tended to come (though see Hesse 1995) from within one particular branch of philosophy often termed Analytic Philosophy (Frodeman 1995). It was also within this branch that the New Archaeologists found themselves when they turned to Hempel (Fritz and Plog 1970; Watson, Leblanc and Redman 1971). It is important to emphasize the varying positions of the different philosophical commentators on archaeology, and many of them would resist categorization in these terms. The position of Wylie is described in the following box. But despite this variety, archaeology would have followed a very different path if it had absorbed greater influence from the Continental Philosophy tradition.

Mediating between objectivism and relativism

Many writers have argued recently that archaeology needs to move beyond the debilitating split between a belief in the objectivity and independence of positivist science on the one hand, and on the other hand, the view that the past is entirely constructed in the present so that all views are equally valid and 'anything goes' (e.g. Wylie 1989). For Trigger (1989, 777) the social sciences as a whole are marked by 'an increasingly vociferous confrontation... between, on the one hand, an old-fashioned positivist certainty that, given enough data and an adherence to "scientific" canons of interpretation, something approximating an objective understanding of human behaviour can be achieved... and on the other hand, a growing relativist scepticism that the understanding of human behaviour can ever be disentangled from the interests, prejudices, and stereotypes of the researcher'.

Wylie (1989; 1992; 1994) has argued that a medium way between extreme positivism and hyperrelativism can be found. She claims that archaeologists need to 'recognise, without contradiction, *both* that knowledge is constructed and bears the marks of its makers, *and* that it is constrained, to a greater or lesser degree, by conditions that we confront as external "realities" not of our own making' (1992, 21). The move from either/or dichotomous thought to both/and inclusive thought in archaeology will become a key theme in later parts of this volume.

Wylie argues that a 'mitigated objectivism' occurs in gender archaeology. Fotiadis (see also Little 1994), however, judges that Wylie's attempt at a middle way never escapes either/or dichotomous thinking. It is certainly the case that Wylie writes that evidential constraints can challenge political and theoretical presuppositions (1992, 16). She seems to suggest that independence and truth survive. She appears to treat the production of truth in archaeology as essentially intellectual, maintaining a distinction between truth and politics.

> While I would agree with Fotiadis' critique of Wylie, it is in my view extremely difficult to write about a middle way of 'guarded objectivity' (Hodder 1991) which accepts objectivity and subjectivity at one and the same time, and Wylie should be commended in her attempt. But the debate too quickly becomes a matter of emphasis and language. In my view it is not possible to resolve the identity of, and tensions between, object and subject except in practice. What matters is whether we can develop archaeological techniques, as those attempted later in this book, which are adequately integrative.

Analytic Philosophy includes a range of specific positions including the Vienna School and later versions of logical positivism. It takes as a starting point the view that the scientific method differs from other types of thought. The scientific method has three characteristics (Frodeman 1995). First, it is objective, that is separate from personal, cultural, political or metaphysical commitments. Thus the facts discovered by science are distinct from the values held by the scientist. Equally, and this is a point I shall return to, the process of *discovery* is thought to be distinguishable from the process of *explanation*. Where insight comes from and the workings of the imagination are thought to be less significant than the logical procedures used to justify a scientific claim. It does not matter where an idea comes from. What is important is how testable the theory is. Observations and theories are seen to be distinct. Facts are not themselves theory-dependent. There is an unproblematic distinction between description and evaluation.

Second, in at least some forms of positivism, it is argued that scientists can only fruitfully talk about observables. Thus, before space travel became possible, one could not usefully talk about the other side of the moon since it was not observable (Dunnell 1992; cf. Smith 1955). Wylie (1982) has remarked on the irony of this – that a discipline which cannot 'see' past societal systems should embrace a philosophy so devoted to observables. Third, science is thought to consist of a single set of procedures applicable to all fields of study. There is only one way to do science.

While I would argue that most of the philosophers who have commented on archaeology derive ultimately from the tradition of Analytic Philosophy, few would agree with all these three points. This is because Analytic Philosophy has been challenged from within by writers such as Quine (1992) and Popper (1992) and has undergone much internal change and debate. In addition, there have increasingly been attempts to deal with the tradition of Continental Philosophy, especially after the impact of Kuhn in 1970.

Within the 200 years (for example since Hegel) of Continental Philosophy, it has been argued that science is not unified and that the scientific method (as described above) is not the only or even the best way to know about the world. It has tried to identify other ways of knowing (such as dialectics, phenomenology, hermeneutics, existentialism). For much of its history Continental Philosophy has been less concerned with the natural sciences and more with society, culture and the personal. But since Kuhn, there has been wider discussion in the natural sciences too of the notion that knowledge is not value-free but is embedded within human interests, and there has been more general acceptance of the existence of a plurality of scientific approaches.

Another way of looking at the distinction between Analytic and Continental philosophies, and between the natural and cultural disciplines, is to describe a difference between those sciences which use a single and a double hermeneutic. The natural sciences are said to use a single hermeneutic. They work within the single framework or perspective provided by the questions and knowledge of the scientist. This framework of understanding confronts a physical world; so the problem is one of testing against data. In the social and cultural sciences on the other hand, the framework of the scientist confronts a world that can talk back. There are two frameworks of meaning and the problem is one of translation between them, of interpreting one framework of meaning in terms of another. Shanks and Tilley (1987) have argued that archaeologists work within a fourfold hermeneutic and in this they emphasize the extent to which archaeology involves translating and interpreting across cultural boundaries and across vast distances in time. The overall difference between the single and double hermeneutic supports the distinction between objective Analytic and interpretive Continental traditions. It emphasizes the fact that each has grown up in response to different sets of questions, anchored in either the natural or sociocultural and historical sciences.

Because of the philosophy-led approaches identified above, archaeologists may know what they should be doing. But in practice they may be overwhelmed by the conflicting advice from philosophers of different traditions and they may come to suspect that philosophy in archaeology, far from being prescriptive, is parasitical. Indeed, perhaps that is as it should be. Philosophers are realizing that different scientists work differently, dependent on the different types of question asked, the different types of criteria used, and the different goals of research (Frodeman 1995, 962). It may thus be the case that archaeologists, and perhaps even different types of archaeologist, use distinctive methods. Perhaps, for example, archaeology, because it uses the methods of both the natural and cultural sciences, straddles the divide between the single and double hermeneutic methods. Perhaps we should not be led by what philosophers tell us we should be doing and should concentrate on what we do (Shanks and McGuire 1996). But I would argue that as archaeologists we have rarely explored what we DO do. We may realize that in practice the traditional accounts do not work, but there is very little evaluation of how archaeologists DO come to conclusions they are happy with.

Another way of looking at the questions of whether archaeology is like other sciences and whether it is internally homogeneous is to consider whether it is an experimental science. One of the most distinctive aspects of the discipline – at least of excavation itself – is that it is destructive. Of course there are many techniques today which are non-destructive, such as geophysical prospection (magnetometer survey etc.), infra-red or X-ray photography. But excavation itself involves the removal of deposits in order to record them. As a result it becomes impossible to repeat the procedure. Digging is thus not like a laboratory experiment which can be repeated at different times and in different laboratories.

Perhaps the differences here are not as great as they might seem. It is widely recognized in the natural sciences that observation can transform what is being measured or observed. Archaeological observation and measurement provide just an extreme case of the same process – the process of observation destroys what is being recorded. And in any case, it might be argued, many aspects of archaeology do allow experiment. Take experimental archaeology (e.g. Coles 1979) itself. Ancient kilns can be reconstructed and the effects of different firing temperatures can be monitored. Bones and sherds can be abraded and trampled in environments simulating varied depositional and postdepositional contexts in order to monitor their effects on artifacts. Certainly, there are difficulties here in knowing whether the past and the experimental situations are concordant. But at least archaeology is in these cases following an experimental procedure. The same could perhaps be said of ethnoarchaeology.

As noted above, it has been argued that if archaeologists cannot test theories in the past, they can at least test theories in the present. Certainly ethnoarchaeological research burgeoned under the positivism of processual archaeology. It was thought possible to use ethnographic information to test theories about the relationships between material culture and society, and these bridging arguments were termed Middle Range Theory. For Binford (1977), Middle Range Theories are the statements which link the static archaeological record in the present with interpretation of the dynamics of what went on in the past. The present material remains act as evidence for claims made about past dynamics. Middle Range Theory provides the link between statics and dynamics because it describes and understands the formation of the archaeological record, using general theories about use, discard and post-depositional processes. For Binford, the record is seen as in a continual process of change (1981), and Middle Range Theories are not seen as being of a particular type; any theory can function as a Middle Range Theory depending on the question being asked. Schiffer (1987), on the other hand, is more concerned with defining types of Middle Range Theory, such as c- and n-transforms (cultural and natural transformation processes). In a persuasive argument, Tschauner (1996) suggests that both processual and postprocessual archaeology use general bridging principles and both in practice give some emphasis to the use of independent sets of information in building accounts of the past.

Kosso (1991, 624–5) argues that the use of Middle Range Theory in archaeology is paralleled in the natural sciences. He uses the example of observing the interior of the sun. The detector-clicks caused by beta emissions from radioactive argon produced by neutrino interactions provide evidence for solar processes. The neutrinos or clicks tell us about the sun's interior only because of a theoretical linking argument. These Middle Range Theories are built from theoretical neutrino physics, radiochemistry, etc.

However, rather than concluding that archaeology uses positivist, natural science procedures, Kosso (ibid., 625) suggests that Middle Range Theory and the natural sciences on which it is based use hermeneutic procedures in which data are themselves influenced by theories. Middle Range Theories are tested and justified by appeals to observational evidence. But there is a circularity here, for Binford as well as for the astro-physics example. Theories in general (including Middle Range Theories) are confirmed by appeal to observations, and observations in general are understood and verified with the support of theories. Observations are theoretically influenced claims about specific situations. Theories are claims which go beyond particular perceptions of observations. Individual observations are interpreted by appeal to theories which are themselves put together and supported by observations. 'This is exactly the structure of the hermeneutic circle . . . Middle Range Theories are hermeneutic tools' (ibid., 625).

So, if all the sciences, including archaeology, use some form of hermeneutic procedure (see further chapter 3), what is the basis for the common-sense realization that there is a difference between the humanities and the natural sciences? Why is it easier to build Middle Range Theories about n- rather than c-transforms? For 'natural' processes we assume that variables interact in universal ways. Thus, regardless of cultural and historical context, wear marks made by material x on material y will remain constant. It is more difficult to say the same for cultural transforms. How material x is deposited in culture y will vary according to, and will be manipulated by, human agency.

The differences being described here can be seen in one of two ways – as qualitative or quantitative. We have already seen the qualitative argument. The difference between the single hermeneutic (natural science) and double hermeneutic (humanity) approaches is seen as qualitative in that something radically different occurs when human agency is involved. We cannot generalize easily nor can we construct universal c-transforms about human behaviour because human intentionality intervenes. Culture limits the applicability of the natural sciences to human behaviour, because of the ability of humans creatively to transform their worlds. 'And so,' the qualitative argument goes 'there is a qualitative difference between the humanities (including the social sciences) and the natural sciences.' 'But,' counters the quantitative protagonist, 'you are just creating a mystique around human behaviour. The differences between the humanities and natural sciences are just a matter of degree of complexity.' According to this complexity argument, as systems become more complex they become less easy to predict. As more variables are considered, so their complex interaction creates behaviour which seems chaotic or non-linear (McGlade and van der Leeuw 1997). This is true of both physical systems and human systems. The difficulty of generalization in the humanities is not, according to the quantitative view, a product of the special character of human culture, but results from the enormous amounts of variables involved – from the physical and genetic to the social, psychological, aesthetic and so on.

Whatever the underlying reasons, it is clear that archaeology incorporates a wide range of forms of argumentation. For simpler, mainly natural processes, some form of general Middle Range Theory does often seem applicable, and it does seem possible to test theories in ethnographic and experimental contexts. For more complex, natural and cultural processes, the argumentation involves greater uncertainty and more of an emphasis on fitting together bits of evidence in order to comprehend specific situations. This latter process will be explored in the following chapters.

Conclusion

For some time now it has been clear in archaeology that Analytical Philosophy, positivism and experimental science can no longer act as banners behind which a unified discipline can be assembled.

Many of the activities within archaeology can be described as using hermeneutic procedures. But, as we will see in chapter 3, hermeneutics accepts an interaction between pre-understandings, method and result. Research develops in a dialectic manner and there is thus little support for the notion of a unifying methodology or body of theory. While hermeneutic thought might itself offer a unifying theme, any such move is undermined both by the fact that some aspects of archaeological research do have strong experimental components and by the fact that hermeneutic procedures are not restricted to archaeology or to science in any general sense. They also form a part of daily practice and of 'non-scientific' thought. There is little here of substance to create a unified method and theory for archaeology.

3 How Do Archaeologists Reason?

In the previous chapter it was shown that many of the descriptions of a universal scientific method, based on hypothesis testing, demonstrate fundamental weaknesses. Much of archaeology appears to use methods not well described as positivist, and even those that do such as experimental archaeology and ethnoarchaeology also have hermeneutic or interpretive components. It is necessary at this point then to outline in greater detail what is meant by a hermeneutic procedure. The main principles of hermeneutics are outlined in the box on p. 32. But it is perhaps more helpful to explore how interpretation in archaeology really works through a series of examples. We have already begun to see how it works by looking at what is missing in self-styled hypothesis-testing examples. But I now want to consider more detailed examples of what happens when archaeologists reason.

The problem is – and this is a point to which I will return in chapter 5 – it is extremely difficult to document archaeological reasoning processes. This is because the empiricism and positivism espoused by archaeologists have tended to encourage an apparent separation between fact and theory. There is supposed to be a controlled and linear process from hypothesis to test to conclusion. Data are supposed to confront theory in a direct and verifiable manner. There is little room here for the description of subjective thought processes, hunches and mistakes – the serendipitous processes of the practice of archaeology. Most reports of excavations have been 'cleaned up' – the debates

and intuitions condemned to the margins, present if at all in acknow-
ledgements, asides, or in diaries lost in archives.

This inability to see 'what really went on' in the 'shelter' of archaeology (see Preface) is one of the most important critiques of the legacy
of processual archaeology and early contract archaeology. The archives
produced over recent decades have increasingly become problematic
since they are not sufficiently contextualized within a reasoning process. Many are extremely difficult to use. Diaries are often not present
and unless one can talk to the individuals who were involved in the
original excavation it is often difficult to make sense of large amounts of
highly formalized data. The provision of a reflexive context must
become one of the main aims of methodology so that it is possible to
make sense of archaeological fieldwork after the event.

Another way of making the same point is to say that archaeological
method has become highly 'textualized'. This has always to some
extent been the case, but in recent decades it often seems as if the
recording process has come to determine the digging process. Of
course, as so many have pointed out, a badly recorded excavation is
worse than no excavation at all. Since excavation is destruction, the
record has to be as accurate as possible. The site becomes the text. But
as recording systems have become more formalized, excavation often
seems to proceed as if the ground was being looked at through the
recording system. Rather than the recording system serving the interests of knowledge acquisition, the relationship is reversed and we dig in
order to record. Thus we may dig rigidly in single contexts because we
are using a 'single context recording system' (see p. 93 below) or we
leave sections or baulks in certain locations so that we can produce the
necessary cross-profiles at the required points. With the standardization
of recording at all levels of analysis, we tend only to record what the
forms (the recording system) require us to record. We tend, therefore,
not to express worries, doubts, impressions, debates, inconsistencies.

The problem with any text is that it is difficult to understand when
severed from its context of production. Because of the constraints of
early computers, and because of changes in the work practices of
contract archaeology, recording systems have had to be highly formalized. Within such systems little information was provided on the wider
context within which data are produced. The site had become a text,
but one without its context of knowledge production. So, in order to
understand how archaeologists reason in practice and in order to try
and penetrate the positivist screen of silence to find out 'what really

goes on' it will be necessary to turn to some examples of archaeological enquiry either from those known personally to me or from those which have emerged in the interstices of field reports and discussions of field methodology.

In considering examples of actual archaeological field reasoning, I wish to argue that rather than testing hypotheses against data, in many field contexts archaeologists are engaged in processes of inference which have the nine characteristics discussed below. I do not wish to imply that the examples used are good or ideal. Rather, they are I believe fairly typical of what goes on routinely in both field and laboratory contexts. It is only by establishing in this and the next chapter what archaeologists actually do, that we can begin to move on and consider some of the ways in which the diversity of archaeological practices can be recognized and built upon.

Hermeneutics

Hermeneutics deals with the theory of interpretation, particularly the interpretation of texts, but more generally with the deciphering of a system of signs. It began in the early-nineteenth century as a means of deciding between different readings of the Bible and other texts. Initially it was argued that, when properly applied to a text, objective knowledge could be obtained. But in the twentieth century, hermeneutics has come to reject the notion that facts can be independent of theory. Rather, there is a subtle interplay between what is in the text and the perspective brought to the text by the reader. Heidegger (1927) argued that all human understanding, including the natural sciences, is interpretive. Not only books but the natural world and all human action are 'texts' to be read (Ricoeur 1971). By this it is meant that in all areas of discovery, the data are never entirely objective or simply 'given'. Rather, we always have to 'read' the object of study in terms of our tools, concepts, expectations and values. This does not mean that objects are completely determined by our preconceptions; objects assert their own independence (Ricoeur 1971; Hodder 1991). Three important components of hermeneutic understanding are the *hermeneutic circle, pre-understandings, and the historical nature of knowledge* (Frodeman 1995). According to the *hermeneutic circle*, the meaning of a part derives from its relationship to a whole, while the whole is understood from the relationship between the parts. This dialectic process occurs at many levels so that a whole at one level becomes a part at another. Thus in archaeology the whole of a site is understood in relation to its parts (the pits, ditches, houses) but the site is itself a part within a region or the whole of a settlement system. This circle of part-whole relationships is not vicious – we do not just impose a whole from our a priori assumptions. Rather, the objects of study can cause us to change our ideas about the whole or about the relationship between the parts. The circle can best be described as a spiral (Hodder 1992). The second point is thus essential – we have to come to the data, and always do, with a set of *pre-judgements*. These are the means by which science progresses because they lead to enquiry and to a perspective from which to look at the evidence. It is only by asking questions that the data can correct us and lead us to discover new knowledge. Our prejudgements typically consist of definitions of terms (e.g. type series), criteria to identify which facts are significant, goals and expected answers, tools (from trowels to mass spectrometers), methods and skills (such as floating procedures for recovery of charred seeds), and the social and political structure of the discipline, excavation team etc. *The historical nature of knowledge* derives in part from the view that our pre-judgements have a lasting effect. Our starting point influences our conclusions and the future trajectory of research. But many sciences are also historical in another sense: rather than building universal laws, the primary concern is with the specific causal circumstances surrounding a particular event.

First, archaeological reasoning often seems to work by integrating parts into a whole. It is based on *whole-part relationships*, on coherence and on 'fitting'. As Barker (1982, 217) argued, 'the ultimate aim of excavation is to draw together the very varied strands of evidence into a coherent whole' and he gave several examples (ibid., 180). Quoting E. M. Forster's dictum 'only connect', Barker argued (ibid., 146) that the most important need in archaeological excavation is to establish relationships, including features and finds, from sculpture to pollen. There seem to be two strands to such claims. The first is that an argument has to be presented that is not internally contradictory – all the different parts fit into a coherent whole. The second strand is that all the different types of data have to be accounted for by the argument.

Collingwood (1946) used to make a distinction between coherence of argument and correspondence with data. Both these strands of research and analysis are part of 'wholeness' but in practice they are difficult to distinguish from each other. As an example of this I will reconsider the interpretation of the Haddenham causewayed enclosure (Hodder 1992) in the southern Cambridgeshire Fens in Britain and dated to the earlier Neolithic.

As soon as the site was identified on air photographs it was categorized as a causewayed enclosure (figure 3.1). This immediately meant that when we approached excavation in 1981, we came with a large amount of pre-understandings (see box on p. 32). The data which we found were initially perceived and interpreted into the whole with which we began. The pre-understandings with which we began concerned, first, a debate about the ritual nature of such monuments in the British Neolithic. While it is recognized that some such enclosures may have had occupation, stock management or defensive functions, they were also used for burial and other rituals involving feasting and 'special' activities. The notion of 'structured deposition' had come

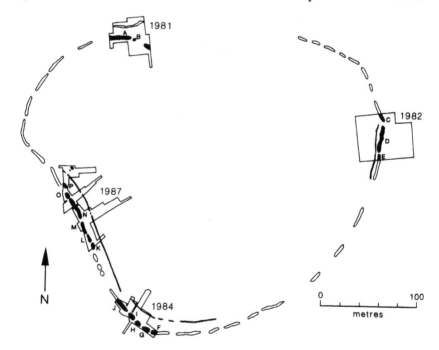

Figure 3.1   The ditch sections (A to P) excavated in different years at the Haddenham causewayed enclosure.

to be discussed in relation to deposits of pottery, axes, human bone and skulls in the ditches (Edmonds 1993).

A second set of pre-understandings concerned archaeological theories about social evolution. It had generally been accepted that in the earlier Neolithic one was dealing with relatively non-complex societies – those with segmented, decentralized organization (e.g. Renfrew 1973). Thus we expected that the segmented ditches (interrupted by gaps or causeways) somehow reflected a segmentary society. In general terms, we expected a low degree of social complexity but a lot of variability between different segments of the enclosure.

These pre-understandings predetermined how we 'saw' the data in the first year of excavation in 1981. The air photographs suggested that in the area of excavation we should find two parallel ditches. We found the northernmost of the two ditches fairly easily on stripping off the ploughsoil. It was peat-filled and very clearly cut into the light grey prehistoric soil. It did not matter at that stage that a double ditch could not be identified on the air photograph to run all the way around the circuit of the enclosure. After all, one of our starting assumptions had been that there should be variability between the different parts of the enclosure because of the presumed segmentary nature of society.

We interpreted other aspects of the data from the northern ditch in relation to our pre-understandings. For example, in the deepest part of the ditch a concentration of large animal bones appeared above a quantity of waterlogged wood. Skull, mandible, pelvis and scapula were the main body parts represented and there was little pottery or flint associated. This seemed to us clear evidence of ritual – structured or placed deposition (cf. Hill 1995).

Our belief that we were digging a ditch of the causewayed enclosure was supported by intersubjective agreement amongst those with the highest credentials. Several eminent Neolithic specialists visited the excavations during this period and pronounced their verdict. The deeper part of the ditch with the animal bone concentration was a typical ditch end, and the narrowing of the ditch beyond was evidence of the existence at some point of a causeway. A small undiagnostic sherd found in the ditch was probably Neolithic. Emboldened by this external support we felt justified and content that a whole had been reached which made sense of all the data in terms of current understanding of this class of enclosure.

There were however, some niggling doubts. The main problem which became more and more acute was 'where was the other, internal ditch?' However much we carefully cleaned the subsoil and checked the air photographs, it was not where it should be. The northern ditch had been so easy to see. Why could we not see the other one? Further trouble emerged in the shape of a small hearth. This was not visible at the top of the prehistoric soil, but it was visible a few centimetres down. This implied that the surface of the prehistoric soil had been heavily leached and discoloured, probably during peat coverage. Indeed acidity tests showed that pH levels increased from 4 to 6 with increasing depth through the prehistoric soil.

Something clearly was not right. The whole which we had constructed could not explain all the evidence that was emerging. Why was the northern ditch so clearly visible on the surface of the prehistoric soil, filled with peaty soil, while other prehistoric features had been heavily leached during their coverage by peat? Why could we not in all honesty really identify clear causeways in the northern ditch? Further problems emerged. Some of the animal bones from the ditch turned out to be horse – and yet horse was not supposed to occur in the earlier Neolithic in northwestern Europe. And we still could not see the southern of the two parallel ditches. We dug deep soundings by machine to try and pick up the line of the other ditch. But we could not see it in these trenches.

It turned out that we could not see it because we did not know what we were looking for. This is an excellent example of the limitations of the view that archaeologists just observe what is there. To a certain extent you cannot see 'what is there' until you know how to look for it. This was the view of Flinders Petrie discussed in chapter 2. In fact the southern ditch was clear in the sides of the machine-cut trenches. But it contained no peat, and it was much bigger than our train of thought, which had understood the shallow northern ditch to be the causewayed enclosure, had led us to expect. So we could not 'see' the ditch. But once the contradictory evidence had become so compelling that an alternative was demanded, we searched until we found another 'whole' which would make more sense of the bits of evidence we had collected. We realized that there may have been leached features not visible at the surface of the prehistoric soil. We looked more carefully where the southern ditch should have been on the air photographs. And we at last 'saw' the evidence – an enormous ditch filled with gravel and lenses of clays and silts as in the surrounding gravels but leached and invisible at the top of the prehistoric soil.

The new whole could now be put together. The northern ditch was not, except in the area of our excavation, fully parallel with the southern ditch. In fact its location by the Neolithic enclosure was by chance. We later obtained a radiocarbon date indicating a late Iron Age to Roman date. The horse was thus explained, the undiagnostic sherd redated, and there really were no causeways. The concentration of animal bone was interpreted as butchery waste rather than ritual deposition (though see Hill 1995 for a further counter argument on ritual deposition in late pits and ditches). As for the southern ditch, this was much more the size that was common on other causewayed enclosures. And there were clear causeways this time. Much other evidence began to fit in too. For example, environmental reconstruction was beginning to suggest that peat growth and the onset of a fenland had started very late in this part of the Fens. Thus it was impossible that a Neolithic ditch of any type, never mind a shallow one, could have been waterlogged at this location.

But the main way that the new whole came to be put together was through further excavation around the circuit of the enclosure. The details of this process of interpretation can be found elsewhere (Hodder 1992). Suffice it to say in this context that what gradually emerged in excavations of the ditch circuit in 1982, 1984 and 1987 was a coherent interpretation which made sense of increasingly large amounts of diverse data. Ditch segments A to P were excavated (figures 3.1 and 3.2). The new interpretation held onto the idea of ritual in the early phases of use since only ritual seemed to make sense of repeated and deliberate recuttings of the ditch segments, and of apparently placed deposits of human bone and polished axes in relation to those recuttings. The new whole also held onto the idea of variability but recast it in terms of social differentiation. As more ditch segments were excavated it became clear that some were much more elaborate than others. Variation occurred on a number of dimensions. The longer ditch segments, and those segments adjacent to the longest ditch segments, tended to have more recuts, more special placements and a higher density of finds (figure 3.2).

This type of variation recurred across different data sets. For example, a palisade was found to run round the enclosure inside the causewayed ditch. The degree of elaboration and recutting of the palisade kept in step with the variation around the ditches of the enclosure, as did variation in the density of finds. The same could be said of the interior itself – variation in intensity of use seemed to occur in zones or sectors which

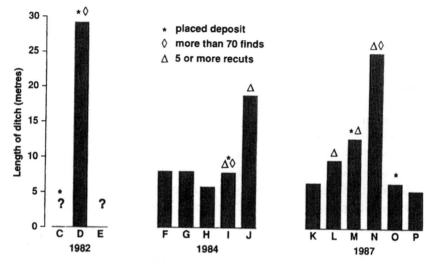

Figure 3.2 Lengths of the Haddenham enclosure ditch segments in relation to nature of deposits, numbers of finds and recuts.

correlated with variation in the residues in the palisade and ditches. The pattern even extended to the analysis of the finds from the ditches. For example, the more elaborate and longer ditch segments turned out to have higher percentages of cattle bones (Hodder and Evans 1999).

More and more evidence seemed to fit together in terms of the idea of variability around the enclosure. What were the causes of this variation? One idea suggests social competition. The main difference between ditch segments is in terms of the amount of soil that has been removed, and in terms of the amount of maintenance and recutting of the ditch. Perhaps social groups competed with each other in terms of the amount of labour that could be mobilized and called upon over periods of time. More successful groups could also deposit more prestigious artifacts and perhaps also gain more access to cattle for feasting. Other evidence which fits into this new whole which was constructed concerns through-time variation. Gaps between ditches were continually narrowed, closed, widened or opened. The overall process seemed to involve the varying fortunes of groups in their abilities to mobilize labour and resources. As one moved round and round the different types of data, pre-understandings came to be reworked in terms of new frameworks or wholes (figure 3.3).

I believe this is a typical example of how archaeologists work. It is difficult for me to substantiate the claim since few publications report

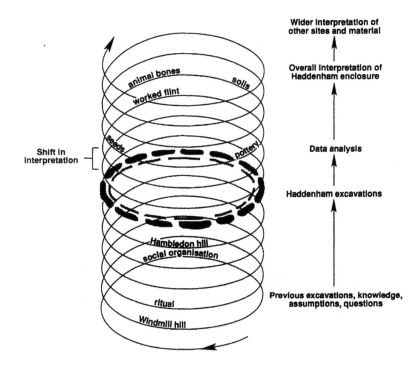

Figure 3.3 The hermeneutic spiral and the Haddenham causewayed enclosure.

on the mistakes and blind alleys down which they went. As already noted, it is difficult to discern how archaeologists do reason. But it is my impression from informal accounts of fieldwork that the type of process outlined at Haddenham is common. In general I would claim that most archaeology is heavily dependent on these types of accommodative arguments (despite Binford's 1989 criticisms of the limitations of such ad hoc procedures). In general, we contextualize and fit together all the bits of evidence available. When bits do not fit we worry at them and try to reduce the inconsistencies. Sometimes the individual parts of an argument seem to work but the whole does not fit together. An example of this from the Haddenham case might be when all the bits (such as the date of the pottery and the ritual deposit in the northern 'Neolithic' ditch) seemed to work individually but the argument as a whole could not explain the lack of a southern parallel ditch.

Perhaps the search for coherence and wholeness is best illustrated by a further field example, one which concentrates on stratigraphical relations. Here again the distinction between coherence and corre-spondence is difficult to make. In the Haddenham case the whole embraces both argument and data. People said they could 'see' cause-ways which were not there. They could 'see' Neolithic pottery which was Iron Age or Roman. They could not 'see' a ditch which was clearly visible in the sides of a trench because they were expecting the wrong sort of ditch. So we cannot separate the coherence of theoretical argument from correspondence with the data. The latter is constructed within the former. But equally the theoretical argument can be con-fronted by data that does not fit. The relation between theory and data is thus dialectical. Theory and data depend on but can contradict each other.

In the following case taken from Çatalhöyük (see box on p. 119), we again see the link between coherence and correspondence within the whole of an argument. We also see the attempt to reduce inconsisten-cies in perspective. To set the scene, we need to look at the plan of Building 1 in figure 3.4. During the excavation of this building in 1996 we came down onto a series of floors at B within the walls C, D, etc. Our first impression was that the floors at B ran up to and were later than (and used contemporary with) wall C. We were fortunate in that a later pit F had cut though wall C and floors B. This meant that we could 'test' the idea that the floors were later than the wall. Observation showed that the test could be verified. The C floors did indeed run up to the wall as suggested in inset L (figure 3.4).

But as more evidence was put together, it did not 'fit'. We came to realize that the floor at B' was earlier than rubble beneath D. Wall C clearly abutted and was later than wall D. Thus, as we understood the building, the B floors were later than wall C which was later than wall D. And at the same time the B' floors, which were the same floors as the B floors, were earlier than wall D. The evidence did not make sense. It did not fit together into a coherent whole. How could floor B be both later than (used contemporary with) wall C and earlier than it?

The breakthrough came when we realized that all the evidence would fit together if we just made one move and argued that wall C had been cut into and was later than the B floors. We went back to look at the section (profile) in the side of the F pit. With new eyes we could see what we had missed before. There was indeed a break between the B floors and the C wall. Our mistake had been to assume that the floors on either side of wall C were contemporary. But in fact they were not. Floors were added in to the north side of wall C after the south side had

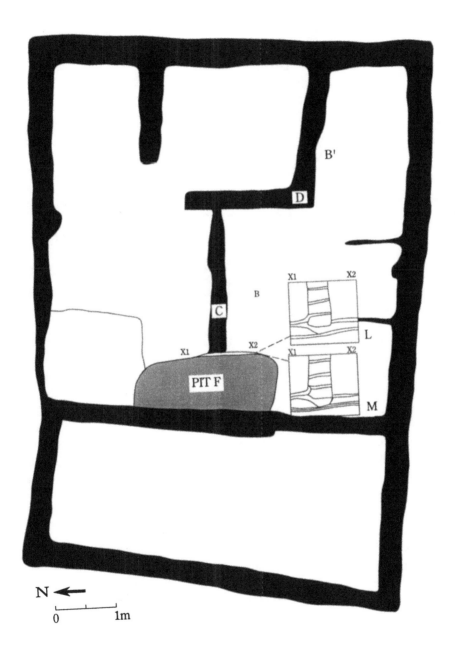

Figure 3.4 Plan of Building I in the North area of excavation at Çatalhöyük East.

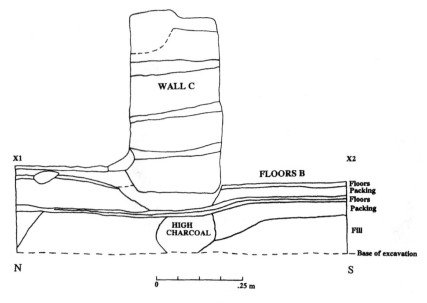

Figure 3.5 Section (profile) showing relationships between Wall C and floors B in Building I (see figure 3.4).

gone out of use. We redrew the section in F to show the break between the B floors and wall C, and to show the evidence which we could now see of a wall-slot cut through the B floors (figure 3.5 and inset M in figure 3.4). The evidence had changed and a coherent whole had been produced. There is correspondence and coherence to the new argument, but it is difficult to separate the two since the data (the relationships in the profile at F) were themselves constructed within the whole.

I have focused here on field examples, but the same can be said of non-fieldwork examples. On p. 90 I describe examples of work on burial interpretation that follow part-whole procedures. A further example of work on gender amongst the Hohokam is provided in the box on p. 44.

It is often said that the whole is more than the sum of its parts. In my view this is often because of the interdependence of correspondence and coherence. It is not enough to bring all the data into line, make them all correspond, and then say 'that's it'. What is clearly also needed is an argument which links the data together into a coherent whole. There is always the need to go beyond summing the parts and create an understanding. There is thus a need for creativity and this will be discussed further below. Some other general characteristics too will be explored below. These derive from the fact that the whole that is constructed will of course vary with the parts that are included in the analysis. The whole will depend on the parts that are brought into relation with each other. As a larger area is searched for comparisons and influences so a larger scale of analysis is undertaken; the same is true for different time scales. Archaeologists are able to approach the data in a multiscalar way, searching for different wholes that might make sense of the data at different spatial and temporal scales. Equally, different types of context or whole can be produced by including different types of data – for example, subsistence, social or ritual data. So the discussion of wholes must involve multiple types of context. And clearly, how these decisions are made about how to link data together and at what scale will vary with the interpreter. Different people will see different relations as significant. Thus archaeological research is also multivocal.

Another aspect of the interpretive process that will be examined below derives from the emphasis on multiple scales, contexts and voices. If there is so much variation and if interpretation is thus historically embedded (Trigger 1984), the implication is that interpretation can only ever be momentary. This is why in figure 3.3 I have indicated a spiral rather than a closed circle – we do accommodate our arguments and move on. This vision might be disturbing for some in that it implies that there is little stability in our interpretations. The 'conclusions' we reach at the end of fieldwork would always have been changed if we could have gone on to consider more data or more ideas. Where we stop in the excavation process will also be an arbitrary point in our interpretive process. I know that if I had spent another year at Haddenham new discoveries would have forced a change of interpretation. Most archaeologists recognize that if they could have spent another day, week, month on the site, they would have come to different answers. The 'wholes' we describe are both final (they account for known theories and for the data so far collected) and provisional (they will be altered as new data and new theories are considered).

In searching for 'coherent wholes' in interpretations of the past, it is important not to confuse methodological and substantive coherence. By this I mean that when we fit parts into a whole we are using a method. That method does not imply that the whole we construct for the past need be of any particular type. The substantive nature of the whole we construct may involve systemness and integration. But other theoretical positions will expect the substantive whole to be societies with internal conflicts and contradictions. It may often be the case that as more data are collected for complex societies in the past, the wholes that are constructed need to be nuanced and non-systemic. An example is given in the box below. Here the method involves constructing an argument which makes a coherent whole. The argument is constructed and made plausible by considering more and more types of evidence which all seem to fit together to make a coherent case. But beyond this methodological point the content of the argument itself involves tensions, contrasts and contradictions. This is not a holistic or systemic view of society. A comparable example of identifying a whole which has contradiction as its main focus is provided by McGuire and Saitta's (1996) analysis of South-western puebloan societies in North America.

Gender among the Hohokam

Crown and Fish (1996) argue that there is evidence from burial and settlement data of increasing social differentiation in the shift from pre-Classic to Classic amongst the Hohokam. In order to assess the impact of the emergence of an elite on women, they look at a variety of different classes of data.

Production

Crown and Fish assign specific tasks to Hohokam men and women on the basis of cross-cultural analogy and burial associations. The appearance of comales (griddles used to make tortillas) in the Classic period suggests an increased workload for women in corn preparation. At least part-time specialists may have been involved suggesting increased differentiation among women.

Domestic architecture

During the Classic period there was increased walling of domestic compounds and groups of houses. The increased seclusion and internal integration produced by the walling allowed greater differentiation among women within the compounds but cut them off from wider networks of power and knowledge.

Ritual space

Platform mounds appear in the Classic period. They have evidence of both ritual and domestic use on the tops. Evidence of female activities also occurs here and again supports the notion of increasing differentiation among women.

Burial goods

Hohokam women were not buried with the same degree of energy expenditure as men; they were more often buried with utilitarian objects than the men. The calculated 'values' of the artifacts in female graves show increasing differentiation from pre-Classic to Classic.

Putting all these strands of evidence together suggests a coherent whole – that there was a simple increase in differentiation among women from pre-Classic to Classic. So at one level, the influence of women diversified alongside that of males. But one bit of evidence above does not fit – the increased segregation and seclusion of women behind walls. Thus rather than a simple systemic whole, Crown and Fish construct a more complex argument about a contested society. They argue as follows. (a) The influence of most women within the public sphere declined. The walls suggest that they were unable to gain access to knowledge and community activities. (b) An increased role of women in production resulted in an increased and more diverse status within the corporate groups indicated by walled compounds. These contrasting processes (a and b) are argued to be inter-dependent in that the emergence of an elite was based on women's production. The control and seclusion of the increased importance of women became of greater concern.

The second aspect of archaeological reasoning to be described here is that it works by *analogy and comparison*. In a sense this is just saying that the wholes put together at one level or in one sphere have to cohere with larger and more inclusive wholes and with disciplinary knowledge and cross-disciplinary knowledge. Archaeologists tend to restrict their discussion of the use of analogical argument to consideration of ethnographic analogy (Orme 1981; but see Wylie 1982). Wylie (1985) has made the distinction between formal and relational analogies, the first based on comparisons of form and the second based on an understanding of the causal relationships between variables (see also Hodder 1982c). Ethnographic analogies are generally used in archaeology for three purposes. First, as a source of ideas in order to broaden the horizon of possibilities about how the past might be interpreted. For example, a broad anthropological reading suggests how kinship, exchange or ritual can be organized in pre-capitalist societies. Second, as a buttress to an argument about what happened in the past in a particular case. Thus it might be suggested that women in the past were probably central to the domestication of plants because in a large proportion of foraging societies today, plant gathering and processing are carried out by women (Watson and Kennedy 1991). Third, the ethnographic present may be used to 'test' ideas about the past. Thus it might be claimed that hunter-gatherer settlement systems can be divided into 'foraging' and 'collecting' systems (Binford 1980). In the former, hunter-gatherers adopt a seasonal round, moving to resources and leaving once the resources are consumed. In the latter, hunter-gatherers make use of central places where they store food and from which they plan task-oriented forays into the landscape. In a cross-cultural survey Binford demonstrated that the different settlement systems correlated with the seasonal availability of resources. 'Foraging' systems were found in environmental contexts with high productivity and year-round resource availability. 'Collecting' systems were found where productivity is low and resources are only seasonally available.

I would argue that the apparent 'test' in this example is false because we cannot be sure that the societies being grouped together are really comparable. All that is really happening, in this and in all types of ethnographic parallel, is that information is being transferred from society to society on the basis of similarities and differences. Making comparisons and drawing conclusions on the basis of similarities and differences is more robust in experimental archaeology. Here, it is more possible to hold variables constant and conduct experiments in laboratory-like conditions. A wide range of examples is given by Coles (1979) and the success of this approach has been apparent in studies of site-formation processes. In such cases, information is transferred from one context to another because it can be assumed that the physical and biological laws of nature hold constant across time and place. The movement of artifacts of different sizes down slopes of different degrees can be assumed to be the same 10,000 years ago as today (e.g. Rosen 1986).

But it is not only in ethnoarchaeology and experimental archaeology that we see arguments based on analogy and comparison. In fact, argument using such means is pervasive in archaeology, and everywhere the problem is: when we move beyond the natural properties of the record, how can we decide whether different cultural contexts are similar enough to allow transfer of knowledge from the one to the other? Take, for example, the traditional culture-historical approach which describes cultural similarities and differences in terms of invasion or diffusion. Clearly here the argument is built up from analogy and comparison – if the pottery or architecture in places a and b are similar, then we can transfer information from one to the other, and we do so by saying that both a and b were produced by the same people or by people in close contact with each other. But, always, the argument has to evaluate whether the contexts are similar enough to allow the transfer. Perhaps the temporal and spatial distances between a and b make contact implausible; perhaps there are local continuities which suggest indigenous rather than exogenous development.

The same emphasis on analogy and comparison is seen in systems analysis. The notion that a cultural system is like an ecological or biological system involves transferring information from one domain to another on the basis of perceived similarities and differences. It might be assumed that the different components of cultural systems function in relation to each other in the same way that the organs of the body regulate each other; indeed, this analogy is the basis for many functionalist perspectives in archaeology and the social sciences (Hodder 1982b). Analogical arguments are also used within systems analysis. For example, it is often argued that the ritual subsystem functions in relation to the social or subsistence subsystems. A change in one subsystem relates to changes in another. In other words, information can be transferred from one subsystem to another on the basis of some claimed similarity (that both are in the same system, or changes are contemporaneous, etc.). But, as ever, the problem is whether the objects being compared are similar enough to allow transfers of information across context. The same problem dogs the application of Darwinian theories in archaeology (e.g. Dunnell 1989). Is it relevant to use analogies with genetics in order to understand cultural transmission (Shennan 1989)? Can the two contexts really be compared?

Most, if not all archaeological argument from artifact typology to evolutionary theory, is based on analogy and comparison. In all such cases, information is transferred from context a to b on the basis of similarities and differences. But an underlying problem is that we cannot be sure, in the realm of cultural behaviour, that contexts are sufficiently similar for the transfer of information. We know that the same thing can have different meanings in different contexts. In language, we work out the different meanings for the sound 'saw' from contextual clues. In bodily signalling, the same gesture (two fingers held up, palm to face) can mean different things in different contexts ('victory' on the European continent, a 'sexual insult' in Britain). The same straw hat means very different things when worn in a butcher's shop, in a punt on a river, or on the stage with cane and spats. The evaluation of similarities and differences has to be balanced against the interpretation of context.

At all stages from the identification of classes and attributes of objects to the understanding of high level social processes, the archaeological interpreter has to deal simultaneously with two areas of evaluation. First, the interpreter has to identify the contexts within which things had similar meaning. The boundaries of the context are never 'given'; they have to be interpreted by the archaeologist. Of course, physical traces and separations might assist the definition of contextual boundaries, such as the boundaries around a village or the separation in time between sets of events. Ritual contexts might be more formalized than or may invert mundane contexts. But despite such clues there is an infinity of possible contexts that might have been constructed by indigenous actors. The notion of context is always relevant when different sets of data are being compared and where a primary question is whether the different examples are comparable; whether the apparent similarities are real.

Second, in conjunction with and inseparable from the identification of context is the recognition of similarities and differences. The interpreter argues for a context by showing that things are done similarly, that people respond similarly to similar situations, within its boundaries. The assumption is made that within the context similar events or things had similar meaning. But this is true only if the boundaries of the context have been correctly identified and are stable. Many artifacts initially identified as ritual or cultic have later been shown to come from entirely utilitarian contexts, and vice versa (Hill 1995). The interpretations of context and of meaningful similarities and differences are mutually dependent.

It is important to emphasize that the identification of contexts, similarities and differences is not a matter simply of describing 'objective' data such as artifact similarities or boundaries around settlements. The identification of contexts, similarities and differences is itself an interpretation based both on the patterned remains and on the behavioural and material culture theories deemed appropriate by the archaeologist. Applying general theory to particular cases is itself a matter of analogy and comparison. It involves the transfer of information within and across contexts on the basis of similarities and differences. But our expectations and pre-understandings play a central role in the recognition of pattern.

A third aspect of archaeological reasoning is that it depends very much on *pre-understandings*. The importance of these was clear in the field examples from Haddenham and Çatalhöyük given above. At Haddenham these pre-understandings meant that we initially misunderstood the date and function of the northern ditch. At Çatalhöyük one significant pre-understanding was that a building such as Building 1 would be occupied as an entity – we did not expect that floors in different parts of the building would be of different dates. This led us initially to assume that the floors on both sides of wall C were contemporary and in use with (later than the construction of) wall C. It took a long time to overcome these initial taken-for-granteds.

In trying to identify the types of pre-understanding that are common in archaeology, the following might be suggested.

1   Our initial definition of the object of study. We might start with a definition of complexity, or social structure, or settlement. Or the origins of agriculture – these act as themes which pull apparently unrelated bits of evidence (seeds, bones, ceramics etc.) into relationship with each other.

2   Criteria to identify which facts are significant and which are not. These are often general ideas about what causes change (e.g. we may only look at subsistence data) – or the very category 'subsistence' data itself. In looking at a section/profile we are trained to 'read' it in a particular way, noticing some things (e.g. major soil colour changes) but not others (minor lenses or differential drying out).

3   Our idea of the goal of the enquiry and our notions of what will count as an answer. We tend to know what we are looking for, and we need to be able to recognize it when we find it. For example, we may have the goal of understanding past subsistence behaviour and only accept answers based on economic or environmental variables. And we might assume that such information will be gained by

particular types of analysis of animal bones, carbonized seeds, sediments and soils.

4   Tools. These very much determine what we can find. For example, different types of trowel are used in the USA, UK and Japan. In different traditions, different types of sieving techniques and different types of seed machine are used. In some traditions only dry sieving may occur, and then only selectively or not at all. As well as field tools there are computers, microscopes, chemicals etc. Different tools allow and promote the gathering of different types of data.

5   Methods and skills. These include the ability to make a plan or map, collect samples, how to hold and use the trowel or shovel, how to use statistics. In archaeology, many of the field skills are not thought to be teachable except in practice – they have to be learnt as part of practical knowledge.

6   Social structure. This includes the relations between participants in the research team. It includes gender issues and more particular instances such as the domination, distance and respect expected by certain East European professors. It includes situations such as the dependence of a US graduate student on the support of his or her professor. Networks of colleagues in the academy, professional institutes, unions etc. are also relevant.

7   The wider social, political and funding context. Projects have to be justified in terms of wider issues and these may include destruction of the heritage, increasing tourism through heritage, the reclaiming of traditional knowledge (e.g. Erickson 1988) or even global warming. The funding context particularly affects the types of question that can be asked. At a global scale it is apparent that some regions are unable to participate in research and debate because of lack of institutional support and funding. Many regions feel marginalized from debate because of this global context (e.g. Olsen 1991).

In a sense this emphasis on pre-understandings is closely related to the processual archaeology emphasis on asking questions and testing theories and on problem-orientation. But there the emphasis was placed on testing theories (chapter 2). Where the ideas came from, their wider context, was deemed less relevant. Within the view presented here, where the ideas come from does matter because the pre-judgements and the questions asked have a lasting effect on the conclusions reached. In order to understand the answers you have to understand the questions asked and the methods used.

A fourth aspect of archaeological reasoning which derives from the third is that it is often, at least partly, *data-led*. This may seem opposed to the emphasis on questions and pre-understandings. In both the Haddenham and Çatalhöyük field examples above, it was problems that emerged *within* the consideration of the data which led to a search for alternative interpretations. This does not contradict the importance of pre-understandings and of the questions asked. Rather, it suggests that the pre-understandings do not determine what is discovered. After travelling round the hermeneutic spiral (figure 3.3), the excavator ends up in a different place – led there at least in part by the data that have been encountered.

The data-led emphasis also derives from the fact that, on the whole, archaeologists have learned that they can only ask certain questions of certain types of data. As discussed in chapter 1, different types of site are approached with very different sets of theoretical baggage. It would be considered folly to try and point provenience all sherds from an urban site in northwestern Europe. The task would be too enormous. On the other hand, it is considered acceptable and even necessary to point provenience all struck flint from a Palaeolithic living floor. Climate change is a major issue in Palaeolithic studies but is rarely an issue in Romano-British archaeology. Investigators ask very different types of question in different contexts. Their research is often data-led rather than being problem-oriented.

There may be some occasions in which research is entirely question led. Some of the research conducted by the palaeoeconomy team led by Eric Higgs (1972; Higgs and Jarman 1975) was sometimes so focused on subsistence data and site catchments that it paid scant attention to lithic or ceramic data or to the sites in a social setting. In some highly controlled laboratory experiments, or in field surveys in virgin areas, it may be possible to follow an almost entirely problem-oriented approach. But this is rare. In most cases, archaeologists try to be sensitive to the problem at hand in creating holistic arguments.

This emphasis on date-led inquiry differs from the notion that data offer 'resistances' to theories (Shanks and Tilley 1987). In my view this latter notion gives too much attention to pre-understandings. It implies that, with some resistance, archaeologists impose their subjectivity on the object world discovered through excavation. The problem with all such discussions is that they oppose subject and object in a Cartesian fashion (Knapp and Meskell 1997; Rowlands 1984). In this volume I wish to get away from the dichotomous view that the past is *either* subjective *or* objective. Analysis of actual archaeological field-work suggests that it is *both* subjective *and* objective. By this I mean that we construct the past from our own perspectives (pre-understandings), but we are also led by our experience of the data to new understandings. I will argue that we try to escape dichotomous thinking.

Fifth, *method is interpretation dependent.* From the above points it is clear that archaeologists approach the survey or excavation of different types of site in different ways. If they interpret the site as a Romano-British villa they will use a different methodology and call in different special-ists from a Palaeolithic open site. In the example of Higgs' palaeoeco-nomists too, the methods used derived from pre-understandings which interpreted all sites in economic terms.

In general terms, the methods used by archaeologists vary from site to site and from problem to problem. In deciding how to dig and sample a pit we tend to make assumptions about whether it is a refuse pit or a burial, for example. A specific example is provided by recent work at Çatalhöyük. In Space 107 a layer was discovered with a cluster of large animal bones, obsidian, pottery, shell, burned brick and stone etc. – and a lot of charcoal. Depending on our interpretation of this we would treat it very differently. If it is an activity area then we would plot everything very carefully and take a lot of chemical and micromorphology samples to identify a 'floor' etc. If it is a midden dump we would only plan and dry sieve and do flotation and take one archive sample. The specialists from their different perspectives agreed that it was probably dump – there were no signs of obsidian production or use, and no signs of bone breakage or special activity patterns. The wide range of types of mater-ial, some burned and some not all fitted into a dump picture. On this basis we followed a less intensive sampling method.

No archaeologist can claim to dig a site entirely or to obtain all the information from it. Sampling is an essential characteristic of archae-ological research. But what should we sample for, and how intensively? These fundamental questions underlie many aspects of method. For example, they underlie issues to do with sieving (screening), flotation, sectioning, quadrat excavation, scientific analysis, recording of finds and so on. Once the excavation of a particular block of soil has taken place, it cannot be repeated. The sampling must therefore be carefully constructed. And the sampling strategy depends on what it is that the archaeologists think they are excavating.

One of the problems with many sampling strategies is that they are largely pre-set or a priori. By this I mean that they are worked out in advance according to general guidelines such as that x per cent of sites should be excavated, or x per cent of floor deposits and x per cent of midden deposits. I will discuss in chapter 11 alternative sampling strategies that are more sensitive to the specific data and their interpretation.

A sixth aspect of reasoning in archaeology is that it is very dependent on *narrative*. This is closely related to the part-whole idea – that a theme has to be provided which makes sense of the data and which serves to provide a coherent 'story-line'. It is also related closely to pre-understandings – a perspective has to be found from which to make sense of the data at the beginning.

Spector (1993) has argued that even a catalogue list may contain hidden narratives which need to be open to critique. She discusses data from a historic site at the nineteenth century Little Rapids site in Minnesota at which there is evidence for contact between colonial and Native American (Eastern Dakota) groups. She argues that a typical catalogue of such material would divide metal from bone artifacts and place metal and other trade items linked to European contact in front of Native American and local products. So even a catalogue contains a narrative. Spector argues that alternative narratives need to be constructed which are more inclusive of the Native American voice. Indeed, the need to include Native American oral traditions in archaeological interpretations is now widely argued (Cohen and Swidler 1997; Nicholas 1997). Many feminist writers have suggested that more emphasis should be placed on narratives which place people into the past and which are more sensitive to alternative perspectives (Tringham 1991; Joyce 1994; Kus 1992). For a wider discussion of narratives in archaeology see Hodder (1989) and Tilley (1989b).

My concern here, however, is more to concentrate on the way in which narratives are a routine, if largely unrecognized, aspect of archaeological inquiry. A clear example is provided by the way in which archaeologists draw sections or profiles. If an untrained crew member or student is placed in front of a section and told 'draw what you see', the product is often gobbledygook! There are limitless numbers of lines, lenses, changes in colour and texture than can be observed on any complex section. The untrained eye has no way of discerning the relevant patterning in the soil. A section drawing acceptable to the discipline will result only when the draughtsperson has in mind some sequence of events – that 'here is a layer which was cut by a ditch which

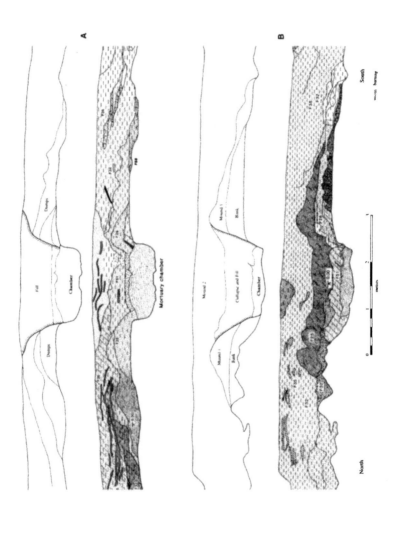

Figure 3.6 Cross-sections (profiles) through Haddenham long barrow, and two interpretations (A and B) of the sequence of events.

later filled up and then became filled with peat before the whole lot was finally sealed by alluvium'. In other words, the section or profile can only be drawn by simultaneously constructing a narrative of the unfolding of events through time.

Figure 3.6 provides alternative narratives for sections cut through a Neolithic long barrow at Haddenham in the Cambridgeshire Fens (Hodder and Shand 1988). The prehistoric soils in this area became very leached after coverage by peat and water. Since draining, the sites have been rediscovered but it is often difficult to discern the interfaces between layers in the discoloured soils as they are excavated and recorded. In the field, it was possible to see different things in the sections. The differences related to two different narratives (for a fuller account of which see Hodder and Evans 1999). On the one hand (interpretation A in figure 3.6), it could be argued that the mound was built around and over the wooden burial chamber as one drawn out event. According to this view the banks around the burial chamber were just the first phase of the dumping of soil for the mound as a whole. The burial chamber was open from the top in a complete mound. On the other hand (interpretation B in figure 3.6), it could be argued that the burial chamber was initially located within earthen banks. This small construction was then destroyed and filled in before the overall mound was constructed. So rather than a single event we have a sequence of events. This second narrative accords better with existing hypotheses about Neolithic burial ritual in similar monuments (Kinnes 1992). But it could not be denied on site that the first narrative made perfect sense of the data – the whole was equally persuasive.

The above example indicates clearly the central role of story-telling in archaeology. Having a story in mind is necessary to help us think while we dig, think of alternatives. On many archaeological excavations, the director or area supervisors will give site talks or tours, perhaps on a weekly basis. These often function to create a sense of community and achievement, but they are also opportunities to put varied pieces of the excavation into a narrative. Having stories or narratives in mind helps participants on a field project put their parts into a whole. Having stories in mind also leads us to raise questions. It is an essential part of the archaeological process. It has to take place *at the time of digging*. This is because archaeological excavation is destructive and non-experimental – we cannot repeat the experiment of the excavation. How we dig depends on the stories we are telling ourselves at the time of digging (see point 5 above).

It might be argued that I am just being provocative. 'Why use words such as narrative and story-telling when you are simply talking about the need for hypotheses and research questions – a need with which everyone would agree. What is the difference between a hypothesis and a narrative or story?' In my view, the answer to this takes us back to the notion of part-whole. A hypothesis is simply a proposition – it may be taken from anywhere and has no necessary relation to the wider contextual understanding of the site being investigated. Indeed, one of the critiques of 'hypothesis-testing' as a strategy for archaeology (see the Higgs example given as part of point 3 above) is that it can lead to the use of a narrow perspective inappropriate to the particular data at hand. Narratives are also propositions, but the emphasis on story-line implies a need to situate the particular proposition within a wider argument. Narratives have beginnings, middles and ends. They have to take account of a wider set of considerations – there has to be an overall whole and a coherence between stories told at different levels. The trouble with the term 'story' is that it implies a lack of concern with links to data and this is not advocated here. Rather, a term is needed which both takes account of the need to link interpretations to data and of the wider structure of the account being told. Perhaps 'narrative interpretation' fits this dual role best.

Perhaps most important, the emphasis on narrative or story-line implies narrating or telling *to* someone. Archaeologists have to produce different accounts for different audiences. The notion of narrative takes us beyond the idea of pure knowledge to a recognition of archaeology as a practice within society.

The construction of narratives is part of the public responsibility of archaeologists. It is not enough to say to a wider public that a site is dated to 8000 BC or that it has 45 per cent domesticated animals and 80 per cent chert. Many sections of the wider public which funds archaeology in varied ways want to have the past interpreted for them in terms of some sequential narrative. Why is a site at this time period and with these amounts of domesticated animals and chert important? Why is it significant? In answering such questions for a wider audience, archaeologists are required to 'tell a story', not in terms of Auel's 'Clan of the Cave Bear', but in terms of a responsibility both to the information recovered and to public interpretation. There are thus forces both within and outside archaeology which require archaeologists to write narratives.

A seventh aspect of archaeological reasoning is that it is *multiple and diverse*. In the example given above of the use of narrative in the interpretation of stratigraphy at the Haddenham long barrow, different interpretations were espoused by different people, perhaps because of different pre-understandings. Different people 'read' the past in different ways and this is one of the themes behind the idea that the archaeological record is like a 'text' which has to be 'read' (Patrik 1985). But whether the text analogy is accepted or not, we have already seen in chapter 1 (box on p. 10) that different types of archaeologists, different specialists and experts in different periods or areas, will tend to conduct their archaeology in different ways. Those more engaged in analytical methods linked to the natural sciences (dating, phosphate analysis, petrographic analysis and so on) often use universal codes and definitions, they conduct experiments and test hypotheses. Those more engaged in methods linked to the humanities may take a more interpretive or hermeneutic approach (as defined in the box on p. 32). We have seen how a Romano-British villa is approached differently from a Palaeolithic lithic scatter. Certainly, research excavations often have different agendas and different methods (for example in terms of sampling and analysis) from contract archaeology.

As we will see in chapter 9, this diversity partly results from the diverse global society in which archaeologists increasingly live and work. But it also results from the fact that archaeology has both academic and professional arms, and from the ways in which the discipline sits astride the humanities and natural sciences. Those archaeologists who see themselves as historians or as serving history may work in different ways from those who see themselves as in part physicists or chemists. The archaeologist writing up a site, attempting to integrate reports from a variety of different specialists, will often feel like a 'bricoleur', needing some degree of 'do-it-yourself' knowledge of a wide range of specialisms, fitting together different pieces of evidence into a synthesis.

This emphasis on diversity is not the same as that on 'multiple working hypotheses'. The critique of the latter partly stems from the critique above of the tendency for processual 'hypotheses' to be fragmented and decontextualized. But it is also that the notion of 'working' implies that the different hypotheses will ultimately be resolved. In practice, archaeologists often find that resolving one hypothesis simply opens up further questions and issues. I argue here that hypotheses are always embedded in narratives that people want to tell. We need later in this book to replace multiple working hypotheses by multivocality.

The eighth point concerns *productive tensions* (a term introduced to me by Carolyn Hamilton). So far I have implied that the archaeological process can be seen as a matter of fitting data and theory, parts and wholes. But much of the time, theories at different levels may not cohere. The other side of the coin of the search for coherence is that research often focuses on the places where there is lack of fit and on the tensions between competing views and perspectives. These tensions and contradictions are productive in that they lead research on.

It used to be argued by some archaeologists (e.g. Clarke 1972) that archaeology went through phases of 'normal science', interrupted periodically by revolutionary change. The experience at least of archaeology over the past 30 years contradicts this view. The notion that 'everyone agrees' with a unified set of aims and objectives for the discipline has been criticized in chapter 1. What has become much more normal in archaeology is diversity and debate. 'Normal science' seems in archaeology to involve the production and reproduction of differences. In a fully dialectical (Hegelian) view, the tensions never are resolved – as soon as a coherent synthesis is attained new antitheses are exposed. Whether we argue that contradictions are 'natural' or whether we say they can be resolved, they are undoubtedly a prevalent and central part of productive archaeological research.

Thus, inconsistencies are often resolved only temporarily and provisionally. A set of stratigraphical relationships may be made sense of in a particular solution, but in the process of reaching a coherence data which do not fit may have been glossed over or explained away, and these sacrifices to coherence always provide an opening for doubt and critique. A solution may be found to a particular stratigraphical problem – but this does not deal with the underlying difficulty that at the micro-level there are sequences of events which cut across our definition of bounded layers (see chapter 6). At the micro-scale, artifacts may be deposited at the boundaries or surfaces between two layers which properly should be associated with neither of them. Much of the time we ignore this level of imprecision, but there is an underlying contradiction between scales of analysis which is unavoidable.

The tensions are often productive. In the stratigraphical example, the issue of whether artifacts on the surfaces of layers are *in* or *below* the layer above may lead to careful micro-analysis of the sedimentological process, of the treatment of layer surfaces (is there evidence of a gap in time before the deposition of the upper layer, is there evidence of trampling onto the surface of the lower layer, and so on). The tension may lead to new research in the attempt to find a resolution.

The ninth point deals with *evaluating 'fit'*. In the end we are left with the problem of what makes a good hypothesis or a satisfactory answer in conclusions. I have defined how archaeologists reason and come to conclusions, but how do we choose between alternatives – what makes one say 'that's it' – and how do we respond when someone says 'no it isn't'?

This last point refers to the dependence on corporate agreement – we need others to agree and support our claim. Indeed, some might argue that this intersubjective agreement was ALL that was necessary. From one angle this is saying that a fact becomes proven or objectively verified when other people replicate the results. True replication is extremely rare in archaeology – there is always some doubt about whether comparable cases really are similar. One can go and dig a similar site, but not an identical one. The same is true of excavation units or artifacts. Thus replication is partly a matter of judgement and intersubjective agreement. From another angle the dependence on intersubjective agreement implies that truth and objectivity are based on power and authority – truth depends on who you can get to agree with you!

To reduce truth and objectivity solely to intersubjective agreement is dangerous and inaccurate. Social, political and ideological factors undoubtedly play a role in the evaluation of hypotheses and judgements in archaeology. But there have been too many cases in the past of large parts of archaeological communities agreeing to ideologically manipulated versions of prehistory (Arnold 1990) for us to accept intersubjective agreement as the sole arbiter of truth. There has to be the opportunity to challenge consensus viewpoints, for archaeologists to say 'the dominant view is wrong'. Indeed, the history of the discipline is replete with examples of heterodoxies which have become orthodoxies (such as the rise of processual archaeology in North America, or more specifically the acceptance of radiocarbon dates in Europe, or changing views about the origins and spread of agriculture, or about whether unilinear evolution is applicable to the rise of the state).

While not denying the importance of social factors, it remains important to distinguish the criteria archaeologists use in evaluating the fit of theories. We have seen that the idea of 'testing' is inappropriate in archaeology because the data are partly constructed within theory and because most archaeology is not an experimental discipline. The need to shift from 'testing' to 'fitting' was described in chapter 2. But how do we evaluate the fit between theory and data? Why are some interpretations more plausible than others? How does confirmation occur? The answers to such questions have been discussed in qualitative research across the humanities and social sciences (Denzin 1989; Lincoln and Guba 1985; Denzin and Lincoln 1994). Differences occur in archaeology primarily because it is not normally possible to interview the people who produced the archaeological record, and because material culture, by its very nature, straddles the divide between a universal, natural science approach to materials and a historical, interpretive approach to culture. There is thus a particularly marked lack of agreement in the archaeological community about the appropriate basis for confirmation procedures. An interpretive position can and should accommodate scientific information about, for example, natural processes of transformation and decay of artifacts.

Confirmation in archaeology mainly concerns the criteria for assessing coherence and correspondence. Coherence is produced if the parts of the argument do not contradict each other and if the conclusions follow from the premises. There is a partial autonomy of different types of theory, from the observational to the global, and a coherent interpretation is one in which these different levels do not produce contradictory results. The partial autonomy of levels of theory is apparent in the ability of archaeologists to look back at and reinterpret sites on the basis of the same evidence (e.g. Barrett et al. 1991 in their re-working of the excavations of Pitt-Rivers). Earlier observations can be used to allow different interpretations – the different levels of theory (observational and social reconstruction) are partially autonomous. This point is parallel to the claim made by processual and positivist archaeologists that arguments must be tested using independent theories such as Middle Range Theories (Tschauner 1996). However, in my view, different arguments and levels of theory are only partially autonomous, and the emphasis should rather be on fitting multiple strands of theory and evidence.

Certainly, some of the strands of evidence that are woven together refer to widely found theories external to the particular case under consideration. Thus, as well as internal coherence there is external coherence – the degree to which the interpretation fits theories accepted in and outside the discipline. Of course, the evaluation of a coherent argument itself depends on the application of theoretical criteria, and I have already noted the lack of agreement in archaeology about foundational issues such as the importance of a natural science or humanistic approach, or about whether 'independence' of arguments can be claimed. But, whatever their views on such issues, most archaeologists seem to accept implicitly the importance of simplicity and elegance. An argument in which too much special pleading is required in order to claim coherence is less likely to be adopted than is a simple or elegant solution. The notion of external coherence could also be extended to the social and political issues identified above.

The notion of correspondence between theory and data does not imply absolute objectivity and independence, but rather embeds the fit of data and theory within coherence. The data are made to cohere by being linked within theoretical arguments. Similarly, the coherence of the arguments is supported by the fit to data. On the other hand, data can confront theory, as already noted. Correspondence with the data is thus an essential part of arguments of coherence. There are many aspects of correspondence arguments that are used by archaeologists. One is the exactness of fit, perhaps measured in statistical terms, between theoretical expectation and data. Other arguments of correspondence include the number of cases that are accounted for, their range in space and time, and the variety of different classes of data that are explained. However, such numerical indications of correspondence always have to be evaluated against contextual relevance and interpretation in order to determine whether the different examples of fit are relevant to each other.

Other criteria that affect the success of archaeological theories include fruitfulness – how many new directions, new lines of inquiry, new perspectives are opened up. But much depends too on the trustworthiness, professional credentials, and status of the author and supporters of an interpretation. Issues here include how long the interpreter spent in the field and how well she or he knows the data: their biases, problems, and unusual examples. Has the author obtained appropriate degrees and been admitted into professional societies? Is the individual an established and consistent writer, or has he or she yet to prove her or himself? Does the author keep changing her or his mind?

In fact, the audience does not respond directly to an interpretation but to an interpretation written or staged as an article or presentation. The audience thus responds to and interprets a material artifact or event. The persuasiveness of the argument is closely tied to the rhetoric within which it is couched (Gero 1991b; Hodder 1989; Spector 1993;

Tilley 1989b). The rhetoric determines how the different components of the discipline talk about and define problems and their solutions.

The confirmation of archaeological theories depends, therefore, on inter-subjective agreement, and on temporality. Different arguments will hold sway at different historical moments. If what we already know explains things then we may not search for alternatives – we mainly do this when standard accounts do not work any more. But equally, our assessment of an adequate explanation will change because of wider social and political factors (e.g. Trigger 1984). There can be no universal 'cookbook' for confirming archaeological interpretations. The tendencies I have described are variously appropriate in specific historical contexts.

Conclusion

By looking at the practices of archaeologists, by looking at what they (or at least some of them) do rather than at what they think they ought to do, it has been possible to characterize some components of the reasoning processes involved. First, it would appear that archaeological practice cannot easily be described as based around the testing of theory against data. Such a description is under-mined by the recognition that the data are themselves 'seen' through theory and pre-understanding. To some extent we 'observe' what we want to or are trained to observe. On the other hand, archaeologists are led by the data in certain directions. They do seem to accommodate their views to their experience of the data. Therefore, rather than talking of 'testing', it is better to describe the archaeological process as based on 'fitting'. Archaeologists seem to work by fitting theory and data together until a coherent whole is reached.

Second, this fitting process works best if it aims to be non-dichotomous. It does not help to say that the data are either subjective or objective. It is more productive to acknowledge that the data are both constructed by us and that they objectively help to constitute our subjectivities. Both/and is better than either/or in a number of domains of archaeological method. The archaeologist searches for both coherence and at the same time for inconsistencies because it is the parts that do not fit an argument that lead research forward. The archaeologist works with both parts and wholes, with both similarities and differences.

Third, both in terms of the data and our perspective there is a lack of fixity – there is always change. We have perhaps got used to the idea that different theories have to be 'spatialized'. By this I mean that different groups and communities will interpret the past from their different perspectives, situated in relation to different national, ethnic or local interests. General evolutionary theories have increasingly struggled to account for regional variation (Yoffee 1994) and diversity of trajectory. We have seen that multivocality and different audiences are central parts of the archaeological enterprise. But as well as this 'spatialization' of archaeological theory, fluidity is created by a con-comitant 'temporalization'. As pre-understandings engage in a dialectic relation with data-led enquiry, and as solutions are sought to the tensions between different parts of arguments, so there is continual flow and movement. As narratives are written at different scales and in relation to different audiences, and as those audiences and their inter-ests in the past change, so archaeological intrepretation has to be seen as part of a historical process.

This same point about fluidity and diversity can be made by recon-sidering the metaphor of 'reading the past' (Hodder 1986). The notion that the archaeological record can be considered like a text to be read invites the parallel notion that the record/text has to be translated so that it can be read. Certainly this is an attractive metaphor from many angles (cf. Geertz 1973). The emphasis on translation suggests the need to make sense of the past both in 'other' and in 'our' terms. It implies that our interpretations are largely constructions. The past is made sense of in terms 'we' can understand. But on the other hand, the emphasis on translation exaggerates the importance of pre-understand-ings. It underlines the ways in which interpretation is theory-led and downplays the ways in which it is data-led. In addition, it involves notions of domination and control – the past is translated into our terms. Rather than attempting to understand the past in terms of interpretations which might confront and disrupt dominant perspect-ives, translating suggests domination in two respects. First, it implies dominating the past in the sense of imposing interpretations on it which are not sensitive to locality, time and difference. Second, it implies that certain individuals in the discipline can translate the past *for* others – they place themselves in a dominating position in the interpretive process. So, rather than translation we might talk of mediation. The archaeologist mediates between past and present, neither simply describing data nor simply translating it into 'our' terms. The archaeologist as mediator provides information, ideas, images to a diversity of audiences from a diversity of pasts.

The archaeologist cannot stand outside that process. But the archaeologist should not translate or read 'the past' for others. Rather, the emphasis should be on the archaeologist mediating between past and present (Shanks and McGuire 1996). Actively engaged in current issues, the archaeologist contributes to a debate, providing narratives which resonate with contemporary concerns. The archaeologist has to be critical of the ways in which present interests imprint themselves on the way the past is interpreted. Between past and present, archaeologists have to be sensitive to a wide range of contemporary interests while being sensitive also to the evidence available.

A dialogue about the relationship between data and theory

Tester: It seems to me that there is no real difference between hypothesis testing and the hermeneutic circle. Both 'testing' and 'fitting' involve going back and forth between theory and data. Isn't the hermeneutic circle or spiral the same as the feedback loop between theory and data?

Fitter: There do seem to be similarities. Both hypothesis testing and hermeneutic fitting accept that the data are 'theory-laden'. Both involve moving backwards and forwards between data and theory.

Tester: Yes, but I believe that the theory-ladenness of facts can be resolved by using skills, method and objective procedures. However biassed one's interpretations, one needs to be able to check them against the data using rigorous and replicable techniques.

Fitter: But for us hermeneutic fitters there is never a moment at which objective data confront subjective interpretation or theory. I don't believe archaeologists ever 'test against' the data. For me, the data are always both subjective and objective. I want to retain the tension of data and interpretation; I don't think it can be resolved except provisionally. The data are always part of the interpretation as is shown in figure 3.6.

Tester: OK, so I believe in opposing objectivity and subjectivity, and you don't. But surely you can see the need to use Middle Range Theories or 'measuring devices' which are independent of your interpretations. Surely this makes science more secure?

Fitter: That sounds fine, but how do you decide which measuring device to use? How do you know which one is relevant to your data? These issues of relevance and choice, discussed in this chapter under the heading of analogy and comparison, mean that the Middle Range Theories are neither independent nor objective.

Tester: Well, it is rather like the doctor who has a hypothesis that you are ill. She uses a thermometer, which is based on independent sets of knowledge, to test her hypothesis. Archaeologists use independent arguments about the formation of the archaeological record.

Fitter: But my doctor recently gave me advice based on alternative medicine. The trouble with your medical example is that some people do not accept the relevance of medical science to their illness. This problem is exacerbated in the humanities – it is difficult to think of independent measuring devices that we would all agree on to 'measure' whether a building was a shrine. In my view even the doctor works by fitting lots of pieces of evidence together.

Dialectical thinker: I agree with the fitting view so far, but there are clear similarities between your 'fitting' ideas and the type of dialectical thought embraced by some Marxists today, such as McGuire (1992) and McGuire and Saitta (1996). We dialectical thinkers also focus on the data as both subjective and objective.

Fitter: I agree that the fitting and dialectical views often appear indistinguishable. But sometimes there is a difference in emphasis. McGuire and Saitta (1996, 199–200) endorse the generalization and prediction seen in processual archaeology. I think these emphases probably derive from the materialist associations of much dialectical thought. Despite the rhetoric of even-handedness, dialectical thinkers sometimes retain a materialist and objectivist stance.

Dialectical thinker: So don't you accept the need for generalization and prediction at all?

Fitter: Generalization of course; but not prediction. The latter smacks of determinism and material or objective causality.

Dialectical thinker: In that case, I agree there is a difference. Your view is too open-ended for me, and in any case, I believe it is possible for dialectical thinking to transcend the objective/subjective divide.

4 Interpreting Material Culture

We have seen in the last chapter that interpretation in archaeology seems to involve 9 characteristics. In the most general of terms these 9 characteristics describe a process in which there is a fluid and non-dichotomous relationship between the archaeologist and archaeological data. Archaeological research involves a 'fitting' (not a testing) process which is both data and question (perspective) led so that subject and object are interrelated. The fitting process is unstable and diverse.

Some other characteristics of reasoning in archaeology can be explored. These further lead to emphases on interactivity, fluidity and diversity.

Interpretation and description What is the difference between description and interpretation? This debate in archaeology seems to revolve around the roles of uncertainty and selectivity. In a helpful discussion of 'interpretation', Tilley (1993, 1–5) points out that the term is mainly used in contexts in which uncertainty exists. In discussing where interpretation begins and ends, he uses the example of describing a book. If I count the number of words in the book, have I interpreted it? Most people would probably say not. If I say the book was written in English, does this count as an interpretation? Again, probably not. If I describe the contents of the book, the situation becomes more blurred. And certainly, by the time I argue that the book is stylistically complex, ironic or depressing, most people would accept that interpretive statements were being made. These latter statements seem interpretive because they involve a selection of information in relation to prior knowledge. No description of anything can be exhaustive, but as the thing being described becomes more complex, more selectivity is required and more uncertainty that different people will come to the same conclusions.

Tilley also gives archaeological examples. Counting the numbers of potsherds on a settlement site does not seem to involve interpretation. But once I start to say that the high frequency of sherds is unusual for this type of site, or that the sherds can be classified into types based on shape, colour, temper, decoration etc., then interpretation does seem to be involved. When statements are obvious we deny that interpretation is involved. But once judgement and selection are involved in the linking together of things to make (new) sense, then we accept that interpretation has occurred. It is part of the aim of this book to demonstrate that interpretive judgements are present in all areas of archaeology, even down to making catalogues, doing laboratory experiments and excavating features in the field. In all these activities we make selections of information in relation to pre-understandings. In all these activities we have to accept that other people might make different selections and come to different conclusions.

Descriptions seem obvious and undisputed. Interpretations involve the selection of information according to certain criteria, and they involve judgements that can be contested by others. However, all description involves selecting and ordering information. As we increasingly recognize in the discipline the complexity of archaeological and material culture data, we open the door to the view that description involves selection, judgement and interpretation. We can only look at things from particular perspectives and with particular questions in mind. For example, we initially approach artifacts normally at macroscopic level. At other scales of analysis, different descriptions result. In the choice of scale interpretive decisions are made.

All description involves an interpretive component. But equally, all interpretation involves trying to link sense to data. Interpretation is always interpretation of something. Thus it is always partially a description. Once again, we need a non-dichotomous approach. The link between description and interpretation is so close that in anthropology an interpretive approach is associated with the idea of 'thick description' (Geertz 1973). For Foucault (1977) too, interpreting or explaining an event involved a description of the minutiae of events.

As already said, these descriptions involve selecting and ordering. And they also involve expressing an account in some narrative mode. Thus a 'thick description' would be one in which interpretation was essential but in which care was taken to come close to the rich specifity of events.

This recognition of the dependence between interpretation and description is very much at odds with archaeological practice. For example, most excavation coding forms separate out 'interpretation' from 'description'. Thus a layer, unit or context may first be 'described' in terms of soil characteristics, and dimensions and volumes may be measured. The artifacts found in the deposit may be listed and their locations described. An interpretation follows which may say that the layer is 'the fill of room 397 above floor 26'.

There are two points which can be made about this common archaeological practice. First, the separation between description and interpretation is false since even the 'description' has interpretive components (for the same point in relation to the recording of standing buildings see Grenville 1997). For example, any archaeologist who has used codified soil descriptions will recognize the subjectivity involved (does this wet soil feel gritty, does it have 2 per cent or 5 per cent inclusions of less than 0.05cm size etc.?). Even the filling of a bucket is interpretive. Archaeologists might be asked to count the numbers of measured bucket-fulls of soil taken from each excavated deposit. But what exactly is a full bucket? – slightly mounded with gaps around the edge, shaken down, etc. etc.? Some interpretation is involved in the most descriptive statements.

Second, the social context in which description takes place also leads to complex interpretive decisions being made. For example, Gero (1996) uses the ethnomethodological perspective of Garfinkle (1967) to demonstrate that our knowledge of the past is embedded in the social practices of archaeological fieldwork. Dry descriptions of archaeological data mask the interpretive process. 'Formal accounts (including final site reports) deliberately obscure the practical organization of knowledge construction' (Gero 1996, 257). References to the contextual conditions of knowledge construction are 'removed' from the text which 'reports' the 'evidence'. The accounts are generalized and impersonal, to make it seem as if anyone would have come to the same conclusions. What is left out is the personal, heterogeneous and contingent process that lies behind 'description' (see box on p. 69 for an example of the effects of such biasses).

Interpretation cannot easily be separated from description. Indeed, good archaeological science depends on carefully made and well-grounded interpretation. Data 'descriptions' are in practice of little use in themselves (Grenville 1997). In looking through data sheets, archaeologists tend to turn first to the 'interpretations' before being able to make sense of the 'descriptions'. It is only when a deposit is 'interpreted' as 'a well packed sub-floor fill' that the detailed soil 'descriptions' make sense. It is the interpretive component in data that makes the data useful. In selecting and grouping archaeobotanical samples from excavated units for detailed analysis, the analyst is dependent on the interpretations of the deposit as 'floor', 'fill', 'pit layer', and so on.

Data 'description' and gender bias

Study of the excavation process at the Palaeo-Indian site of Arroya Seco in Argentina (Gero 1996) provided two examples of andro-centric 'descriptions' of archaeological data.

1   A dominant male on the site team made larger soil pedestals for artifacts to stand on than a female fieldworker. This practice led to his artifacts being noticed by the director and a special feature photograph being taken. Little special attention was paid to the female artifact pedestals. For the male, Gero argues that the construction of these data is part of the assertion of power.
2   Male fieldworkers tended to outline soil stains with trowels and to draw them on maps with clear boundaries; women tended to be less definite in their representation of stains. The description of clear boundaries indicates a greater mastery of knowledge within the discipline.

In these examples, 'description' is seen as part of complex social strategies. Gero concludes that rather than being neutral, 'objective science' is actually exclusionary, divided by gendered practices. She suggests the need for an inclusive science.

Interpretation and explanation   In my view interpretation includes, but is broader than, explanation. But it should be emphasized that reference is being made here to the particular way the term explanation has come to be used within archaeology. 'Explanation' is closely associated with processual archaeology. Its aim is to identify causal mechanisms, and it involves demonstrating that a particular event is an example of a general class of events. For archaeologists such as Binford (1989), explanation involves 'if – then' clauses. It involves identifying certain variables as primary, independent or determinant. Within post-processual archaeology too, there was recognition that behaviour is influenced by acknowledged and unacknowledged/unrecognized conditions (Shanks and Tilley 1987), and these could be termed causes. But there was also recognition that reference to such causes does not lead to a sufficient account. This is because there is more to human behaviour than causal relationships. There are intentions, narratives, understandings (Hodder 1992; Johnson 1989; Richards 1991; 1996). Many archaeologists today, of whatever theoretical persuasion, recognize that an adequate or full account of human behaviour must go beyond a description of causal mechanisms in order to interpret the framework of meanings within which people acted and made sense of events in the world around them (for an alternative view see chapter 8 and Barrett 1994).

The general and the particular   As already noted, explanation has normally been seen in archaeology as involving relationships between particular events and general understanding. Interpretation also involves selecting information in relation to a general pre-understanding, but in the case of interpretation more importance is given to the uncertainty of this process. More emphasis is placed on discerning whether a particular case *is* an instance of a general pattern, and more emphasis is placed on re-interpreting general understanding in a specific context.

A contextual approach involves interpreting general categories in relation to particular instances, transforming the generalizations in the process. But what is the appropriate scale at which the particular should be understood? Should it be the individual person or site, or the locality, region, or cultural group which is seen as the relevant unit for analysis? Before the development of mapping and high-speed communication, knowledge may have been highly circumscribed and individuals may have been acting within very partial frames. Barrett (1994) has argued that archaeological entities such as the Beaker Culture are at too large a scale to have been perceived by anyone at the time. Rather, these large-scale entities can be seen as the unintended by-products of smaller scale processes. Many of our explanations and interpretations have been at too broad a scale. We have often reified large-scale categories which are best understood at the local and highly contextualized level. Meskell (1996) has suggested that we need to focus more on individual bodies and has criticized others who have claimed to discuss agency in archaeology but have in fact seen individual bodies as constructed by larger forces (see also Johnson 1989).

This emphasis on the very small-scale and particular is important. It cannot be the case that in the fleeting moments of social agency all the large-scale structures are in some sense 'present'. As I make a pot, struggling to keep the walls upright, or as I write these words, there is not the time for all the material and conceptual structures in which I am enmeshed to play a direct role. Certainly I can monitor the effects of my actions, but my monitoring is itself a partial and ill-informed view. So, at one level, it is important to consider individual actions and small-scale events as separate contexts, worthy of interpretation in their own right. Such consideration may often be difficult in archaeology, but there is undoubtedly the possibility of considering individual agency in historic archaeology and in some prehistoric archaeology (see chapter 8 for a fuller discussion and a prehistoric example). But there are unacknowledged conditions and unintentional effects of my actions. Whatever I intend or however I monitor my actions, there are broader processes and interactions of which I can only be dimly aware. So attention must also be paid to the larger forces within which individual actions are embedded. A multiscalar approach is thus needed which looks at the interaction between individual events and larger scale processes however the latter might be defined. Once again the diverse character of archaeological inquiry comes to the fore.

The creative imagination   If it is accepted that there is some looseness between individual and small-scale events and large-scale processes, if action is not entirely determined by causal mechanisms, and if the complexity of social systems means that unpredictable, non-linear relationships occur, then it follows that interpretation of events must involve a creative component. Interpretation involves selectively linking events and materials and individuals with larger scale processes. It involves recognizing that general understanding may have to be re-formed in order to make sense of a particular case. The uncertainty in interpretation seems to put creativity centre stage. Creativity also plays an important role because of the need to find new solutions which resonate with changing data and changing perspectives.

On the whole, the role of the creative imagination has been played down in archaeology (but see Mithen 1998). As in many sciences, the imagination is seen as unpredictable, fanciful and misleading, opposed to the rational. It might be recognized as a source of insight but it has to be controlled. Because the attempt has been to escape intuitive and speculative thought in archaeology, the emphasis has been placed on the testing of ideas rather than on their generation.

As Sue Thomas (1996) has argued, this is a false and unfortunate dichotomy which can only limit the vibrance of the discipline. Indeed, it is now widely accepted that both subjectivity and objectivity are central to the success of archaeology as a science (Rowlands 1984). S. Thomas (1996) shows that in fact there is an increasing need for and use of imagination as disciplinary knowledge increases. The more archaeologists know about a given situation in the past, the more the solution has to be imaginative and creative. Imagination in archaeology operates in relation to disciplinary norms and disciplinary knowledge. The subjective and imaginative side of archaeological research is not simply personal or ad hoc. It is informed by disciplinary rules and knowledge.

Imagination and creativity are needed in order to ask questions of the data (Trigger 1998, 102). The whole research process, as we have seen, depends on posing questions, taking a perspective through which sense can be made of the data. But imagination and creativity are also central to finding answers and solutions. They are the key to the problem-solving process that is archaeological interpretation. Making sense of events in the past can never be a matter of following rules since there is always a uniqueness to historical circumstance. Imagination is needed in making relevant comparisons, in accounting for exceptions, and in finding a narrative that accounts for more of the data.

The notion that the 'whole' (the interpretation) is more than the sum of the parts suggests the need for a creative act in going beyond the parts in order to conceive the whole. Even in the most deterministic of views in which human behaviour is seen as predictable according to general rules, a creative moment is needed in recognizing that a particular case is an example of a specific general rule. The whole is always more than the sum of its parts.

'Their' meanings and 'our' meanings   When we interpret structures and actions, are we interpreting the meanings, purposes and intentions which 'they' had in their heads? Are we getting at their (internal) under-

standing or are we only able to describe from the outside, in our own terms? (This dichotomy between 'their' internal meanings and 'our' external descriptions is often wrongly linked to 'emic' versus 'etic'.)

A useful example is provided by White and Thomas (1972) in their attempt to classify stone tool assemblages from the Highlands of Papua New Guinea. A classification of the tools in terms of formal types was unsuccessful. The tools were divided according to the position of the retouch in relation to the long axis, so that a series of end, side, end and side, etc. tools were distinguished. The occurrence of these classes, however, exhibited no consistent patterning in assemblages across space and time. For example, few trends could be seen through strati-graphies or in terms of regional patterning. Consistent patterning was, however, observed when the tools were re-classified according to eth-nographically documented criteria. In the Highlands, ethnographic observation suggested that stone tools were indigenously classified according to the use of the edge. The main criteria were factors such as the number of edges that were used, and the size, angle, retouch and curvature of the edges.

What this example implies is that a description that approximated the indigenous classification will produce systematic patterning in the record. However, the possibility remains that a classification that does not approximate 'their' view might also produce coherent patterning. White and Thomas (ibid.) also point out that we should not take for granted the existence of an indigenous classification that is not con-tested by different groups in society. We should also not assume that individuals have one indigenous view that can be accessed consciously and explained to the analyst. I want to argue that, particularly for material culture, it is difficult to accept a simple dichotomy between 'our' and 'their' perspectives.

To understand an indigenous perspective we would often assume that it is necessary to talk to people. Western social science has long privileged the spoken over the written and the written over the non-verbal (Derrida 1978). But when material culture meanings are con-sidered, 'what people say' is often very different from 'what people do'. This point has perhaps been most successfully established over recent years by research stemming from the work of Bill Rathje (Rathje and Murphy 1992; Rathje and Thompson 1981). In studies in Tucson, Arizona, and elsewhere, Rathje and his colleagues collected domestic garbage bags and itemized the contents. It became clear that, for example, people's estimates about the amounts of garbage they produced were wildly incorrect, that discarded beer cans indicated a higher level of alcohol consumption than was admitted to, and that in times of meat shortage people threw away more meat than usual as a result of hoarding behaviour. Thus a full sociological analysis cannot be restricted to interview data. It must also consider material evidence separately from questionnaires.

It might be countered that material culture can indicate indigenous perspectives because it is like a language that can be 'read'. Some material culture is designed specifically to be communicative and representational. The clearest example is the material object, such as this book, which is a written text itself. But direct communicative signalling is also seen in various signs and symbols such as the badges and uniforms of certain professions, red and green stop and go traffic lights, smoke signals, and images of Christ on the cross. Because this category of material culture meanings includes written texts, it is to be expected to be organized in ways similar to language. Thus, as with words in a language, such material symbols are often arbitrary. For example, any design on a flag could be used to indicate a nation as long as it differs from the designs on other flags and is recognizable with its own identity. Thus the system of meanings in the case of flags is constructed through similarities and differences in a semiotic code. Miller (1982) has shown how dress, like language, is organized both syntagmatically and paradigmatically. The choice of hat, tie, shirt, trousers, shoes, and so on for a particular occasion is informed by a syntax that allows a particular set of clothes to be put together. On the other hand, the distinctions among different types of hats (bowler, straw, cloth, baseball) or jackets constitute paradigmatic choices.

The metaphor of language has been widely applied to material culture, both in archaeology and in other disciplines (e.g. see Tilley 1990). Initially it may seem to be the case that the pot appears to 'mean' in the same way as the word *pot*. Recent work has begun to draw attention to the limitations of this analogy between material culture and language (Hodder and Shanks et al. 1995). Many examples of material culture are not produced to 'mean' at all. In other words, they are not produced with symbolic functions as primary. Thus the madeleine cookie discussed in Proust's *A la recherche du temps perdu (Swann's Way)* was produced as an enticing food, made in a shape representing a fluted scallop (Hodder 1991). But Proust describes its meaning as quite different from this symbolic representation. Rather, the meaning involved the evocation of a whole series of childhood memories, sounds, tastes, smells surrounding having tea with his mother in winter.

Many if not most material symbols do not work through rules of representation, using a language-like syntax (Sperber 1975). Rather, they work through the evocation of sets of practices within individual experience. It would be relatively difficult to construct a grammar or dictionary of material signs and symbols except in the case of deliberately representational items, such as flags and road signs. This is because most material symbols do not simply communicate. Rather, their meanings are grounded in the experiences and practices of life. Insofar as members of society experience common practices, material symbols come to have common evocations and common meanings. Thus, for example, the ways in which certain types of food, drink, music, and sport are experienced are embedded within social convention and thus come to have common meaning. A garlic crusher may not be used overtly in Britain to represent or symbolize class, but through a complex set of practices surrounding food and its preparation the crushers did come to mean class through evocation and association. Bloch (1995) has shown that the carvings on wooden buildings in Madagascar do not 'mean' in terms of communication; rather they play a functional role in emphasizing the social importance of the house.

Because objects endure, have their own traces, their own grain, individual objects with unique evocation can be recognized. The specific memory traces associated with any particular object (a particular garlic crusher) will vary from individual to individual. The particularity of material experience and meaning derives not only from the diversity of social life but also from the identifiability of material objects. The identifiable particularity of material experience always has the potential to work against and transform society-wide conventions through practice. Because of this dialectic relationship between structure and practice, and because of the multiple local meanings that can be given to things, it would be difficult to construct dictionaries and grammars for most material culture meanings. It is difficult to argue that there is one indigenous meaning, or that all indigenous meanings can be understood through language.

The importance of practice for the social and symbolic meanings of artifacts has been emphasized in recent work on technology (Schlanger 1990; Dobres 1995). Each technical operation is linked to others in operational chains (Leroi-Gourhan 1964) involving materials, energy, and gestures. For example, some clays are better for throwing than others, so that the type of clay constrains whether a manufacturer can make thrown pots or hand-built statuettes. Quality of clay is related to types of temper that should be used. All such operational chains are non-deterministic, and some degree of social choice is involved (Lemonnier 1986; Miller 1985). All operational chains involve aspects of production, exchange and consumption, and so are part of a network of relations incorporating the material, the economic, the social, and the conceptual and even moral. Latour (1988) provides examples such as modern speed bumps (termed 'sleeping policemen' in Britain) which force people to be socially responsible and moral by not driving too fast outside schools, although in fact the reason for not driving fast is that one does not want to break one's car on the bumps. In archaeology it is widely argued that monuments or artifacts which involve a large amount of time, energy or labour to produce are appropriate indicators of high status; the link between the signifier (such as the monument) and the signified (high status) is not arbitrary or simply representational.

There are thus at least two different ways in which material culture comes to have meaning. The first is through rules of representation. The second is through practice and the mutual implication of the material and non-material. Whereas it may be the case that written language is the prime example of the first category and tools the prime example of the second, language also has to be worked out in practices from which it derives much of its meaning. Equally, we have seen that material items can be placed within language-like codes. There is some support from cognitive psychology for a general difference between the two types of knowledge. For example, Bechtel (1990, 264) argues that rule-based models of cognition are naturally good at quite different types of activity from connectionist models. Where the first is appropriate for problem solving, the second is best at tasks such as pattern recognition and motor control. It seems likely then that the skills involved in material practice and the social, symbolic, and moral meanings that are implicated in such practices might involve different cognitive systems than involved in rules and representations.

Bloch (1991) argues that practical knowledge is fundamentally different from linguistic knowledge in the way it is organized in the mind. Practical knowledge is 'chunked' into highly contextualized information about how to 'go on' in specific domains of action. Much cultural knowledge is non-linear and purpose dedicated, formed through the practice of closely related activities. The practical world involves social and symbolic meanings that are not organized representational codes but are chunked or contextually organized realms of activity in which emotions, desires, morals, and social relations are involved at the level of implicit taken-for-granted skills or know-how.

It should be emphasized that the two types of material symbolism – the representational and the practically associated (or phenomenological) – often work in close relation to each other. Thus a set of practices may associate men and women with different parts of houses or times of day, but in certain social contexts these associations might be built upon to construct symbolic rules of separation and exclusion and to build an abstract representational scheme in which mythology and cosmology play a part (e.g. Yates 1989). Such schemes also have ideological components that feed back to constrain the practices. Thus practice and representation interpenetrate and feed off each other in many if not all areas of life. Structure and practice are recursively related in the 'structuration' of material life (Giddens 1979; Bourdieu 1977).

The diversity of types of verbal, written and material meanings within any society suggests that it is naive to assume that archaeologists can reconstruct *the* indigenous meanings in the past. People often find it difficult to translate from practical and sensory meanings to verbal meanings. We learn practical knowledge by repetition and the monitoring of the results of action. Much work in psychology shows that practising of skills and routines leads to 'automization'. By this I mean that we become adept social actors without necessarily being able to bring practical knowledge into conscious thought with any ease. The knowledge or know-how becomes difficult to access with conscious thought. Certainly practical routinization may initially involve conscious manipulation in relation to a social environment and social goals. But once routinized, there may be only partial links to conscious thought. Thus when 'we' are interpreting 'their' meanings we are dealing with skills about which people may not have been articulate – and which in fact may have become partially disengaged from conscious thought.

This last point undermines the dichotomy between 'our' and 'their' thought. We learn how to behave in the practical world through practice and routinization. As already argued, the routines we learn are embedded within social convention. Our personal experience of associative meanings, the thoughts and emotions which are embedded in our practical engagement with the world, are at least partly the product of the objective conditions within which we live. They are thus 'outside' ourselves, as much as they are 'inside' ourselves. A similar point is argued in relation to language by poststructuralist writers (Bapty and Yates 1990). We think about the world through a language that is already written for us.

This discussion demonstrates that there were many types of meanings which 'they' had in the past. Even if 'we' could talk to 'them', they would be no more able than we are in our contemporary lives to verbalize all the levels of non-discursive meaning which lie within their actions and statements. It is our role as observers to attempt to understand the links between actions, events, symbols and the material conditions and social conventions within which they are embedded. Both 'they' and 'we' have to interpret action.

Conclusion

I have argued here that there is a diversity of types of meaning in society. There have been successful attempts by archaeologists to interpret conflicting and contested meanings in the past (Brumfiel 1991; Hastorf 1991; Ferguson 1991). But it should not be supposed that if we could talk to people in the past that the difficulties of interpreting diversity of meaning would be resolved. Indeed, anthropologists, historians and sociologists have, to some extent, to work like archaeologists. Many types of social meaning are practically involved in the material world. They are not spoken and are thus hidden, but they are not arbitrary and unavailable for study. To the contrary, the non-arbitrary material relations of much social meaning open up the possibility of grounding interpretation in the 'thick description' of social life. It is thus possible for the anthropologist, historian or sociologist to 'excavate' meaning in the practices of social life, without depending entirely on the spoken world. For archaeologists themselves, often, ironically, trying to be like anthropologists, historians or sociologists, the important point is that meaningful material practices leave residues on which the creative imagination can dwell, using the techniques described in chapter 3, so that interpretation can occur.

Given the diversity, instability, complexity and multi-levelled character of material meanings it is clear that an interpretive approach is needed which is open to alternative readings of the same evidence.

Interpretation has to be sensitive to the particular as well as to the general. Imposing general rules without careful evaluation of their relevance to the local situation is clearly inadequate. There is thus a need to focus on archaeological method. A basic requirement for such a method is that it be able to adjust to changing contexts and circumstances. Rigidity of approach is unlikely to be able to accommodate to diversity in the topic of study. An approach is needed which can reflect upon itself, probe its own taken-for-granted assumptions, and adapt to changing circumstance. In the following chapter I wish to begin to explore the possibilities for a reflexive method in archaeology. Indeed, the rest of this book will be a response to the position established in the first four chapters that archaeological research in practice is diverse, fluid and non-dichotomous. What methods can be used in order to enhance these characteristics of archaeological enquiry?

5 Towards a Reflexive Method

Most accounts of method in archaeology accept that at some level the data are constructed in theory – they are 'theory-laden'. This was true of many culture-historical archaeologists who responded to the theory-ladenness of data by sticking as closely as possible to the facts. Processual archaeology certainly accepted the notion that the data are constructed through interpretation. The response was to emphasize testing and independence of middle range arguments. The theory-ladenness of facts is also recognized in realist accounts (see box on p. 23) and dialectical accounts (McGuire and Saitta 1996; McGuire 1992 and see box on p. 64).

It is unfortunate that archaeologists in their practices have not been as sophisticated as in their theories. In practice, archaeologists have ignored or side-stepped the issue of theory-ladenness. As already noted, many excavation record forms still separate description and interpretation in the way advocated by Barker (1977; 1982). Carver (1989, 669) argues that this tradition in Britain extends back to Pitt-Rivers, such that 'English excavators, particularly, believe that there ought to be a science of retrieving archaeological evidence which has nothing to do with the interpretations that are subsequently made'.

This same separation of data description and theoretical interpretation continues in much modern excavation, which is underlain by the following scheme in which the data are seen to consist of objects (ceramics and lithics for example) and contexts (layers and houses for example).

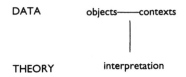

Figure 5.1   The supposed separation of theory and data in archaeology (compare figure 5.2).

Consider the following two statements from Joukowsky's (1980) *A Complete Manual of Field Archaeology.*

> In addition to day-by-day notes, the square supervisor is responsible for a subjective interpretation of the meaning of his or her excavation. This subjective analysis is submitted at the conclusion of his/her work in a particular area and is physically kept separate from the objective facts, so that assumptions are kept distinct from field notes. (pp. 218–19)
> If the earth is from a sterile layer, it can be dumped, but if it comes from an occupation level, the earth should be carried to the screen, spread on it, and sifted so that no telltale signs will be overlooked. (p. 175)

The first statement argues that interpretation should be kept separate from objective fact and that it should occur only after data have been collected. The second statement contradicts this by arguing that the methods used depend on prior interpretation. The excavator has to interpret a deposit in terms of whether it is an occupation level before screening (sieving) is used. How is one supposed to know whether a layer is sterile before it has been screened?

Interpretation occurs at many levels in archaeological research, and in the example just given, it cannot be confined to a higher level. As was shown in chapters 2 and 3, it is generally the case that how we excavate a site is determined by our prior interpretation of the site. For example, decisions will frequently be made about whether to screen on the basis of interpretation. For example, a 'floor' context may be excavated more intensively than one interpreted as 'fill', with 100 per cent water screening only being used in the 'floor' context. In such cases, whether an artifact exists at all within the archaeological view depends on interpretation. Microartifacts may only be recovered because of full water screening of 'floor' contexts. The same artifact from a 'fill' would have less chance of recovery and might simply 'not exist'. Thus the objective existence of an artifact as 'data' depends on the interpretation that has been made prior to and during excavation. How, then, can it be maintained that subjective data interpretation should only occur after objective data description and collection?

Archaeologists have typically dealt with the problem of needing to know what is being excavated before it is excavated by sampling different parts of deposits or sites in different ways, or by taking initial trial soundings (sondages) before full excavation. The assumption in such cases is that any mistake made in the method used to excavate parts of the deposit or site can be rectified when digging other parts of the 'same' deposit or site, or even other sites in the same region or class of site. The problem with this approach is that in cultural deposits we cannot assume that all the sampled parts of the deposit, site or group of sites are similar. In laboratory-based archaeological research or in experimental archaeology it may be possible to repeat experiments, varying conditions in a controlled way, so that different instances of the 'same' phenomenon can be examined. In excavation, whether different parts of a deposit or different deposits or sites are the 'same' is itself an interpretation. Such an interpretation might be best made after excavation but it has to be made prior to excavation if trial soundings of an entity such as a pit or site or of a category such as a class of pit or site are to be made.

This contradiction which lies behind archaeological research designs is again clearly illustrated by Philip Barker's *Techniques of Archaeological Excavation* (1977; 2nd edition 1982), a volume which describes methods which have become common in British field archaeology. On the one hand, Barker accepts that 'interpretation...inevitably begins as features are seen, dissected and removed' (1982, 145). Since recording begins during excavation, and since 'the interpretive element in the recording can never be completely isolated' (ibid., 146), the archaeologist has a great responsibility to interpret *immediately*, as layers are uncovered (ibid.). For Barker, recording is always an interpretation – for example, a section or profile drawing records what the excavator sees rather than simply what is there.

So, on the one hand, for Barker interpretation is prior to or at least embedded within recording and excavation. But it is a very different strain in Barker's account which has come to dominate British field archaeology. This is the contradictory view that this interpretive component should be minimized by separating evidence from interpretation. 'Immediate on-site recovery...should be as objective as it can be' (1982, 147). He suggests that 'in order to minimise the interpretive element in the record' (ibid., 145) neutral terms such as 'feature' and 'context' should be used. He argues for formalized cards and coding sheets – indeed for the whole system of 'objective' data description that has become routine. Subjectivity and speculation become central only at higher levels of interpretation (ibid., 147).

Why was it possible to side-step the centrality of interpretation within 'data description'? Perhaps the answer lies in the need to handle increasingly large amounts of data and the codification implied by computer-aided techniques. Barker (1982, 206) expresses this latter need. He suggests that the excavator may start off with doubt about whether a post-hole might be a root-hole, or a floor a random scatter of pebbles. Although Barker feels that this interpretive doubt should be retained in the excavation report he accepts that it often is not. The reason is that if all such interpretive issues were included in the report it would become too dull because there would be *too much information*. The handling of large amounts of data led to the use of highly codified and rigid computerized recording systems. In order for such systems to work it had to be assumed that data gathering could be separated from and be prior to interpretation. Another important factor was the development of contract archaeology and the resulting system-atization of method. Competitive tendering has often led fieldwork to be undertaken in less time and with less resources. 'Most archaeological reports have become terse statements of reductionist objectivity' (Chadwick 1998). Shanks and McGuire (1996) argue that the management strategies followed by contract archaeologists in the USA led to de-skilling and to a need for standardization.

The key point here is that, as many archaeologists would in theory accept, excavation method, data collection and data recording are all dependent on interpretation. Interpretation occurs at the trowel's edge. And yet, perhaps because of the technologies available to deal with very large sets of data, and because of the rise of contract archaeology, we have as archaeologists taken the position that excavation methods can be separated from and be seen as prior to interpretation. It will be argued below that modern data-management systems perhaps allow some resolution of the contradiction. At any rate, it is time that the contradiction was in some way faced and dealt with.

The data are not 'given' to interpretation. Rather, interpretation is part of the data.

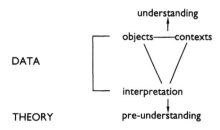

Figure 5.2 The relation between data and theory in archaeology.

Archaeological Data

Archaeological data can be defined as a set of dynamic, dialectical, unstable relations between objects, contexts and interpretations (figure 5.2). The terms object and context are here being used relationally within a nested hierarchy of terms from attribute to artifact to assemblage to type to layer to feature to site to region (figure 5.3). Other terms such as phase could be included. 'Object' refers to a lower level entity (e.g. feature) within a higher level entity (such as a site) termed context. In the following account I refer mainly to objects as artifacts and to contexts as layers, assemblages or features. But it should be noted that similar arguments can be used for attributes (objects) on artifacts (the context of the attributes). The problem of scale or level is the problem of how to decide what is the relevant context for a particular archaeological entity – this is part of the general problem discussed below of linking 'objects' to 'contexts'.

The three parts of the hermeneutic triangle in figure 5.2 can be looked at in the following ways:

At the primary level of data analysis, interpretive *theory constructs objects* in a number of ways. In chapter 1 I discussed emerging problems in the definition of the archaeological object. Particularly at the micro-scale, material 'objects' can be seen to be a function of perspective or scale of analysis. As another example, Munsell charts or type series are developed independently of new object finds and are imposed on them. But in applying these codes we often recognize some 'slippage' and difficulty – some interpretation becomes necessary, and the absolute separation between data and interpretation cannot be maintained. For example, how burnt does a bone/flint have to be before it is classed as burnt? What boundaries should we choose between large and small

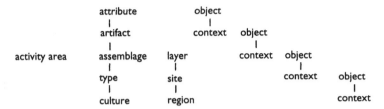

Figure 5.3   One of many possible hierarchies of relationship between objects (lower level categories) and contexts (higher level categories).

sherds, or abraded and unabraded? In answering these questions at the primary level we often do not use object-context relations. We tend to impose a priori assumptions. We say we are just 'describing' the variability and that this is a relatively objective procedure; or we say that we are using techniques proven at other sites or regions; or that there is something universal about the class of object being examined, etc. But ethnotaxonomic work on colour and on ceramic classification has shown that typologies are always to some extent socially constructed (e.g. Miller 1985; Arnold 1971; Baines 1985; Berlin and Kay 1969). Cultural variation in stone tool categorization was described in chapter 4.

Perhaps the clearest example of how theory constructs objects is that whether we find objects at all depends on the methods used which depend on the theories espoused. For example, as already noted, whether we wet or dry sieve and the size of mesh used determine whether small objects will be found. The sieving decisions will themselves often depend on general theory such as 'burnt deposits are more likely to have carbonised seeds'. In all these cases we tend not to use contextual information in interpreting the general or local rules in relation to the objects. We do not make full use of the local, varying information, especially as codification has increased in archaeology.

Theory also constructs context and again we often ignore local, object-based, information in defining contexts. We have long recognized in archaeology that meaning depends on context – for example, whether an object is defined as residual or not depends on other things in the same context (layer, pit etc.). But the boundaries of the context are not 'given' – they are defined theoretically. For example, it has become a widely accepted convention that the minimum context or 'unit' is the soil matrix. But another way of defining context would be to use clusters of artifacts (which may lie within or even cut across soil matrices). In any case the boundaries of soil contexts often have to be interpreted. For example, should all the fine lenses in middens each be separate contexts? Since fine-grained excavation is often not possible, how many lenses should be lumped together to form one context?

There is no fixed entity of bounded earth that can be recorded independently of interpretation. For example, in building 'fill' (material which has been thrown or collapsed into an abandoned building) there may be many small soil boundaries which we ignore during excavation and recording. The same is true of dense middens containing multiple lenses of discarded material. Similar sized lenses when found on a floor in a shrine would probably be dug separately. In some cases, large blocks of soil might be taken and the fine lenses excavated under the microscope. In other words, whether a soil boundary is recognized, or even seen, depends on interpretation. It is a matter of recognizing a soil boundary as significant (at a particular scale).

The boundaries of contexts depend on interpretations of cut relationships – which pit cuts which, and so on. And the grouping of postholes into contexts depends on their interpretation as houses. The problem is, as with objects, that we try to define the contexts a priori. We try to do this 'objectively' without specific reference to the objects found in them. But we recognize the slippage, the arbitrariness in practice – because contexts depend dialectically on theories and objects.

So definition of objects depends on interpretation of contexts and definition of contexts depends on interpretation of objects. There has been a long debate in archaeology about the relative importance of objects and contexts. Montelius' typological division of the Scandinavian Bronze Age in 1885 appeared to depend on a study of objects and their change in form over time. However, in the same early period in the development of archaeology, Müller countered that the systematic placing of an object within a typological series was only possible if we already knew its find context (Müller 1884; Gräslund 1987; Sørensen 1997). In fact, in most archaeological typology some information about context influences the typological definition of objects, whereas the context is defined (in relation to its date or function) in relation to the objects found within it.

So everything depends on everything else in the hermeneutic circle. I should emphasize that I am talking here about what archaeologists do in practice. We all know these complex inter-relationships occur in practice but we often choose to ignore the slippage from the practical

STAGE 1

Stratigraphically A is later than B.
But if artifacts in B are clearly later than A and if there is some uncertainty about the stratigraphical relationship we might, in post-excavation, decide to reinterpret the profile/section as;

STAGE 2

So that B is later than A.
Alternatively, we might decide that we had been wrong about the artifacts in B and reinterpret them as earlier than those in A or as intrusive into B. Thus, we return to;

STAGE 3

Figure 5.4   A simplified example of the fluid relations between objects and contexts in archaeology.

aim of separating interpretation and data description. As an example of what happens in practice, we can look at figure 5.4 and its attached explanation. The stratigraphical relations between layers can be revised by evaluating the dates of the objects – and on wider theories about how the site developed etc. But the dates of the objects can also be revised by re-evaluating the stratigraphical sequence. And consideration of the overall problem of the relationship between objects and contexts depends also on pre-understanding and on the interpretation the archaeologist is interested in developing. So everything depends on everything else in a hermeneutic circle.

This interdependence of objects and contexts within an interpretive framework can be shown in a number of different examples, although most concern the way in which objects are redefined in relation to context.

Example 1 – dating ditches S. Thomas (1997) has discussed a site in which during the excavation the archaeologists had observed from the data so far excavated that parallel ditches tended to be contemporary. This theory was being used to date unexcavated ditches and to direct sampling of unexcavated ditches. The theory was held to even if contradicted by the artifacts found in the ditches. Thus, in this case, artifacts found in ditches were being given meaning (as residual etc.) on the basis of an interpretation of context which was based on the interpretation of the site as a whole which was itself based on the dates of artifacts found in some ditches.

Example 2 – palaeoethnobotany A good example from palaeoethnobotany is provided by Lennstrom and Hastorf (1995). It might be assumed that the charred plant remains in a deposit relate in some way to the use of that deposit, but Lennstrom and Hastorf point out that the charred remains in a feature could be secondary and redeposited. They deal with this problem at the site of Pancan in the central highlands of Peru (650–1000 AD) by intensive sampling of all deposits and by comparison of charred plant assemblages in neighbouring deposits. Thus, if the plant assemblages in neighbouring (including above and below) deposits are similar, the suspicion must be that the plants in any particular deposit were not placed there intentionally, but were part of general background soil contents. Cutting and recutting of pits, for example, would redistribute charred plant remains through various deposits.

Lennstrom and Hastorf note that the soil in some human and animal burials contains plant remains similar to that in surrounding deposits. But in some cases, unique assemblages can be observed. In these cases it can be argued that the plants were placed intentionally in the pits and graves as part of ritual behaviour. Equally, they determine whether plant remains recovered from hearths were in situ by comparison with all other contiguous deposits. In these examples, the meaning of a particular percentage of maize varies according to context. In one case, the maize remains would be interpreted as unintentional. In another, where the percentage differed from surrounding deposits, the maize would be given a different interpretation, involving intentionality.

Example 3 – lithics Lithic specialists have tended to impose basic divisions of their material based on universal assumptions. One of the most widely used is the division between blades and flakes. Conventional wisdom dictates that any flake that has more than a 2:1 length to width ratio is typed as a blade (Inizan 1992, 58). Conolly (1996) has made several criticisms of this approach. The first is that the terms blade and flake are often assumed to relate to different technological processes. Experimental research has shown that blade production requires more pre-planning and may be linked to larger scale and more specialized production (Clark 1987). Clearly, however, these same more structured production processes can produce flakes that do not respect the 2:1 ratio. Second, the lithic artifacts recovered are usually broken and fragmentary so that estimates or interpretations of original morphology have to be made – the full dependence on universal metric criteria becomes undermined. Third, there may be important technical and social distinctions between blades which cut across or do not respect the conventional 2:1 division. Other non-metric criteria such as dorsal scar patterning and edge profiles may be used to classify an individual lithic piece in order to tease out such variation. It is not enough to depend on universal criteria which are insensitive to context.

The distinction between blades and bladelets is a parallel case. An arbitrary metric cut-off point is often used to distinguish small and large blades in an assemblage (Conolly 1996). But Tixier (1974, 7) suggests that the specific metric divisions between blades and bladelets devised by him for the Epipalaeolithic of the Maghreb, should not be used elsewhere without taking into account the technological context of the assemblage to which it is being applied. The division between blades and bladelets is meaningless unless it is related to processes in the production or consumption of these artifacts. For example, the division may be related to technical differences between large and small blades, such as different core types or reduction stages. It may be related to functional differences as when blades are hafted as sickle segments, while bladelets are microliths in composite tools. It may be related to social differences, as when blades are womens' tools, bladelets mens' tools. Thus the distinction between blades and bladelets must be worked out in relation to other, local evidence; and it must be seen as fluid, potentially changing through time and across space.

As a final lithic example, Conolly (1996) takes the definition of tool types. Conventionally, retouched lithic artifacts have been assigned a tool type by reference to criteria such as the blank used, the working edge morphology and the suspected function. Examples include projectile point, flake side-scraper, sickle blade. There are clearly difficulties in assuming that only intentionally retouched pieces were used as tools (Gero 1991a). Unmodified flakes can be hafted as projectile points, and a 'projectile point' can be used as a knife. Use-wear and functional analyses may help to pick up such variation, but there are a number of ways in which the imposition of tool categories must be made sensitive to other or local information. For example, there may be social differences. Thus a 'projectile point' found in domestic contexts may be pressure flaked and used as a knife, while the 'same' object found in a non-domestic context may have been made using a soft hammer and may have been used as a projectile.

Example 4 – burial Parker Pearson (1993) has demonstrated that contextual information relating the dead to the living is necessary for adequate understanding of mortuary remains. He identifies three types of analysis in which burial can be contextualized.

1 *Analysis of spatial and topographic relationships between the abodes of the living and the dead* Parker Pearson reconsiders the Saxe and Goldstein hypothesis that formal, bounded disposal areas for the dead can be linked to societies with corporate groups organized by lineal descent. Closing off the dead is linked by this hypothesis to the control of restricted resources. Morris (1991) has shown in case studies from Classical archaeology that these general terms and ideas need to be reinterpreted in relation to specific historical circumstances. As Parker Pearson (1993) notes, notions of liminality, segregation and boundedness may be applied differently in different societies. In some societies, it may be adequate to separate the dead by placing them below the ground; in others it may be necessary to place them on the other side of running water. In his own work in Denmark, 'the concept of separation should be seen as relative to whatever existed before or after' (ibid., 206). It is only when sequences of changing

placement of the dead can be identified that we can attempt to ascribe meaning to the relationship of the dead to the living.

2 *Analysis of intra-site organization within the abodes of living and dead* – Differentiation among graves can be compared with differentiation among houses to see if, for example, status is represented in one or both domains. In some cases, the world of the dead may misrepresent that of the living. Also, the structure of a settlement may be organized according to principles such as gender (men's or women's houses or activity areas), kin (such as spatial distinction of moieties), status (as in the central placing of a dominant house), or cosmological principles. Comparison can be made with the spatial organization of cemeteries of the same date.

3 *Analysis of the distribution of artifacts and assemblages between settlements, funerary deposits and other contexts* Archaeologists often attempt to ascribe 'value' to grave goods in order to establish degrees of differentiation and ranking amongst graves. There is a danger here of a circular argument as artifacts are scored according to their rarity in funerary contexts or according to the amount of labour invested. Rather than making cross-cultural assumptions so that the same thing always has the same value (because it involves the same amount of labour), cross-contextual analyses allow the symbolic value of artifacts to be assessed more accurately. An analysis of the selection processes for grave goods has been carried out by Braun (1977). He compared the rubbish contexts and grave assemblages from Native American sites of the Woodland Period and distinguished those items in burials which were of significant social value as determined by their rarity in the waste contexts of settlements.

In all these cases, the issue is one of 'redefining the archaeological object' (see chapter 1). The accepted division of the archaeological domain into pottery, lithics, animal bones, burials or whatever, has proved too restricting. We have taken these categories as self evident, at least partly because their material nature gives them an apparent 'objectivity'. But there is a need to break out of the constraints imposed by this false objectivity and explore new 'objects' which cut across the old definitions and which may be productive in new ways and directions. The examples above show that the same material object may mean different things in different contexts. Meaning is relational. Archaeological interpretation is limited by the common practice of separating out certain classes of object (ceramics, lithics, burial) and considering them on their own. At certain levels of analysis, archaeologists recognize the need to break out of these limiting categories in order to examine cross-cutting concepts. Themes such as burning, or domestication, or decoration can be explored which cut across existing categories and allow a wide range of different types of data to be involved.

Interpretation at the Trowel's Edge

This interpretive linking process occurs at all levels, including in the process of digging itself (Bender et al. 1997). As the hand and trowel move over the ground, decisions are being made about which bumps, changes in texture, colours to ignore and which to follow. This is a practical bodily interpretation. It is influenced by one's interpretation of what is happening and by what one is finding. If an artifact flicks out, we interpret whether it came from this layer or that.

But we have seen that how we excavate (trowel, shovel; sieving or not; the placing of sections) depends on an interpretation of context (e.g. this deposit is worth wet sieving because it is the only example of a late Neolithic hearth). But the interpretation of the context depends on knowing about the objects within it. So ideally we would want to know everything that is in a pit *before* we excavate it! This is the hermeneutic conundrum: 'interpretation is only possible once interpretation has begun' (Scruton 1982).

The way archaeologists have dealt with this is to pretend that excavation and the coding of objects are objectified, neutral and systematic. We all know they are not but we turn a blind eye, which is to some extent justifiable. We have to start somewhere. We cannot just sit watching the pit in a crisis of hermeneutic doubt.

In practice we have to excavate without knowing what we are excavating, and we have to define contexts without understanding them, and we have to choose traits without knowing what the types are. But archaeologists have perhaps gone too far the other way – towards a very codified and generalized and decontextualized analysis (for a similar point regarding the recording of standing buildings see Grenville 1997, 4). This may have been necessary as people began grappling with very large data sets using relatively crude techniques. But the technologies are now beginning to catch up with the problem – they increasingly allow a methodology which is hermeneutic, fluid and interpretive.

On the one hand, a fixed definition of objects and contexts is required in archaeology. This is because (a) excavation destroys evidence. While we can return to the excavated artifacts to remeasure and redefine them into new categories, this cannot be done with soil contexts etc. Thus it is important for the archaeologist to assume that the contextual relationships are fixed. This is a sense of security based on insecure foundations and ways have to be found round this problem. Fixed codification is also needed because (b) sites, features and artifacts have to be compared. Cultures, phases etc. have to be defined on the basis of comparing like with like. Thus it is important to know how many naviform cores are found at which sites and at which phases in the Near East. Such comparison is essential for constructing spatial and temporal as well as functional and other patterning. But it can be recognized that such comparisons may be based on arbitrary distinctions which have no meaning in terms of behaviour or society. It is more productive to construct comparisons by comparing like with like. If two artifacts look the same, as we have seen this does not necessarily imply that they have the same meaning. For example, the 'same' artifact type may appear at very different dates in different areas. So chronologies etc. are not built only on the basis of a fixed relationship between type and meaning – we allow for spatial-temporal (contextual) lag in building up chronologies. And this sensitivity to context has to be applied more widely.

So a methodology is needed which incorporates a fluidity in the relationship between object, context and interpretation. This fluidity is a necessary and integral part of archaeological work, especially in the excavation process. It is necessary to foreground interpretation here since interpretation determines excavation and sampling strategies.

Some of the new technologies for introducing relationality and fluidity will be described in chapter 7, but for the moment we can evaluate some simple steps that many have already taken. One example is 'single context recording', the context here referring to a locus or a unit of soil. This method was introduced, after experiment elsewhere, in the Department of Urban Archaeology in London in 1975. It involves the recording in the field of individual units of bounded soil matrix which are described on separate forms ('context sheets') and from which artifacts and samples are kept separately (normally a layer or arbitrary layer). Typically, also, each context (or unit, layer, or cut) is planned individually. The original aim of introducing such a decentralized recording system, at least in Britain in the 1960s and 1970s, was to democratize the excavation process – so that excavators of individual features (contexts) could carry out their own recording and planning. The sole right to record was wrested from the hands of the director or site supervisor. The method was linked to the rise of a more professional and developer-funded archaeology in which higher levels of training and skills in field specialists could be expected. The technique thus encouraged more participation, more multivocality, since some 'interpretation' was required in the writing up of context records. Interpretation was put more in the hands of the person excavating – at the trowel's edge. The technique also has the effect of allowing a flexibility in the building up of wider plans and phases. These higher level entities can be defined and redefined in terms of combining and recombining the individual context information. They allow the higher level entities to be deconstructed and rebuilt rather than being fixed and determining. In these various ways, 'single context recording' encourages a variety of interpretation at different levels. It has its disadvantages if one is searching for a fully interpretive approach. In particular, single context planning produces plans in which units of earth are decontextualized, shown separated from other units around them. The approach allows a flexibility in the fitting together of units into larger contexts, and in this sense it foregrounds and opens up the excavation and recording process. But at the same time it provides a method which is codified so that the 'context sheets' can be entered into computerized data bases.

Another attempted step towards fluidity is to introduce categories into the recording system which promote interpretation in the field. For example, many archaeologists in Britain now use a recording event, context or unit category termed a 'cut'. This is used to describe the past event of removal of soil (for example in digging a pit or ditch or wall foundation) before infill. The existence of such a category helps to encourage the excavator to decide on interpretations of events in the field. For example, a boundary between floors can be interpreted in a number of different ways – was one floor simply placed on another, or is there evidence of a cut – either a truncation by recutting before the upper floor was laid, or a wearing away of the lower floor during use?

It might be objected that terms like 'cut' are too rigid and do not encourage a wide range of interpretations. The problem with allowing a wide range of interpretive descriptions on record sheets is that it complicates later computerized search and retrieval. It may thus be better to have a hierarchy of terms from the very general and codified to the more specific and idiosyncratic. For example, it may be helpful to have on context sheets an 'event' category, which can be subdivided into 'positive' events (such as building a wall, filling in a pit) and 'negative' events (such as cutting or wearing away), themselves divided into different types such as (positive) room fill, natural layer, midden and (negative) recut, erosion, wear. These lower-level terms may be more in need of redefinition and reinterpretation during the post-excavation process. In these ways, the excavator is encouraged to make interpretations at a range of different levels.

But the remaining problem is that large amounts of data have to be handled so that a certain amount of codification is needed. After all if two very similar layers were called 'midden' on one recording sheet and 'dump' on another, or if freedom is allowed in the use of idiosyncratic labels, later computerized retrieval of information might be very difficult. Large scale projects which develop over time need to keep tabs on what has been excavated. The knowledge needs to be easily available and retrievable.

This tension between coding and interpretation will be discussed further in chapter 7, but tackling this problem is at the core of any attempt to introduce a fully reflexive method. This is because the coded form (the 'context sheet', the 'locus form') bears little relation to the process of excavation. It records what archaeologists think they have found. It assumes objective data set apart from the process of discovery. For example, the form in figure 5.6 contains no information whatso-ever about how the context was excavated. The forms hang in the ether, 'objective' accounts of what was 'observed'. They are often largely filled in after the excavation of a particular unit or locus has been completed. They provide an interpretation of what was seen, but separate from what was done. In fact, however, what was seen is related to what was done. The interpretation of a unit or locus depends on how that unit was excavated. The description of what was 'objectively' there develops within a process of working at the soil. What is found depends on how the archaeologist searches and works. The 'objective' data emerge within a process of discovery.

Thus, rather than locus forms and context sheets which purport to record what was found, it is important to embed claims about the observed record within the narrative of discovery (for one attempt to deal with this issue see Bender et al. 1997). Ideally, archaeologists should write narratives as they dig, describing what part of a feature they dug first and why, what serendipitous problems they met, 'what happened next', so that data and conclusions can be set within the process of archaeological activity, not separated from it. Many field recording forms do already include contextual information such as weather conditions, implements used, date, and so on. There is the opportunity, therefore, for a fuller account, with narratives replacing or adding to forms.

Retrieval of information from such narrative accounts would provide a major challenge, and some groups of archaeologists are today experimenting with possible solutions. Some of these solutions may involve new technologies (see chapter 7), such as photographic or video records linked to spoken narratives which are digitized into a data base. Alternatively, it may be possible to link data forms to diary narratives (see chapter 7). Another possibility may be to provide lists of keywords or key topics that must be included in excavation narratives and which then allow computerized search and retrieval. One way or another, the writing of narratives rather than the filling in of forms may become, or return as, a central focus of archaeological data gathering.

Other practical steps to achieve greater participation and openness have been experimented with at the Turkish Neolithic site of Çatalhöyük (see Hodder 1997 and box on p. 119). As on many 'excavations abroad', it is necessary for many of the non-field project specialists to be present on site. But it is possible to turn this necessity into a virtue and have ceramic, faunal, lithic, archaeobotanical, micromorphological etc. specialists present within excavation trenches and taking part in the primary interpretive process. This interaction is achieved by tours and individual visits every one or two days, and it is now planned to have primary processing of faunal remains and perhaps other artifact categories in the excavation area rather than in the field laboratory. The aim of all this interaction across specialisms is twofold. The first purpose is to contextualize specialist information within the particular characteristics of the site. Thus, rather than assuming what burned bone looks like universally, the identification of burned bone can be informed by the interpretation of context. For example, if the bone comes from a deposit which is, on other evidence, heavily burned, then it too is more likely to have been burned. In this way, general knowledge about what burned bone looks like can be accommodated to specific evidence for burning at Çatalhöyük. The second purpose of the tours is to empower and inform members of the excavation team by surrounding them with information. Thus, the more that is known about the artifacts as they come out of the ground, the more is immediate interpretation facilitated. In this way methods and recording techniques can be adjusted. This type of interaction may often be difficult because it involves breaking down barriers and boundaries between field and laboratory expertise. In some contexts it may involve conflict between field professionals and academic or laboratory personnel. But the end result is beneficial in that excavation and sampling strategies can be enhanced by an informed interpretation of what is being excavated and sampled. On small scale projects, similar integrative effects may be obtained by merging the roles of non-field and field specialists. For example, faunal specialists may be involved in field excavation, at least on a part-time basis, and increasingly field staff seek training in other areas of professional expertise.

A good example of the beneficial effects of this type of interaction on site is the following, again from Çatalhöyük. During the excavation of a cut feature which had vertical sides, the excavators suddenly began to worry that perhaps they were taking out the wrong deposits. They began to feel that 'perhaps we have got the whole thing the wrong way round' – they were worried that rather than digging out the fill of a large pit, they were actually digging out the deposits into which the pit had been dug. Now in such a situation it would help the excavators to know *as they dig* what the relative date of the pottery in the two contexts is. In fact, the ceramic specialist initially thought that the pottery in the supposed pit was earlier (Level VIII pottery) than what it was dug into (Level VII pottery). So the doubts of the excavators were initially strengthened. In the end everything came right and both sides decided that the excavators had been correct in the first place. The ceramics were redated and the two sets of data coincided – a satisfactory 'whole' was created.

The destabilization of taken-for-granted assumptions and the critique of universal codes is also encouraged at Çatalhöyük by the presence in the field team of an anthropologist whose concern is to study the various aspects of the context of production of knowledge. Carolyn Hamilton worked with us during the 1996 and 1997 field seasons and used participation techniques to try and expose some of the assumptions we were making, some of the contradictions we were not facing, and some of the potential for alternative interpretation. Hamilton's aim has been to participate in and contribute to the excavation process and her presence quickly came to be far from marginal. Her work interdigitated with ours so completely that very many of our interpretive and methodological ideas ended up deriving from discussion with her. The presence of a team member dedicated to questioning leads to a greater understanding of the processes in which we are engaged. The

Figure 5.5 Circulating knowledge at the trowel's edge at Çatalhöyük. Those discussing the interpretation of a layer in Building 2 include the excavator (in trench), excavators from other parts of the site, archaeobotanists, micromorphologist, faunal specialist, lithic specialist, and a member of the video documentation crew.

anthropological work not only makes the account of the production of knowledge (for example, on video or in diaries, see chapter 7) by team members more complete. It also means that the knowledge itself is informed by a greater awareness of alternative interpretations. Hamilton also had a privileged access into our thoughts through individual interviews and was able to point out for us parallels and comparisons between team members. Again communication and interactivity were enhanced. The benefits to the project are tangible both in terms of results and working relations.

Recursive Archaeology

One way of summarizing the approaches described above is to say that they involve a move from a linear to a recursive, reflexive or circular process. Most discussions of archaeological field methodology describe it as a linear process. For example, Renfrew and Bahn (1996, 106–7) refer to the step-by-step methods adopted by the Museum of London.

Reproduced here in figure 5.6, this scheme appears as mechanical. The linearity of such schemes is made possible by the assumption that description can and should be separated from interpretation. But in practice a much more complex process hides behind this linear formalization. Sharer and Ashmore (1993) generally describe field methodology as a sequence of retrieval-recording-analysis-interpretation. But they also point out that processing and classification are best done while fieldwork is still going on. This allows the archaeologist to look at the data as they are coming out of the ground and to suggest areas or problems on which to concentrate. For example, there may be evidence of a little-known period on which excavation could focus.

I have argued in the same vein that it is false to claim that description can be separated from interpretation. The result of this argument is that I have tried to describe mechanisms in this chapter which allow for a complex process of feedback, interaction, and circularity. Ideally, the aim is to circulate around different types of data, continually adjusting one type of data in terms of the others until a satisfactory argument has been built. Figure 5.7 is an attempt to capture this process in terms of a diagram. The procedures keep returning back on themselves. Loops occur within loops. Excavation of one unit takes place in relation to the excavation of other units, all of which takes place within the wider context of changing understanding of the site as a whole.

Figure 3.3 expressed a similar point about a still wider context. Here the excavation of a causewayed enclosure site at Haddenham in eastern England (chapter 3) is part of a spiral of knowledge which extends outwards to the region and to more general and theoretical understanding of, for example, ritual and social organization. Archaeological research is a complex, multistranded and multiscalar process. Its path ways and outcomes are unpredictable. There is continual flow and transformation.

Conclusion

This chapter has sought to enhance the ways in which archaeological reasoning is diverse, fluid and non-dichotomous. In particular, it has focused on archaeological practice and method. In the area of field methods a contradiction was observed between what archaeologists say in theory about practice and what they do in practice. In earlier chapters I had argued that in practice archaeologists use a diverse set

CONTEXT RECORDING SHEET / **MUSEUM OF LONDON**

| Grid Square(s) 110 – 115 / 210 | Area/Section B | Context type DEPOSIT | Site Code XYZ | 89 | Context 138 |

DEPOSIT
1. Compaction
2. Colour
3. Composition / Particle size (over 10%)
4. Inclusions (under 10%) occa / mod / freq
5. Thickness & extent
6. Other comments
7. Method & conditions

1) VARIES FROM LOOSE TO COMPACT
2) DARK GREYISH BROWN
3) SAND (40%) SILT (60%)
4) FREQUENT LARGE FRAGMENTS OF POTTERY AND TILE ; FREQUENT MEDIUM AND SMALL FRAGMENTS OF BONE , OCCASIONAL MEDIUM AND SMALL FRAGMENTS OF LEATHER, SMALL FRAGMENTS METAL , AND WHOLE OYSTER SHELLS (ALL INCLUSIONS WELL SORTED)
5) THICKEST AT NORTH (25mm) SLOPING DOWN TO THE SOUTH / EAST (10mm) THE LOWER BOUNDARY TO THE NEXT HORIZON IS IRREGULAR
6) OCCASIONAL LENSES OF ORGANIC MATERIAL
7) WEATHER DRY , EXCAVATED WITH MATTOCK.

PTO

CUT
1. Shape in plan
2. Corners
3. Dimensions/Depth
4. Break of slope- top
5. Sides
6. Break of slope- base
7. Base
8. Orientation
9. Inclination of axis
10. Truncated (if known)
11. Fill nos
12. Other comments
Draw profile overleaf

Stratigraphic matrix

| 121 | 135 | | | | | | | | |

This context is | 138 |

| 154 | 157 | 148 | | | | | | | |

Your interpretation : Internal (External) Structural Other (specify)
A DUMPED DEPOSIT , (PROBABLY REFUSE)

Your discussion :
LARGE QUANTITY OF POTTERY AND BONE PLUS OTHER MATERIAL , AND WELL SORTED NATURE SUGGEST IT IS A DUMP OF REFUSE MATERIAL.
(MIGHT BE ASSOCIATED WITH STRUCTURE [95])?

Context same as :   PTO

Plan nos : P 138 (X 2)	Site book refs	Initials & date NH 24/8/89
Other drawings : S/E	Matrix location : C3	Checked by & date SP 2/9/89
Photographs : ☐ Card nos :		

Levels on reverse
Tick when reduced and transferred to plans : ☑
Highest :   Lowest :

Finds (tick)

| None | Pot | Bone | Glass | Metal | CBM | Other BM | Wood | Leather |
| ☐ | ☑ | ☑ | ☐ | ☑ | ☑ | ☐ | ☐ | ☑ |

Environmental samples
Sample nos & type : ②③ BULK SAMPLE FOR SIEVING – FISH BONES etc.

Other finds (specify) : 1 WHOLE CERAMIC VESSEL
Finds sample (BM) nos :

Checked interpretation :

PTO

| Provisional period | Group | | Initials & date |

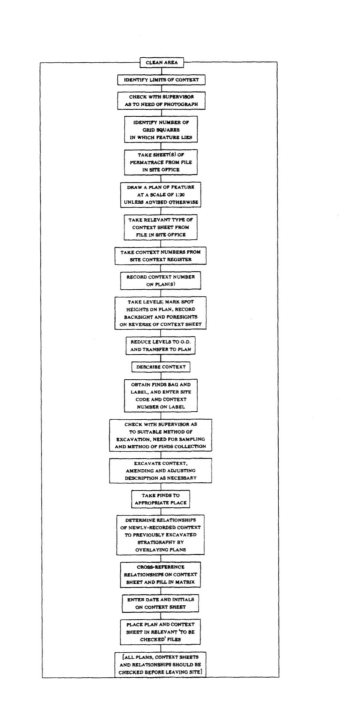

CLEAN AREA

IDENTIFY LIMITS OF CONTEXT

CHECK WITH SUPERVISOR
AS TO NEED OF PHOTOGRAPH

IDENTIFY NUMBER OF
GRID SQUARES
IN WHICH FEATURE LIES

TAKE SHEET(S) OF
PERMATRACE FROM FILE
IN SITE OFFICE

DRAW A PLAN OF FEATURE
AT A SCALE OF 1:20
UNLESS ADVISED OTHERWISE

TAKE RELEVANT TYPE OF
CONTEXT SHEET FROM
FILE IN SITE OFFICE

TAKE CONTEXT NUMBERS FROM
SITE CONTEXT REGISTER

RECORD CONTEXT NUMBER
ON PLAN(S)

TAKE LEVELS; MARK SPOT
HEIGHTS ON PLAN, RECORD
BACKSIGHT AND FORESIGHTS
ON REVERSE OF CONTEXT SHEET

REDUCE LEVELS TO O.D.
AND TRANSFER TO PLAN

DESCRIBE CONTEXT

OBTAIN FINDS BAG AND
LABEL, AND ENTER SITE
CODE AND CONTEXT
NUMBER ON LABEL

CHECK WITH SUPERVISOR AS
TO SUITABLE METHOD OF
EXCAVATION, NEED FOR SAMPLING
AND METHOD OF FINDS COLLECTION

EXCAVATE CONTEXT,
AMENDING AND ADJUSTING
DESCRIPTION AS NECESSARY

TAKE FINDS TO
APPROPRIATE PLACE

DETERMINE RELATIONSHIPS
OF NEWLY-RECORDED CONTEXT
TO PREVIOUSLY EXCAVATED
STRATIGRAPHY BY
OVERLAYING PLANS

CROSS-REFERENCE
RELATIONSHIPS ON CONTEXT
SHEET AND FILL IN MATRIX

ENTER DATE AND INITIALS
ON CONTEXT SHEET

PLACE PLAN AND CONTEXT
SHEET IN RELEVANT 'TO BE
CHECKED' FILES

[ALL PLANS, CONTEXT SHEETS
AND RELATIONSHIPS SHOULD BE
CHECKED BEFORE LEAVING SITE]

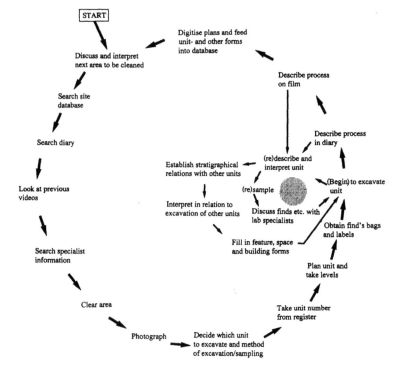

Figure 5.7   The recursive excavation process used at Çatalhöyük.

of strategies in the field and laboratory. These methods were summarized in chapters 3 and 4 as hermeneutic and interactive. But in what they say in theory about practice, archaeologists often paint a very different picture. Rather than accepting a non-dichotomous account, they argue that the theory-ladenness of facts can be overcome by objective methods. They erect a subject/object opposition and emphasize the importance of codification and standardization at the expense of sensitivity to context and question.

In response to these contradictions, this chapter and this book so far have suggested the following arguments.

1   It is important to accept and no longer ignore in practice the widely agreed theoretical point that interpretation is involved in the construction of data. Data description and interpretation cannot be radically separated in practice. Much of archaeology is not an experimental science and we can rarely test theories against data. Rather we construct interpretations in a fitting process.

2   Meaning is relational – everything depends on everything else, as when stratigraphic relationships partly depend on the dating of artifacts and vice versa. The parts are understood in relation to the whole and the whole is constructed from the parts.

3   Meaning is both general and local. The faunal specialist with a wide range of general knowledge about what burnt bone looks like might still say 'we need to find out what burnt bone looks like at this particular site'. We should not impose codes insensitive to context.

4   Emphasis has to be returned to the point of excavation. The excavator should not be seen as a technician. The person excavating should have the fullest possible knowledge and the widest range of possible narratives. No one else can ever have the same opportunity to deal with the tension of interpretation and data. This emphasis on the act of digging is essential because (a) excavation is destructive, (b) the method of excavation used depends on interpretation. What you find partly depends on your interpretation of what you are going to find.

Some will argue that I am simply advocating relativism (see boxes on pp. 23 and 159), that I am claiming that there is no objectivity at the level of data collection, and that this chapter is just a pernicious extension of postprocessual ideas into a realm which has been happily free from subjectivity and interpretive bias. Certainly I am arguing that interpretation occurs at all levels of archaeological enquiry. I hope I have demonstrated clearly enough that interpretation is not something which happens after description. It cannot be marginalized and ghettoized in ivory towers. It happens at the trowel's edge.

Complaints about the introduction of subjectivity into an objective area of archaeological work are caught within the object/subject opposition which has been so well critiqued by Rowlands (1984; see also Lampeter Archaeology Workshop 1997). In fact, as we have seen repeatedly already in this book, 'objectivity' is always framed within questions and theories. To say that data are objective is not to say that they are beyond argument, dispute or reinterpretation. It is only to say that they provide evidence to support a theory. This is not to deny that, looked at from another (subjective) point of view, the data could also provide (objective) evidence of alternative theories.

I was very struck by an example of this during the 1996 season at Çatalhöyük. In the field sections or profiles we observed what we termed 'faultlines'. These appeared as discontinuities in horizontally layered walls or floors where one block of layers had slipped down-wards. What had caused these diagonal fault lines (Hamilton 1996)? Three interpretations were developed. One view was that they had been caused by earthquakes. Evidence in support of this view was the existence of earthquakes in the area and the clean nature of the fault lines themselves. Another view was that the slippage occurred during construction of the walls. The evidence for this was that the 'bricks' were often over 1 metre in length and were very thin and irregular. They must have been made *in situ* on the walls, the clay put on wet between wooden boarding. Perhaps the boards were sometimes taken off too early, causing slippage. The third interpretation was that the faults were caused by pressure from leaning walls and roofs. The evidence for this argument was that at least in one case the walls in question could be shown to have moved far from the vertical. This would have exerted enormous pressure and fault lines. Proponents of each interpretation would argue their case passionately. And each would use evidence in ways which they saw as objective and un-problematic. Each would say 'can't you see, it's so obvious'. Each wanted to use the fault lines as unambiguous evidence of their theory. In the injunction 'look! can't you see' appeal was being made to an assumed objectivity. When in fact what was happening was that the world was being perceived *as evidence* for something – that is both as objectively there and as subjectively constituted.

And this is my claim generally in this chapter and in this book. In clawing back interpretation into the data construction process I do not assert that 'all the data are subjective' or that 'archaeology can only be relativist' or 'anything goes'. Far from it. What is needed is a redefini-tion of the debate. Rather than subject versus object the central issue is the use of data as evidence for interpretation.

6   The Natural Sciences in Archaeology

Scientific analysis is often opposed to interpretive archaeology. As was discussed in the first three chapters in this book, it is possible to argue for a diversity of approach within the discipline. Positivist, experimental approaches closely allied to the natural sciences are part of this diversity, as are hermeneutic, interpretive approaches allied to the humanities, and empiricist, realist, dialectical or pragmatist accounts. In this chapter I want to pursue further the distinction between interpretive and natural science approaches. The couching of this dichotomy in terms of a single and double hermeneutic (p. 25), implies that at some level both approaches can be described in hermeneutic terms. I wish to explore further the differences and similarities between the two approaches and to incorporate, rather than to marginalize, natural science methods within a diverse interpretive archaeology.

I wish to start with the example of geology. This is especially apt as an example of the role of the natural sciences within archaeology because historically archaeology in the nineteenth century modelled itself on geology. As Daniel (1962) has fully documented, the geological sciences were central in the establishment of the antiquity of stone tools in river gravels in Europe. These sciences also played an important part in establishing key archaeological concepts such as stratigraphy. 'Nor does there appear to be any reason why those methods of examination which have proved so successful in geology, should not also be used to throw light on the history of man in prehistoric times' (Lubbock 1865, 2).

It is also an apt example because geology and the earth sciences still play such a central role in archaeology, for example in the study of cave sediments, in the sourcing of stone axes, in geophysical prospection, and in geoarchaeology as a whole. There are several apparent similarities between archaeology and geology. They have similar foundational 'laws', particularly those of uniformity and superposition. Both have similar problems – especially incompleteness of data and gaps and poor resolution in the stratigraphic record; a lack of experimental control; and enormous time spans so that direct observation is difficult or impossible.

It may thus come as a surprise to archaeologists that Frodeman (1995) describes geology as a hermeneutic science. To anyone who has prized open the thin layers of schist rock looking for fossils, the notion that the geological record is 'read' like a book will make sense. Frodeman argues that geology follows hermeneutic principles (see box on p. 32) because examining an outcrop is not simply a matter of 'taking a good look' (ibid., 963). Rather, the geologist has to read or interpret the outcrop by assigning values to various aspects of the outcrop, judging which are significant and which are not. A geological student has to be taught to make sense of clues of past events and processes. In terms of the *hermeneutic circle*, understanding of the outcrop (the whole) is based on an understanding of the individual beds (the parts), which are in turn made sense of in terms of their relationship to the whole outcrop. The importance of *pre-judgements* is also clear in geology. 'To approach the Western Cordillera with concepts like *ophiolite complexes* and *accretionary terrains* will affect what one sees in the field' (Frodeman 1995, 964). Geology is a *historical science* like cosmology, palaeontology and human history. The historical nature of these enquiries derives from three factors.

First, since the pre-judgements have an influence on (though they do not determine) what is discovered by geologists, it follows that geologists at different historical moments will ask different questions and come to different conclusions. Their results are historically situated. Second, laboratory experiment can have a limited role in the discipline. As Latour and Woolgar (1986) have shown, even in the experimental sciences such as physics and chemistry, social and historical factors play a role. But the aim in experimenting with, for example, chemical reactions is not to describe specific historical conditions that affect a particular reaction, but rather to create an ideal and general situation. Thus the chemicals used have been assayed for purity. Each chemical reaction is seen as an instance of a general principle. But in geology, at least part of the enterprise is to chronicle the particular events that occurred at a given location. Geologists do identify general laws (e.g. Walther's law) but at least part of the interest is in individual outcrops or events (the Western Interior Seaway, the lifespan of a species). Because of the singularity of these events, hypotheses are not testable. 'Although the geologist may be able to duplicate the laboratory conditions of another's experiment (e.g. studying the nature of deformation through experiments with play-doh), the relationship of these experiments to the particularities of Earth's history (eg the Idaho-Wyoming overthrust belt) remains uncertain' (Frodeman 1995, 965). Rather than using only experiment and modeling, geologists also support arguments by using other strategies common in the historical sciences, such as reasoning by analogy. Uniformitarianism assumes that present-day geologic processes operate in a manner similar to those in the past. Despite changes in the way geologists view principles of uniformity (Gould and Lewontin 1979), arguments by analogy with the present remain important.

A third historical aspect of geological enquiry concerns the centrality of narrative. As in human history, geologists define entities, themes or ideas around which data can be organized. Examples are the Laramide orogeny, the Cretaceous Western Interior Seaway, the Bridge Creek Limestone, and the species *Mytiloides mytiloides* (Frodeman 1995, 966). These central themes provide the coherence necessary for an intelligible narrative to be built out of seemingly disconnected events. Geologists do not simply work by subsuming events under predictive generalizations. Rather, they try to integrate events into organized wholes which have an overall structure or story. So the examination of the Greenland Ice Sheet Project ice core is explained and justified by our concern with global climate change, and the study of black shales is funded because of the larger narrative of its relevance to hydrocarbon exploration.

In conclusion, Frodeman argues that while geology depends in part on the deductive-nomological methods of the experimental sciences, it should not be seen simply as using a lesser or derivative version of the mode of reasoning found in physics. Instead geological reasoning provides an outstanding model of the techniques of hermeneutics and history. Geologists use a variety of techniques to solve their problems.

As our understanding of the social component of laboratory work progresses (e.g. Latour and Woolgar 1986) it becomes possible to situate the natural sciences within the contextual archaeological enterprise. Archaeological science need not be seen as a separate and foreign sphere. Indeed, in the practices of archaeological research, different types of data are played off against each other all the time in order to achieve a coherent interpretation. Thus, radiocarbon dates are evaluated in terms of whether they make sense in terms of cultural sequence. 'Outliers' are rejected unless some special case can be argued. The history of the impact of radiocarbon dating on European prehistory (e.g. Renfrew 1973) is replete with examples of archaeologists reluctant to accept the new dates until gradually they could be accommodated to a new understanding of the overall culture-historical framework. Maps of phosphate or magnetic susceptibility values on sites have to be examined closely to see whether they are indicating depositional, or post-depositional processes or just 'noise'. The maps are made sense of in terms of a wide range of information dealing with architecture and artifact distributions. For example, does spatial variation in phosphate values correlate with other evidence for the use of space in terms of activity areas, stables, burials and so on? At one level it is simply a matter of integrating scientific and cultural information to make a coherent argument. At another level it is a matter of deciding whether 'the data' make sufficient sense to be accepted and published as data.

I now wish to provide some more specific examples of the ways in which natural science data are part of the same archaeological process of interpretive reflexivity as cultural data. Of course, the distinction here between the natural sciences and the humanities can itself be subjected to scrutiny. It can be argued that our understanding of the natural world is itself culturally mediated. Archaeology, in the following examples, demonstrates this fluidity between the natural and humanistic sciences more clearly than many disciplines.

Geoarchaeology and Harris matrices

In chapter 1 I introduced the problem of how to define 'layers'. These and their boundaries are often taken for granted in archaeology. Of course, there are problems of 'splitting or lumping', but once the decision has been taken to lump lenses into a layer or to split a layer into smaller lenses or layers, it is assumed that the further description of stratigraphic units is objective and routine. The identification of the layer (or unit, context, locus, or spit) is the primary building block of the recording process in archaeology. It is according to these units that

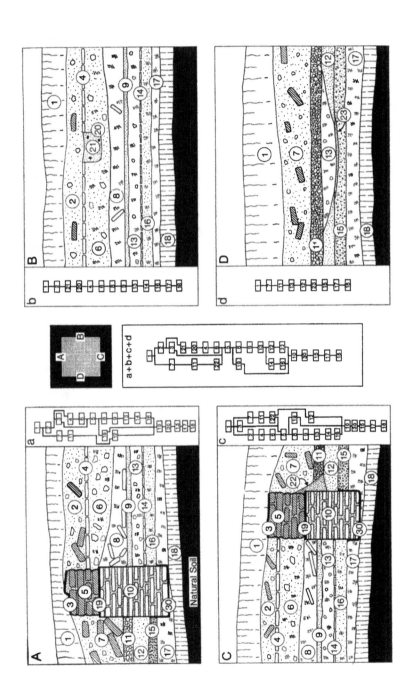

Figure 6.1 The illustration used by Harris (1989) to show how the stratigraphic sequence of a site may be gradually constructed from all the stratigraphic evidence. A stratigraphic sequence is made from each side of a trench (A, B, C, D) and then combined to form the overall sequence.

artifacts are retrieved, soils recorded and analysis and comparison undertaken. For example, the building of a Harris matrix (e.g. figure 6.1) is dependent on the assumption that the primary recording units as identified in the field have a stratigraphic integrity (Harris 1989).

Barham (1995), however, points out that we cannot take for granted the layers and their boundaries as viewed by eye in the field. Most routine description of stratigraphy is visual and therefore restricted to the recording of properties within the visible light spectrum (electromagnetic wavelengths of 0.4–0.7 micrometres (μm)) and with resolutions limited by the unaided eye to about 60 microns. The Harris matrix is built up in terms of this particular perspective. There are now techniques available to archaeologists which allow the recording of layers and stratigraphies across a far wider range of electromagnetic radiation wavelengths. Such techniques include sampling of undisturbed deposits to allow analysis in terms of micromorphology, sediment geochemistry, mineral magnetic susceptibility measures, particle size, and so on. Figure 6.2 gives some indication of the full range of wavelengths which could be applied.

Thus on the one hand, a wide range of techniques is available for exploring stratigraphies at a range of wavelengths. These techniques

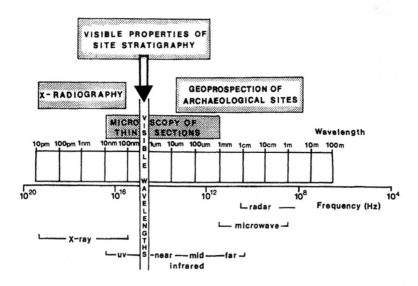

Figure 6.2 Electro-magnetic radiation wavelengths utilized by techniques commonly applied to archaeological sediment context recording, micro-analysis and site geoprospection (Barham 1995, 148).

have been very productive as, for example, in the use of magnetic techniques for sediment description and context interpretation (Barham 1995, 149). The analysis of spectra within thermal wavelengths has allowed the production of age-estimates from Thermoluminescence (TL). On the other hand, the field archaeologist struggles to describe stratigraphy with the eye and with a limited number of aids such as Munsell soil colour charts and soil description manuals. The archaeological data as defined by the visible properties of stratigraphy differ from those defined at other wavelengths. In this case the application of techniques from the natural sciences reinforces the hermeneutic point that the data change when looked at from different perspectives.

There is no problem here as long as the data from analyses at different wavelengths produce compatable results. But very often it may be difficult in the field to determine whether the interfaces between layers or contexts are the result of primary depositional processes or of post-depositional factors (Schiffer 1987). The latter may include decalcification, redox changes, clay translocation or bioturbation. It may only be possible to identify such processes after analysis at wavelengths undetectable by the archaeologist working in the field. Layers and their sequences may be incorrectly defined and inappropriate sampling procedures may be used. The analyses necessary in order to identify such post-depositional problems often take place after excavation in laboratory contexts. But the Harris matrix describing stratigraphical relationships is often left unchanged. 'Re-ordering the matrix to account for such problems, through integration of data from later analyses...is normally omitted' (Barham 1995, 155).

The need, then, is to integrate analyses of a wider range of wavelengths in the excavation process so that a more fully recursive or integrated interpretation can take place. The scientific analyses do not lead to the conclusion that archaeological enquiry is a linear process of theory testing and data acquisition. Rather, we see that different perspectives have to be integrated at all stages. One aid to the problem of defining layers in the field is X-radiography (Barham 1995). X-radiographs are produced by passing X-rays through a specimen (an undisturbed sediment sample produced from a core or monolith) onto photographic film. This is a relatively quick and cheap process and so can be undertaken in the field and can contribute to the primary definition of layers and their boundaries and interfaces. Barham (1995, 168) provides examples of the application of the technique in the field. In some instances the rate and nature of deposition can be inferred and the degree of bioturbation. Laminations and banding invisible to the naked eye can be discerned. Field results such as these not only contribute to the identification and interpretation of layers. They also allow decisions to be made about sampling strategies, for example for pollen and diatoms.

X-radiography of sediments on archaeological sites thus helps to provide a wider range of perspectives in the identification and interpretation of layers and their interfaces. Rather than occurring at a late, 'lab' stage of analysis, and rather than being insufficiently incorporated into Harris matrices, geoarchaeological information can be included in a primary phase of the very construction of data (the layers and their boundaries). It can be involved recursively in a hermeneutic process.

Other examples: soils, wood and sex

Micromorphology (e.g. Matthews et al. 1996) has come to be an essential aid to the understanding of prehistoric soils and sediments. Its use on complex tell sites in the Near East has led to an ability to differentiate between a wide range of activities in different types of spaces (ibid.). One such use of this technique is demonstrated in table 6.1. Here field observations of stratigraphies within buildings are related to micromorphological observations of the same stratigraphies and to interpretations of space. But it is important to recognize that the interpretations of the use of space which are informed by the micromorphological analyses are also dependent on the archaeological evidence for the use of spaces and features. Thus, extremely clean floors can be interpreted as clean/? ritual spaces partly because of the presence on the floors of *Bos* jaw and horn cores and moulded sculptures. Similarly, the interpretation of floors with charred wood and cereal grain as for burning and cooking activities is helped by the presence of a fire installation (hearth or oven). In another example, some micromorphology thin sections from floors at Çatalhöyük were interpreted as indicating puddling. This interpretation was undoubtedly influenced by the fact that the floors in question were placed immediately below the hole in the roof which allowed people, but also rain, to enter. The interpretation of micromorphology evidence is also dependent on ethnographic observations so that knowledge can be built up of the range of activities which leave behavioural signatures in micro-stratigraphies. Overall, the technique of micromorphology is used within a circular and multi-stranded interpretive process in which cultural and natural information play an equal and integrated role.

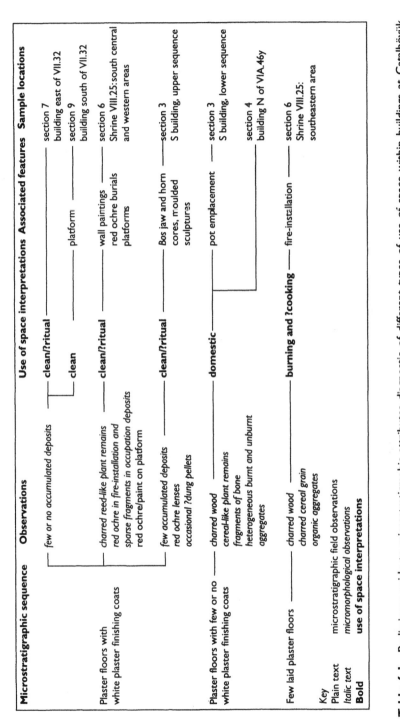

Microstratigraphic sequence	Observations	Use of space interpretations	Associated features	Sample locations
Plaster floors with white plaster finishing coats	*few or no accumulated deposits*	**clean/?ritual**		section 7 building east of VII.32
		clean	platform	section 9 building south of VII.32
	charred reed-like plant remains red ochre in fire-installation and sparse fragments in occupation deposits red ochre/paint on platform	**clean/?ritual**	wall paintings red ochre burials platforms	section 6 Shrine VIII.25:south central and western areas
	few accumulated deposits red ochre lenses occasional ?dung pellets	**clean/?ritual**	Bos jaw and horn cores, moulded sculptures	section 3 S building, upper sequence
Plaster floors with few or no white plaster finishing coats	*charred wood cereal-like plant remains fragments of bone heterogeneous burnt and unburnt aggregates*	**domestic**	pot emplacement	section 3 S building, lower sequence section 4 building N of VIA.46y
Few laid plaster floors	*charred wood charred cereal grain organic aggregates*	**burning and ?cooking**	fire-installation	section 6 Shrine VIII.25: southeastern area

Key
Plain text   microstratigraphic field observations
Italic text   *micromorphological observations*
Bold   **use of space interpretations**

Table 6.1 Preliminary guide to microstratigraphic attributes diagnostic of different types of use of space within buildings at Çatalhöyük (Matthews et al. 1996).

Another example of the importance of integration is wood analysis based on charcoal identification. On the one hand, this technique can be used for palaeoenvironmental and palaeoecological reconstruction (e.g. Davis 1983). On the other hand, it can be used for understanding social and cultural practices and preferences (e.g. Hastorf and Johannessen 1991). But in fact the two aspects of the ancient use of wood are interdependent. Environmental study focuses on variation in species representation through time. But this would be undermined if there were also contextual variations. For example, if the samples for palaeoenvironmental reconstruction come from hearths and house fill and midden – much of the variation in species would be contextual. Equally, however, it is no use talking about cultural selection of wood unless there is some understanding of the availability of such wood-sources in the local or regional environment. In order to understand the environment one needs to understand cultural variation, and in order to understand cultural patterning one needs to know the environment.

Finally, I would like to take the example of sexing human remains. Archaeologists have tended to assume that biological sex should be differentiated from cultural gender (Gero and Conkey 1991; Gibbs 1987). This position has come under scrutiny because of the widespread historical and ethnographic evidence that different societies and people categorize sex differently (Knapp and Meskell 1997). Geneticists have come to recognize that a simple opposition between XX (female) and XY (male) is difficult to maintain. Individuals exist with XX, XXY, XXXY and XXXXY chromosomes. There is actually a continuum of chromosomal variation and a range of different criteria such as genes and sexual organs that do not necessarily coincide in identifying a simple binary opposition (Knapp and Meskell 1997). Yates (1993) provides ethnographic examples of societies in which the sexual organs are not regarded as directly determining the sex of a child. He also refers to Lacan (1977) and Deleuze and Guattari (1984) in arguing that our conceptions of a natural biological difference between male and female are cultural-linguistic constructs. Historical perspectives are provided by Foucault (1981) and Laqueur (1990).

Many archaeologists in earlier generations will have had lingering doubts that the sexing of human remains was objective and straightforward because of the apparent ability of human remains specialists to tailor their sex identifications to whether the artifacts associated with a body in a grave were 'male' weapons or 'female' ornament. More recently, however, clear criteria have been developed for discerning sexual difference on the basis of human remains (e.g. Brothwell 1981; Calgano 1981; Schutkowski 1993), and distinctions are made between sexual dimorphism (in size etc.) and secondary sexual characteristics (Garn et al. 1967; Molleson 1994). The criteria used include skull and dental variation, the size and robustness of the vertebral column, sternum, clavicle, scapula and long bones, and various characteristics of the pelvis such as the angle of the sciatic notch. Many of these criteria concern size, robustness and degrees of variation in form rather than absolute dichotomies. Indeed, Brothwell (1981, 59) points out that the features used to identify the sex of an individual vary with the group being studied (see also Molleson 1994; Thieme 1957). The degree of supraorbital development used to identify European males is found in a number of females among Australian aborigines. Equally, the robustness of female Australian aboriginal bones may be far greater than is generally found in male pygmies. Even within a population group there is considerable overlap in the range of measurements found in the two sexes.

It is possible that people in the past used different criteria to identify sex from those used in the West today, and even that the criteria varied according to age or status. For example, perhaps different sexual criteria were used to define a high status man versus a high status woman than were used to define a low status man. It is certainly possible that more or less male men (on certain criteria) were treated differently. There would thus be advantages in going beyond the simple description of human bodies as male or female. It would be interesting to divide the human remains into more or less male men and more or less female women. It would then be possible to see whether these differences correlated with cultural evidence in the graves. Is there any evidence that robust men were treated differently from gracile men?

But such an approach would still leave the (natural science) identification of the sex of the human remains separated from the (cultural) interpretation of social roles. A more thorough integration of the natural science and humanity approaches would be to include cultural information into the very definition of biological sex. A good example of the interaction between biological and cultural information is the work by Molleson (1994) on the nineteenth-century Spitalfields remains. For these individuals, there are historical records and names from which the cultural attribution of sex can be discerned. This helped Molleson to evaluate her analytical techniques.

It would be possible to study human remains from prehistoric and other contexts in a non-dichotomous way. Rather than first carrying out a 'pure' biological analysis which is then compared to the cultural inventories from graves, it would be possible to introduce the cultural information from the beginning. In this way the analysts can 'read themselves into' a particular population and discover the idiosyncratic ways in which sex was constructed. Of course, it cannot be assumed that the artifact inventories in graves are themselves divided rigidly by sex. Neither the biological nor the cultural data provide a fixed point from which to discern sex. Rather, the process can involve fitting different types of data, working back and forth between the natural science and cultural data until the best accommodation is obtained.

Conclusion

Undoubtedly, there are differences between the different sciences and between the natural sciences, social sciences and humanities. I do not wish to downplay these. The goals and the methods differ. But when brought together in archaeology, these different methods need to work together. I have provided examples in this chapter of research in archaeology which benefits from a recognition that information from the natural sciences can be used in order to achieve a better understanding of social and cultural strategies in the past. I have suggested that the variety of scientific procedures used in archaeology can be accommodated within a generalized hermeneutic approach; by this I mean an approach in which a diversity of strands of evidence are brought together in order to construct a whole. It is often by fitting together contrasting types of evidence that a more complete overall argument can be made.

7 Using the New Information Technologies

The use of natural science techniques in archaeology does not lessen the need for an interpretive approach in which meaning is seen to be relational and diverse. If anything, the use of a wide range of natural science applications in archaeology adds to the diversity and to the recognition that the archaeological record is constructed differently when approached with different pre-understandings and with different observational tools.

One scientific instrument which has had enormous impact on the discipline is of course the computer (Reilly and Rahtz 1992). Initially, the use of large mainframe computers led to the ability to handle very large amounts of data but at the expense of a move towards fixity and codification. Thus, the initial result of the use of computers was away from relationality and diversity. The trend towards codification was enhanced by other changes in the organization of archaeology. The rise of contract archaeology has been a dominant part of this process, together with an increasing professionalization of fieldwork. The result has been an enormous rise in the codification of method and the homogenization of techniques. Accountability, costing, standards, comparability are the key concerns here.

As already noted, codification and systematization are needed in archaeology to cope with large amounts of data, to allow retrieval of data, and to allow comparison of data. But modern computers and software allow a more flexible and fluid approach. It is now possible to conceive of systems which allow retrieval and comparison of large amounts of data but which are at the same time interactive, flexible and relational. In this chapter I wish to explore some of the new technologies to see whether they allow some of the relationality, contextuality and reflexivity discussed in chapter 5.

Outline of some methodological principles

I argued in chapter 5 that an important aspect of archaeological enquiry was that interpretation played a role in the construction of primary data. What this means in practice is that archaeologists sometimes find themselves re-assigning artifacts to categories and to contexts. In the case of re-assigning objects to categories (such as 'blade' or 'flake') it is always possible to go back to the object and re-measure, or to measure new variables. But the same cannot be done for contextual information. It is not possible to go back to the soil contexts which have been destroyed in excavation. As a result, archaeologists have tended to assume that the soil context is sacrosanct, and fixed in the field. But as already noted in the example provided on p. 87, it may be desirable to return to contextual relationships in order to re-define them.

One partial solution is electronic planning and 3D recording of artifact locations and context boundaries (e.g. using Penmap). In such cases, the boundaries of contexts can later be redrawn and artifacts re-allocated to new contexts. It may also be possible to develop the use of high resolution digital photographs which can later be reconsidered and reinterpreted. Alternatively artifacts can be allocated provisionally to arbitrary groupings such as a, b, c which reflect our multiple hypotheses. The data base then records that find x could be in abc, ab, or bc. The finds can later be grouped depending on which hypothesis is preferred, or alternative data bases can be built on the basis of competing hypotheses. It is also possible using this system provisionally to allocate artifacts to clusters of artifacts which may be within or cut across soil matrix boundaries.

Çatalhöyük

Throughout this book the Neolithic site at Çatalhöyük has been used to provide examples. This is partly because it is the location of the field project currently being directed by the author. But it is also used because many of the issues discussed in this volume derive from discussions with members of the project team. The project participants have contributed significantly to the ideas in this book although they would not wish to accept any responsibility for it.

Çatalhöyük East is a 9000 year old site in central Turkey near Konya. It was first excavated by James Mellaart (1967) in the early 1960s. The site quickly received international recognition as fundamental to our understanding of early farming (especially cattle domestication), sedentism and the formation of complex societies, trade, the role of women in early mythologies and societies. In particular, its spectacular wall reliefs and wall paintings both provided an unrivalled window into Neolithic ways of life and thought, and raised questions about the role of early 'art and symbolism'.

Fieldwork restarted at the site in 1993, under the auspices of the British Institute of Archaeology at Ankara and with a permit from the Turkish Ministry of Culture. The first three years of fieldwork have been published (Hodder 1996), and more can be found out about the present research on http://catal.arch.cam.ac.uk/catal/catal.html

A similar point can be made regarding stratigraphic relations (Harris et al. 1993). As described in chapter 6, the Harris matrix approach assumes clear-cut contexts and clear-cut relations. Three-dimensional soil relationships are reduced to a simplified and codified two dimensions – there is considerable abstraction and formalization, and the only relations used are above, below, same as. But understanding the stratigraphic relationships of a context is complex – it depends on interpretation and narrative. For example, we may say this layer is equivalent to that because they are both on the same house floor even though not touching; or we say that this is earlier than that because it is a 'foundation deposit' even though we cannot see the cut; or we say this layer is equivalent to that because of a join of sherds. It is thus necessary to produce alternative stratigraphic relationships based on competing hypotheses and to annotate the different versions with explanatory accounts. In other words, it is necessary to embed the matrix of stratigraphical relations in a narrative. Chadwick (1998) suggests that more interpretive components should be added to a Harris matrix. He points to stratigraphic conundrums that do not always obey the rules established by Harris, for example fills that build up in much earlier capped drains, or pits that are dug through deposits while the latter are still forming.

As noted in chapter 5, getting information back to the excavator as quickly as possible is essential. This may be assisted by some of the currently available technologies. For example, immediate digital data input may allow the quick production of artifact distributions and plans. At Çatalhöyük (Hodder 1996) we have invested in a local, on-site computer network – the terminals of the laboratory and field staff are linked by a hub so that data sheets and plans can immediately be accessed and linked to artifact-based information. Indeed it increasingly seems necessary to have a dedicated 'data-analyst' present with the time and resources to search for relationships between different types of data so that understanding can quickly be fed back to the excavators.

Circuitry and feedback to excavators of information from large data sets can be enhanced by the new technologies. A major challenge at Çatalhöyük has been to construct a data base which allows the maximum amount of flexibility, change and interaction. The system, initially designed by Tim Ritchey and now by Anja Wolle, is a standard relational data base (initially Microsoft Access running on a Windows NT Server machine) in which all aspects of the project are entered – that is, excavation unit sheets as well as the faunal specialist records are on the same data base so that querying across from artifact to context data is facilitated. The aim here is to allow artifact categories (e.g. burned bone) to be evaluated against context information (e.g. whether a deposit or house is burned), and simultaneously to allow context categories (e.g. burned deposit) to be evaluated against artifact information (e.g. whether a bone appears burned).

Another idea is for the data base to retain multiple hypotheses in parallel so that analysis can proceed on more than one basis. For example, different parallel coding systems could be retained for objects/categories/types. Different definitions of 'storage jars' could be retained on the basis of different categorizations of shape, fabric, contents, context (storage room, pit). Analysis of the frequencies of storage jars and the interpretation of contexts could then proceed along different parallel lines depending on the different definitions of storage jars. As further examples, analysis of artifacts could proceed using different definitions of context, different cut relationships, different lumping of lenses into layers etc.

While flexibility and the erosion of the notion of fixed objective categories can perhaps be engendered in these ways, placing large amounts of information into a data base in such a way as to allow efficient retrieval and comparison will always require considerable codification and fixity. It is necessary, therefore, to embed the data base within other information which contextualizes its own production. This reflexivity not only helps us to be critical of the assumptions we make, but it also means that at future dates we or others can look back and understand why we made this or that interpretation, why we used this category or that context definition. It facilitates use of the site archive by later generations.

The contextualizing information can include more than coded forms and texts. The construction of a multimedia data base is essential if a full range of information is to be provided to a wide variety of audiences. Access provides the ability to point to different types of data through OLE, or Object Linking and Embedding. When designing the data base, the field type (e.g. video field or Autocad field) can be set as OLE object, which then gives the flexibility of including data from any OLE aware application.

One of the contextualizing types of data placed on the data base at Çatalhöyük is the diary at present kept by the site and trench directors. With more computer terminals at the site it is hoped to have wider participation in diary writing by members of the project. Keeping some form of diary or running account of an excavation used to be the prime method of recording information. The site or trench note-book is still advocated by, for example, Joukowsky (1980). But in British contract archaeology at least, most have moved to some form of single-context recording with codified forms and prompts. Barker (1982, 147) argued against notebooks of 'prose whose loose format invites the writer to confuse the stages of recording, deduction, interpretation and speculation'. But since these stages are, in fact, inseparable (Carver 1990, 299) it becomes essential, both scientifically and ethically, to record what was being thought when records were being made and methods chosen. We have found at Çatalhöyük that the process of writing a diary in the pseudo-privacy of typing at a terminal leads to highly personal and revealing accounts (even though the entries, as it turned out, were being immediately and avidly read by others on the network). The entries in

Figure 7.1   Video documentation taking place at Çatalhöyük and an example of the digitized database entry (*opposite*).

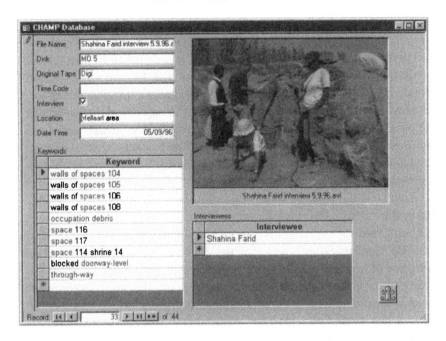

the diary can be linked on the basis of unit and feature number searches to the codified information so that the latter can be set within the context of the production of knowledge. The same aim is identified as a part of feminist practice in archaeology: 'we might consider publishing fuller field diaries that tie investigatory decisions to specific items of new knowledge, to diminish the appearance of knowledge appearing directly and automatically from the field into textbooks' (Conkey and Gero 1997, 429). At the very least, the process of diary writing and reading enhances information exchange and debate within the project.

One of the most important aspects of the context of production of knowledge on an archaeological site is visual (Molyneaux 1997). At Çatalhöyük daily video documentation takes place of group discussion in trenches, individual accounts of excavation progress and laboratory work. In this way team members can point to information they consider relevant, debates can be recorded and illustration provided. These videos are digitized, edited into short clips, and stored on the data base with attached key-words. Thus it is possible to use the data base to retrieve not only field descriptions, Autocad drawings, artifact locations and diary information for any particular unit, but also video about that unit, its discovery and interpretation. The editing process is of course selective, but the visual documentation always includes more 'peripheral' information than texts or forms, and it includes more of the surrounding context within which team members are working and interpretations are made. Indeed, the video documentation at Çatalhöyük, achieved with the collaboration of the Centre for Art and Media-Technology at Karlsruhe, has become very central to our methodology. Not only do the videos allow later critique and evaluation of the construction of data on site, but they also lead to greater information flow about interpretation (as people listen to each other live or on playback in the laboratory) and a greater readiness to submit one's own assumptions to scrutiny. As members of the team pointed out, the everpresent eye of the camera means that thought processes are much more out in the open.

Photographs apparently give an exact impression of what was found on a site. Certainly they have come to be used in archaeology as a prime indicator of 'evidence'. They demonstrate that the claimed discoveries 'really were there'. Along with the site plan, the site photographs provide a final authority. As a result, on many sites much effort is put into preparation and cleaning for photography. Grass is carefully clipped, on some sites excavated pits may be filled with dark soil to make them stand out, and in Japan, the outlines of pits of ditches may be painted white. The evidence is fixed on film for posterity. But of course, the term 'fixed' has a double meaning. On the one hand the photograph fixes the data as evidence. But the whole 'set-up' process implies that the evidence has to be manipulated or fixed in order to be real. The new technologies of digital photography explode the myth of the photograph as evidence more completely. We can now play with the image, manipulating and exploring it digitally. The legitimacy of the photograph is threatened and the distinction between virtual and real is blurred. Similarly the 'setting-up' of the video documentation process described above is very overt. Those involved in explaining what they are doing on screen have to select what they will say, they select shots and filter the argument. It is hard in such contexts to ignore the impression that the objective evidence can be seen in more than one way.

So far I have described site excavation as being undertaken by 'team members'. While on most sites there is a core group undertaking the fieldwork, research and publication, people in the global community may wish to have direct access to a site's data and to participate in its interpretation. For this reason, the data base at Çatalhöyük is being placed on the Web, including drawings and diaries but excluding, for the moment, video clips which require too much storage space for the

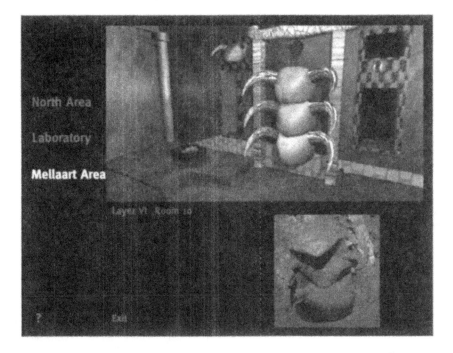

Figure 7.2   Still from a Çatalhöyük CD-Rom. In the upper picture the user can use a mouse to move around a Virtual Reality model of a Neolithic building. By clicking the mouse on features such as the bulls' horns, original photographs from the database appear below to allow comparison between the virtual model and the archaeological evidence.

Internet. The presence of contextualizing information in the data base allows others to understand the process of the construction of the coded information and to be in a position to critique and re-evaluate from alternative perspectives. The 'data' are thus not hoarded by 'the team' until publication but they are immediately part of a public inter-pretation.

Interaction is also enhanced by the use of hypertext in ways parallel to Ruth Tringham's (1994; 2000) 'Chimera Web' for the Balkan Neo-lithic site of Opovo. It can be argued (e.g. S. Thomas 1996) that the use of hypertext and non-linear multimedia data-structures allows some of the decentring of the author and some of the 'writerliness' of texts for which some theoretical statements have called (Bapty and Yates 1990; Spector 1993; Joyce 1994). Since it is possible for each 'reader' of the 'text' to move through it in different ways, there is a greater openness to a wide range of interests and greater opportunities for interactivity and engagement. It is possible in this way to embed a narrative about the site in links to the data base, to visual material, reconstructions and so on at various levels of specialist knowledge. Care must be exercised here, however, as S. Thomas (1996) has indicated. A certain level of archaeological knowledge may be required before the user of hypertext or hypermedia can effectively interact with it. It may be necessary to ensure that part of the hypertext deals with explaining terms and assumptions, so that the tools necessary for interaction are made available and easily accessible.

Virtual reality has already been extremely important in providing a deeper understanding of what it could have been like to move around within and between the buildings at many sites (e.g. Forte and Siliotti 1997; Rick and Hart 1997). This has been achieved at Çatalhöyük by video-length computer animation, but also using Quick-Time VR, VRML and Real-Time Computers (Hodder 1997). A phenomenological or experiential approach has been championed by a current generation of British prehistorians (e.g. Barrett 1994; J. Thomas 1996; Tilley 1994 and see chapter 8). However, in situations with less good or minimal monument survival, or in which there has been substantial landscape change, virtual techniques may allow experiment with alternative forms of interaction between people and the worlds they have constructed round them (for a similar point regarding GIS see Llobera 1996). It may also be possible to use virtual reality to provide a non-specialist 'front end' to a data base. At Çatalhöyük it is possible for users to 'fly' into a CD-Rom version of the site, into individual buildings, 'click' on paintings or artifacts and so move gradually, if desired, into scientific information available from the data base. Potentially, users will be able to move through the site, exploring information, and coming to their own decisions about the 'data' at different levels. For example, one of the problems we have at Çatalhöyük is in deciding whether a building is in some sense a 'house'. Rather than accepting 'our' conclusions on this, the data will be available, as far as that is possible, so that users can come to their own conclusions about the definition of a 'house' at Çatalhöyük.

Publication on-line or on CD-Rom has the potential to allow greater interactive access and greater ability to browse through a site archive. In this way there is the potential to make the archive more accessible both to specialists and to the wider public, and to facilitate the use of contextualized 'primary' data for the exploration of alternative hypotheses. Within such a digital context it is possible for site reports to be written which incorporate multiple views and which contain information about the context of the production of knowledge.

If the new information technologies potentially allow a greater diversity and open-ness of interpretation, it may be felt that the authority of the interpretation by the site director is undermined and that such loss of authority has negative results. Within an open network of information it is certainly possible for alternative interpretations to be disseminated. The interpretation made by the excavator of a site can be balanced by alternative interpretations made by other members of the team. But it is also possible for the excavators' interpretations to be one node within a wider debate. As long as the interpretation by the excavators remains identifiable, wider debates do not threaten the integrity of the initial interpretations. Informed accounts can then be made by other groups and individuals. Alternative interpretations may in the end come to have greater authority than that proposed by the excavators. It is difficult to see why such a process should be seen as negative and undermining except in bastions of traditional academic authority where status rather than knowledge are the key concern.

Conclusion

Simply to introduce the new technologies is clearly insufficient. While highspeed processors on site, hypertext, multimedia and virtual reality may all foster some of the reflexivity, contextuality, interactivity and multivocality that is required, they have to be aligned with broader changes in approach and work practices. The technologies perhaps provide an opportunity rather than a solution.

It may well be the case that some forms of traditional authority in the discipline need to be redefined. As an example, placing so much emphasis on the point of excavation may lead to a re-empowering or re-centring of the field excavator. But it may also involve re-training and re-skilling such individuals so that they can handle the increased amount and complexity of knowledge made available to them during the excavation process. Alternatives might involve breaking the distinction between field and laboratory staff, and providing opportunities for field staff to be also trained as specialists in other areas and levels. More generally, the overall separations between field professional, university academic and laboratory scientist within the discipline do not provide an appropriate context for the necessary degree of interpretive interaction. If interpretation is not to be seen as secondary but as primary to data collection, then so will the institutional divides between data collection, analysis and interpretation be further eroded.

As a further example of the relationship between methodological change and the need for wider accompanying changes in approach, it is possible to consider the impact of widespread data accessibility on the careers of project researchers and field staff. It will often be the case that some aspect of their career development is linked to publication. However, if primary data about the project are immediately widely available, the ability to publish original information may be undermined. Some safeguards and controls on information dissemination may thus be deemed necessary at certain points in the circuitry.

Despite these problems and implications, it can be argued that the end result of a reflexive methodology is an approach with scientific advantages. If more information is available at the point of excavation, choice of sampling and excavation method will be more appropriate to the questions being asked and the problems being studied (Carver 1989, 1990); fuller recording of relevant information will also be possible. If more contextual information is available to those working on materials from the site, there is less danger of inappropriate codes and categories being imposed from outside. If those conducting excavations are open to a wide range of perspectives, they may be more willing to adjust general views to the particularities of the information being discovered. A final scientific advantage might be claimed in the production of archives with sufficient contextual information to make them more usable than those archives based on highly objectified and codified data systems.

8 Windows into Deep Time: Towards a Multiscalar Approach

If it is now increasingly possible to envisage archaeological methods which foreground interpretation, flexibility, multivocality and reflexivity, it is also necessary to consider theories which incorporate these same characteristics. In this and the next chapter I wish to consider some of the wider impact of approaches which look beyond regulation and structure. I first wish to consider theories of change.

For a long time archaeologists have searched for formulaic explanations of change (such that 'x is a function of y + z under certain conditions'). Increasingly such attempts are seen as reductive, and 'explanation' has increasingly been replaced by full 'description' of the complex specificity of local sequences of events. Shennan (1989) has pointed to the apparent convergence of perspectives from opposite ends of the theoretical spectrum. Neo-Darwinian and poststructuralist discussions of change have tended to focus on the individual, on indeterminacy, and on history. Renewed discussion of Darwinian thought (e.g. Dunnell 1989) and ideas of punctuated equilibrium (Gould and Lewontin 1979) on the one hand, and descriptions of historical ruptures (Foucault 1977) on the other, have broken up notions of evolutionary and directional change. Contingency and history are championed in complexity theory approaches (Gumerman and Gell-Mann 1994), and non-linear modelling (van der Leeuw 1989; McGlade and van der Leeuw 1997). Yoffee (1994) has emphasized an evolutionary theory which foregrounds diversity and indeterminacy. At the other end of the spectrum, Barrett (1994) has argued that the major monuments of prehistoric Europe are the unintended outcome of practices which had no overall plan.

The Annales school on the other hand has provided a framework for understanding the relationship between event and the long term. Events are seen as embedded within medium-term social change and long-term environmental and cognitive structures or mentalités. But in such work in archaeology (Knapp 1992, Hodder 1987, Bintliff 1991), the mechanisms which produce the long-term structures are unclear. Examples of long-term continuities abound in archaeology – indeed, the identification of structured pattern over the long term is a particular contribution for which archaeology is well equipped. Bradley's (1990) work on the long-term use of watery deposition in European prehistory, and South American examples of long-term continuities in the use of space (Flannery and Marcus 1983) illustrate this trend (see also Huffman 1984 and Lechtmann 1984). But we remain far from an adequate understanding of what creates the long-term continuities, especially given the emphasis on contingency which is so much in vogue at present (see above). Certainly, memory (Rowlands 1993; Mizoguchi 1992) and the invention of tradition (Ranger and Hobsbawm 1983) play important roles, but neither are adequate mechanisms to explain the construction of long-term continuities even across radical rupture.

Perhaps our problem has been that as archaeologists we have been struggling to find a common language for the different scales of change. We struggle to find an explanation which does equally well for the short-term contingent as for the long-term structural. Perhaps we should accept that the two scales are not commensurate (Kelt, personal communication) and that different types of theory are relevant to the different scales (Preucel and Hodder 1996). This point can be approached by a consideration of the way time has been dealt with in archaeology. Strangely, despite archaeology being a discipline in which time is central, there has been very limited discussion of time (see Bailey 1981; 1983; 1987; Shanks and Tilley 1987), and time has not been seen as central to evolutionary theory. Rather, evolution has been 'spatialized'; time has been treated as space – divided into blocks with relationships between them. This spatial view of time has had consequences for the type of theories that have dominated the discipline. The focus has been on the shift from one block of time to another and on general evolutionary change. Transitions and origins have been the currency of theoretical exchange. Major causal variables have been sought. Societies have been seen as systems. A very different view of change and society is developed if space and society are thoroughly 'temporalized'.

In a temporalized view, the focus is placed on the fleeting moments of time which come and go. These can never be recaptured except partially and provisionally in another time. Moments in time can only be approached and approximated. Time as fleeting means that structure and system can never be fully instantiated in the moment except provisionally and partially. In the practice of the lived moment all the abstractions and constraints and systems cannot possibly be present except in the simplest of terms and most provisional of ways. This is because of:

the complexity and size of the system;
unacknowledged conditions and incomplete knowledge held by actors;
different perspectives and interpretations of appropriate action;
inability to predict all the consequences.

There must, then, always be a disjunction between event and structure. As many have recognized in the social sciences and in archaeology, events must always be underdetermined. One can never adequately explain one level by another; the events and structures are simply not equivalent. A similar point has been made about norm and agency. Kelt (personal communication) argues that very little of what happens in the mind surfaces as consciousness; normative structures cannot be reduced to agency. This disjunction between moments and 'objective things out there' (objects, monuments, systems, norms, structures, histories) which are stretched out in time perhaps helps to explain the difference between causal and interpretive statements. Such statements are not comparable because they refer to different scales. Causal explanation deals with the inter-relationship of variables at a distance, in abstract, removed from the specificity of events. Interpretation in the form of 'thick description' attempts to include accounts of the contingent and historical specificity of events.

Archaeology thus needs to develop approaches to two scales of analysis concurrently. On the one hand the system/structure needs to be examined in order to identify conditions, constraints and consequences; and on the other hand thick/deep descriptions or narrative windows are required which look at how individual events resonate with larger systems and construct change through conjuncture.

The Archaeology of Practice in British Prehistory

One set of approaches which attempts to combine structures with individual agency derives from Bourdieu (e.g. 1977) and Giddens (1979; 1984). These two writers have had a long impact in postprocessual archaeology (e.g. Shanks and Tilley 1987; Parker Pearson 1982; Hodder 1986) and are now increasingly referred to by authors in North American archaeology (e.g. McGuire 1992; Dobres 1995). More recently Giddens' theory of structuration has been applied extensively by Barrett (1994). Both Giddens and Bourdieu have increasingly come under attack in the social sciences (e.g. Turner 1994), the main criticism being that they do not in the end provide an adequate theory of the subject and of agency. In both, the structures which bind us leave little room for transformative action.

There are various responses in archaeology to such worries. One is to turn to dialectical thought. This direction is seen clearly in the work of McGuire (1992) and much of his discussion parallels that described below. However, in my view, the materialist emphasis which remains limits the widespread application of these ideas. Another response to the worries identified above is to turn to phenomenological approaches. For example, J. Thomas (1996), Gosden (1994) and Tilley (1994) have all looked to Heidegger and his idea of 'being in the world'. The main theme here is that mind is not separate from body or nature. Rather, the world in which we live is part of us, not separate. It is always already meaningful. So, for example, Thomas describes material culture as neither essentially cultural nor essentially natural. This anti-essentialism resonates with the emphases on non-fixity and spatio-temporalization in this volume. Thomas sees material culture meanings as relational, historical and always changing. These authors use phenomenology to focus on how the subject experiences the world through the body. In particular, they explore how subjects experience monuments and landscapes as they move through them and carry out practices in them.

These structurationist, dialectical and phenomenological approaches are important in that they attempt to break away from approaches which foreground structures and systems binding people into particular modes of behaviour over time. They seek to undermine the notion of universal oppositions between culture/nature, mind/body, meaning/practice, structure/agent. Rather they place emphasis on the local and the personal – the lived experiences of individuals inhabiting monuments and landscapes. Also they show that the sites and monuments never had one single meaning. Rather the meanings were continually changed through time (Bradley 1993). The site or monument is not a static structure but the product of a long cycle of reordering and renegotiating.

These contextualizing directions lead to radical notions of fluidity and multi-vocality which is why I wish to discuss them here. But questions remain regarding two areas of this recent work in British prehistory: does it provide an adequate account of the *reproduction of structures* and an adequate account of *individual lives*?

Take the example of the reproduction of structures over the long term. The authors being discussed are surely right to focus on the practices through which structures are reproduced. The authors have enriched our understanding of particular monuments by looking at them not as plans seen from above but as places in which people moved and interacted. The monuments can be seen as 'locales' (Giddens 1984) in which routinized actions structure future actions without determining them (Barrett 1994). Such a perspective is important because, as argued above, in the lived experiences of daily practice the large-scale structures and systems cannot all be present as abstract entities. They can exist only in practice. It is thus important to focus on the level of practice in order to understand long-term change.

In theory it is argued by these authors that mind and body should not be universally separated. They are both part of lived experience. Thus in discussing the reproduction of structures, it is presumably relevant to explore both conceptual and material structures. But in the practices of the writings of these authors, the mind/body duality often re-emerges as a meaning/practice duality.

The claim is frequently made by structurationist and phenomenological writers about British prehistory that archaeologists can avoid meaning and empathy and engage in the description of practices. Barrett (1994, 71) argues that in his work 'we have not uncovered what those monuments meant'. In discussing Neolithic and Bronze Age monuments in Britain, practices sometimes appear to become separated from mind. 'Monumentality originated in neither the idea nor the plan but rather in the practice and in the project' (1994, 23). This seems to be denying discursive intentionality, idea and plan too completely. Tilley (1994, 74) writes 'I make no claims to an empathetic understanding' of landscapes. J. Thomas (1996) makes the same point.

For example, the Neolithic Linearbandkeramik 'house was not a structure that possessed a positive meaning, so much as being a means by which the meanings of places and activities might be created' (p. 112). In another context, 'the deposition of artifacts . . . is best seen as part of a performative practice involving sequences of formed bodily movements, in which the meaning of place was evoked and recreated' (p. 203). The implication is that archaeologists can study the practices and the mechanisms for creating and recreating meanings without the need to know what the meanings were. The effects of social action can be understood, it is argued, without interpreting social meanings.

Such a viewpoint effectively recreates a meaning/practice, even culture/nature, dichotomy and long-term structures come to be understood in materialist terms. For example, Barrett (1994) argues that in the British early Neolithic the use of monuments and landscapes is generalized. Thus, a wide range of activities occur at 'ancestral sites'. This pattern is linked to long fallow agricultural systems and generalized rights to community land. In the later Neolithic and early Bronze Age a shorter fallow system implies closer links to the land, the closer definition of inheritance and tenure, and the clearer marking of burial locations on the landscape. Tilley (1994) too argues that the placing of prehistoric monuments in the landscape is related to material factors. The need to control and fix meanings in the landscape is linked to herding and the control of animals, migratory routes and pastures.

These materialist leanings and the denial of the need to consider cultural meanings limit the ability to explain the specificity of the monuments and landscapes. For example, both J. Thomas (1996) and Bradley (1996) describe the ways in which Neolithic Linearbandkeramik houses were centres of experience of the self and of the environment. The daily practices of cutting down trees, moving earth, respecting older houses, living in and using the buildings created a sense of place. People came to 'know' a place as part of 'being-in-the-world'. The similarities of form of Linearbandkeramik houses and megalithic long tombs over vast areas are not seen in terms of a common meaning. Indeed, Thomas argues that the houses or tombs did not have a common meaning. All that was shared in northwest Europe was a 'material vocabulary' (1996, 135). The similarities are presumably produced by the routinization of practices. But why did people keep doing the same thing with their house plans and tomb plans? And why these specific plans?

Rather than viewing people as repeating practical routines related to material need, it would seem necessary to integrate a fuller account of the frameworks of meaning within which practical strategies were developed. The need to consider both practical (phenomenological) and representational meanings was discussed in chapter 4. Other accounts have been successful in explaining the specificity of practices in terms of cultural meanings. For example, J. Thomas and Tilley (1993) have explored the way in which Breton Neolithic tombs have plans which cross-refer to symbolism of the axe and the body. Richards (1996) has discussed the role of water symbolism for henges and other monuments in British prehistory. He has also demonstrated in a detailed study how a series of Neolithic monuments in Orkney use a common symbolism related to the hearth and the house (Richards 1991). In a long-term view of the transformation of conceptual structures in the Neolithic of Europe I have argued (Hodder 1990) that continuities can be observed in the specific forms of houses and tombs. The idea of the 'domus' is seen as practical and material while at the same time conceptual and historically specific. Using such an idea the specificity of practices in monuments can be explained (see also Sherratt 1990).

Another attempt to link practice and meaning over the long term is provided by Treherne's (1995) account of changing bodily life-styles in the European Bronze Age. Why do toilet articles such as tweezers and razors appear at a particular moment in European prehistory? Treherne shows that such articles are related to evidence for increasing individualism, warfare, bodily ornament, horses and wheeled vehicles, the hunt, and the ritual consumption of alcohol. While all these activities are related to the rise and transformation of a male warrior status group, Treherne argues that the key is a changing aesthetics of the body. He describes the 'warrior's beauty' and his 'beautiful death'. This aesthetics is a framework of meaning linked to a set of practices which is quite specific historically and which is part of a distinctive form of self-identity. This life-style crystallized across Europe in the mid-second millennium BC out of roots in the previous few millennia. The institution of the warrior elite was to survive into and in part give rise to an aspect of the later feudal order in Europe.

Treherne's account of long-term structures integrates the material and the conceptual. It is important to note that he achieves this by considering the lived experiences of bodies and selves. 'But surely', it might be objected, 'this is exactly what J. Thomas, Barrett, Gosden and

Tilley are trying to do.' Certainly, and I would concur with the aim to incorporate lived bodily experiences, and ways of being in the world. But I will argue that in fact the bodies constructed by these authors are universal bodies. We have already seen that the bodies they construct are not well situated within specific historical meanings; I now want to agree with Meskell (1996) that opportunities are not taken to explore individual lives.

For example, Tilley (1994) describes a walk he takes between the long parallel banks of the Neolithic Dorset cursus. Much of the account describes the visibility of other monuments along the way. For example, he describes the surprise when the walker suddenly can see a barrow that had been hidden from view. Or 'walking down into the boggy depths of the valley provides a sensation of the entire world being removed' (p. 181) as views are blocked. But how one responds on such a walk would depend on who one is (for example a 'priest' or 'war captive'), on whether the cursus went within or crossed now invisible community boundaries, on the relative social status of the two ends of the cursus, and on a host of other social factors. These social 'meanings' would have a great effect on the perception of the person walking. Even the idea of 'taking a walk' in the country seems peculiarly contemporary. Tilley erects a universal body responding to stimuli in universal ways. All the bodies described by J. Thomas (1996) and Barrett (1994) moving along processional routes or around monuments are universal bodies. The monuments have been appropriated by the archaeologist: 'me as monument'. As Meskell argues (1996; see also Knapp and Meskell 1997), the reconstructed bodies are not located in a specific time and place. It is as if the bodies are transhistorical objects, disembodied beings.

Treherne (1995, 125) makes a related point in relation to Thomas' work. 'Thomas' attention is given to the manipulation of individual bodies, and concomitant notions of subjectivity, through the dominant interpretations of built or acculturated space fixed by hegemonic groups... What he is really concerned with is an external process of subjectification.' So once again, the lived experiences of individual bodies located in a particular time and place are not explored, despite claims to the contrary. There is too little emphasis on subjectivity and self as constructed by individual agents. This lack of focus on individual lives is closely related to the refusal to consider specific cultural and historical meanings. Universal bodies are described in a universal world of material practices.

The wariness of archaeologists in dealing with individuals has been described by Johnson (1989). It is of interest that his remedial example is taken from historical archaeology where texts are used to gain a clear insight into individual lives. Tarlow, too, in her call for a mortuary archaeology which considers emotion, bases her arguments on examples from historical archaeology (1992). Meskell (1998) provides insight into the lives of individuals at Deir el Medina in Egypt in the eighteenth to twentieth Dynasties and shows how individuals negotiate and have an impact on long-term trends. Her accounts depend very much on texts which identify individuals. If it is to be argued that consideration of individuals is central to understanding how long-term structures are drawn upon in the practices of daily life, then prehistory might be seen to be at a disadvantage. We have already seen Treherne (1995) working in a prehistoric context, but even in this example connections to historical literature on feudalism are part of the argument. Knapp and Meskell (1997) suggest that an archaeology of individuals is possible in prehistoric contexts and use as an example Chalcolithic and Bronze Age figurines from Cyprus.

The new archaeology of practice is welcome because it aims to focus on the fluid processes of the reproduction of structures, and on embodiment and subjectivity. The new phenomenology of monuments and landscapes is an important development which potentially allows large-scale trends to be understood at the human scale. But because of a reluctance in some of the work on British prehistory to consider the frameworks of meanings and the practices of individuals, the creation and reproduction of long-term processes is not adequately explored. In my view greater emphasis should be given to those studies which do discuss individual lived experience within historically specific worlds.

Whilst historical archaeologists might be most successful in achieving these aims, we have already seen that there are cases in prehistory which allow windows into the structures and systems through which people lived their lives. As prehistoric archaeologists we can routinely chart the long-term flows of structures and systems. But there are also small windows which open up and allow another dimension. Individual lives come into view. The conjuncture of daily events becomes visible. It becomes possible, bracketed within the vast expanses of prehistoric time, to write a narrative at the human scale. These narrative windows are the key to an understanding of the larger flows. The example I wish to give is the Alpine Ice Man – an interpretive account which shows how an accidental event can play a part in the unfolding of long-term trends.

The Ice Man

Konrad Spindler (1993) summarized the information available at the time concerning the body of a Neolithic 'hunter' discovered in the Ötztal Alps on the Austrian border (see also Barfield 1994; Egg et al. 1993; Goedecker-Ciolek 1994).

The body was partly destroyed on recovery and the site was inadequately recorded. Dated to 3300–3200 BC, the man was probably 35–40 years old, was laying on his left side, with longish dark hair and probably a beard. His body was tattooed, and he wore leggings, a cap, fur or skin garments, shoes and a grass cloak. His equipment included a hafted copper axe, a long bow, a quiver with arrows (two with tanged leaf-shaped arrowheads), various tools, a pannier, a dagger, a net and fire-making equipment.

The man's life was not disconnected from a wider society. He was integrated and linked into exchange networks. His copper axe and finely made clothes indicate that he was not extremely poor and he may have obtained them by exchange. His tattoos, which perhaps had a healing function, are in positions which indicate they were carried out by someone else. The seeds and threshing residues caught in his clothes suggest he had just been down in a valley – perhaps Val Venosta which is only 20 km away or the upper Etsch valley. The shape of his hafted axe occurs on statue-menhirs which are perhaps of a similar date in the Val Venosta. So again the artifacts with him link him into a wider cultural sphere. More generally there are stylistic similarities for the axe, dagger and arrowheads in adjacent cultures. Spindler sees most similarities with early Remedello in northern Italy, and Barfield specifies a 'Civate group' in an area in which collective burial prevails.

It is also possible that there was a dependency between the Ice Man and settled communities in the valleys. Various ideas have been suggested as to his occupation and his reasons for being high in the Alps. As we shall see, there are indications that he was a seasoned mountaineer and that he expected to be away for some time. Perhaps he traded metals, or hunted or was a shepherd. He died near the pass across which sheep and goats could have been brought down from the summer pastures. As settlement expanded in the later Neolithic a wider range of specialized upland resources would have been needed. Sherratt (1981; 1982) has documented this process at the general scale, and there is perhaps some local evidence of extension of settlement in the

Figure 8.1   The discovery of an 'ice man' trapped in a glacier in the Otzaler Alps on the Austrian-Italian border. The 5300 year old body was discovered by hikers, in September 1991. Photo: Popperfoto/Reuter. Reconstruction of his clothing and equipment (Spindler 1993).

late Neolithic (Spindler 1993). People experienced in surviving in upland areas would increasingly have become essential for lowland groups.

We know very little about settlement in the Val Venosta and other nearby valleys, but in general terms we know of settled lakeside villages or defended hill-top sites in neighbouring areas at this time. Such societies needed people who went into the mountains (for stone sources, ores, shepherding, hunting). This gradual encroachment into the uplands is part of a long-term process, involving economic changes such as the increased use of secondary animal products (Sherratt 1981) and the early use of copper. But I want to argue that the unfolding of this process was made up from small-scale events, including the death of the Ice Man, which created conflicts, tensions and dissonance. It is the detailed narrative of this man's death which gives an insight into how the large scale process was played out.

The Ice Man was integrated into a system. But the most remarkable thing for us, looking at his equipment, is his self-sufficiency. This perspective may simply be a bias of our times, but I would argue that even in late Neolithic terms, he was unusually self-sufficient. He carried an extraordinary amount of equipment with him. He had a retoucheur for making his flint tools, spare bits of sinew, and he was in the process of making his bow and the arrows. He had also brought along bits of his broken quiver in order to mend it. He had a pannier probably holding a birch bark container for embers, and a tinder fungus in a belt pouch. Another container was perhaps for liquids. He had an awl, scraper, borer, blade, dagger, axe, net. He had brought some tree bast string to make his bow. He even had his own 'medicine kit' in the form of two pieces of birch fungus attached to his left wrist. He did not have much food with him (probably only a sloe berry and probably a piece of dried meat) but he was able to obtain food using this wide range of equipment.

He was also well dressed for his upland travel. He had fur skins, cap, leggings, upper garment and long grass cloak. And he had probably carried out his own repairs of the clothes – he certainly had the equipment for it. There is evidence that he was a seasoned traveller. His body was lean and he had old fractures to his ribs of a type which often occur in mountaineering accidents. That he travelled a lot is also suggested by the sources of his wooden and plant artifacts – they include 17 species from a wide range of altitudes, and there is also a great diversity of animal products. Part of this variety could have been obtained by exchange, but extensive travel is also possible.

There is, then, evidence of independence and self-sufficiency. The Ice Man's concern with care of himself is also seen in the healants (sloe/ fungus) and tattoos, the location of which on the body suggests 'protection' or healing. He was not an outsider, but he lived an independent and self-sufficient life. And a dangerous one too. Spindler argues that a disaster had occurred producing newly broken ribs so that he lay on his left side to avoid the pain (although it is possible that his ribs were broken in the recovery process). His weapons were unfinished. We do not have to accept the notion of some immediate conflict with lowland groups to see that his life of upland travel involved dangers and at least tension in his relations with lowland peoples. The latter were in part dependent on him − whether it was for herding, wild animals or ores. But yet he was independent and self-sufficient. And in the end he broke the exchange relationships. He 'disappeared'.

Differences between the Ice Man and lowland areas are seen in his clothing (Goedecker-Ciolek 1994). There is no woven material at all, no linen or wool. Wool may not have been available locally yet (Jørgensen 1992), but linen was available in the lakeside villages (ibid.). Linen would have been of little value as the main garment in upland areas, but the total lack of linen is perhaps of note. At the very least a difference between two ways of life is accentuated. In fact the Ice Man has very little from an agricultural world (except by accident, hidden in his clothing). He was eating wild ibex meat and a sloe berry. He had no domesticated meat or bread, and no ceramic artifacts. We know that the axe type occurs on statue-menhirs and thus in a ritual context − but again there is no link to the domestic hearth.

There may always have been people on the margins of society, independent hunters and travellers. But at the particular conjuncture of the late fourth millennium BC, such individuals were becoming more integrated into settled ways of life. Spindler (1993) suggests that in areas such as the Val Venosta clearance occurred first in higher areas and then moved down. At first, people like the Ice Man could remain marginal. But gradually, as dependence on upland resources increased and as secondary animal products became more important for sub-sistence and exchange economies, people like the Ice Man became ever more central.

And yet his centrality was contradictory and full of tensions. The way he lived and died involved independence of the individual, a concern with the self and the body, dependence on wild resources, exchange, death and danger. This life-style gradually came close to (in a spatial sense) lineage- and village-based society in the lowlands. In many parts of Europe the contradictions and tensions which emerged led to the break up of that society and the development of a new way of life based

(a)

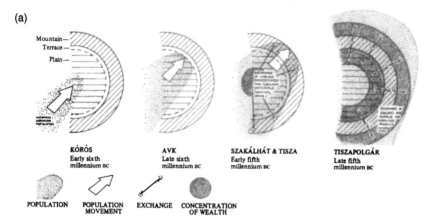

KÓRÓS	AVK	SZAKÁLHÁT & TISZA	TISZAPOLGÁR
Early sixth millennium BC	Late sixth millennium BC	Early fifth millennium BC	Late fifth millennium BC

POPULATION   POPULATION MOVEMENT   EXCHANGE   CONCENTRATION OF WEALTH

(b)

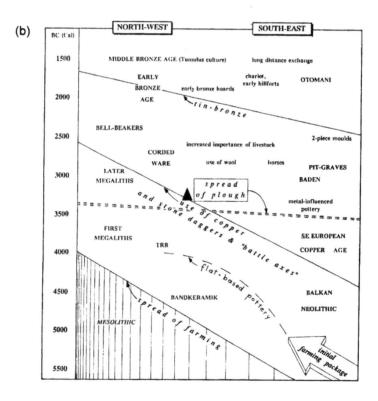

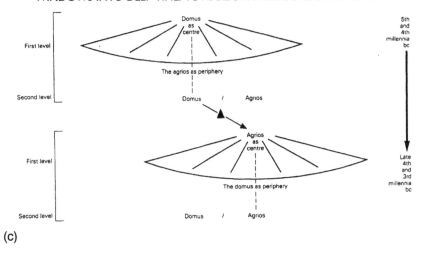

(c)

on a greater emphasis on the individual, particularly on a set of male-associated traits involving hunting, warring and exchange (Sherratt 1981; Treherne 1995; Shennan 1986). The new social form may be close to the Germanic mode of production (J. Thomas 1987). It is this new way of life and its associated beliefs and meanings that I have termed the 'agrios' (Hodder 1990).

All such transformations have been described in the literature as if they unfolded over the long term. For example, Sherratt (1981) has described the Secondary Products Revolution and I have charted a gradual change from domus to agrios (1990). From Childe (1925) to Renfrew (1973) to Shennan (1986) and Treherne (1995) the main characteristic of this change has been the rise of the individual and the appearance of individual burial rites. But these long-term structural transformations are made up from the micro-actions of multitudes of individuals living their lives and gradually transforming the circumstances in which they do so. The life and death of the Ice Man, in however small a way, were part of these larger scale changes. In his life we

---

Figure 8.2 Long-term processes in which the Ice Man's life was embedded. (a) Sherratt's (1982) model for population movement into lowland areas and gradual expansion into upland areas, followed by interaction and exchange between upland and lowland. This process happens at different times between the 6th and 4th millennia in different parts of Europe. (b) Sherratt's (1993, 16) overall chronology for the spread of various characteristics including Secondary Products and individual burial with daggers and battle axes (Corded Ware and Bell Beaker) in Europe. The relative position of the Ice Man at a major transition is marked by a triangle. (c) (*above*) The overall shift from domus to agrios in European prehistory (Hodder 1990, 96). The central location of the Ice Man is again marked by a triangle.

see specialization in an upland and independent way of living. We see the tension of dependence and independence in relation to lowland societies. We see him dealing in a practical way with the contradictions between an old and a new system. In the tragedy of his death we see the breaking of bonds and dependencies. We see the emergence of a set of ideas which conflict with lowland domus-based societies. These new ideas are less about continuity and stability of the domestic hearth, and more about a male-centred ethos of hunting, warring, bravery, exchange and the independence of the individual. The Ice Man's death, whatever the specific reasons, helped to create the impression that this increasingly important way of life was antithetical to societies based on a corporate sense of lineage and dependency and symbolized by the domestic hearth.

The fleeting moment of the Ice Man's life and cold and lonely death provide us with a window through which to peer at the playing out of larger structural and systemic transformations. The find of his body allows a different perspective on these abstract and objective forces. It helps us to see how the structures were mediated and transformed, how they were played out in the practices of personal lives – how individuals performed and transformed the large-scale historical movements.

Narrative windows: a critique

I'm sorry, but much as I can see the point you are making, I found the example of the Ice Man hopelessly uncritical. There is too much sloppy and uncritical interpretation. For example, you have no idea whether the death of the Ice Man was a 'tragedy'. This is just cheap, sensationalist interpretation. By your sloppiness here you are just supporting the view that these narrative windows into past lives always have to be unscientific; just examples of story-telling.

I think that is unfair. I didn't want to write a whole book about the Ice Man. If you want to check the detail you can go and read Spindler and the other references I gave. You will see there that all the assertions I made are supported by evidence available to me at the time. I was using the example just to make a specific point about how archaeology can in some circumstances provide an insight into how the large-scale structural transformations we normally study are made up from the micro-actions of individual lives. We can provide a human perspective.

But you would accept that other researchers could interpret the Ice Man in different ways. They could tell a story that had quite different implications.

Of course, I accept that other interpretations are possible. But for the moment I think my account is plausible and well-grounded. For example, you criticized my use of the word 'tragedy' to describe his death.

Yes, its use seems emotional. There are other possibilities. Think for example of the Inca frozen bodies which are the result of sacrifice. It is also possible that people were relieved at his death.

I did think about such possibilities. But in evaluating them, the evidence did not seem to 'fit'. Of course, the recovery of the body was not initially well controlled, but there seemed to be no evidence of formalized ritual behaviour. I used the term 'tragedy' because the evidence indicated that the Ice Man had had close relationships with other people. In his death, those social links were broken; but because of the manner of his death, it was not possible to use formalized burial ritual to come to terms with the break. The 'tragedy' argument made better sense of the evidence.

I can see your point, but I am still worried about the emphasis you are placing on this rather sensational find. The book by Spindler is the only archaeology book I have seen on sale in airport bookshops throughout the world. The Ice Man has attracted widespread imagination. Is this really the stuff of a scientific archaeology?

There are many reasons for the popularity of the book, but at least one of the reasons is that such finds allow an insight at the human scale. I agree we need to look at the evidence soberly and rigorously, but we should not lose sight of the importance of such evidence for providing an important window into the distant past. Rather than dry descriptions of cultural change, we can gain an interpretation of how individuals worked within and dealt with the contradictory forces that surrounded them. The finds allow a more agent-centred approach; but they also provide a potential for engaging a wider audience in archaeological debate.

OK. I accept that archaeological science must incorporate narrative windows, as long as you accept that your account could have been more carefully argued.

Well . . . OK.

Conclusion

For much of its data, archaeology can only give a general systemic view – it can describe the flow of cultures or systems, the rise of complexity, the collapse of states and inter-regional networks of exchange. The data are often too scanty to allow anything else, and the ability of archaeologists to paint grand syntheses with a broad brush is impressive (for a recent argument in favour of grand narrative see Sherratt 1995). But there are moments in archaeology which capture the public imagination when very rich and detailed information is found – an Ice Man, a Pompeii, a Shang tomb or a Tutankhamun. We should not scoff at this – the popularization derives from a fascination we all share. It invites narrative. It provides a window into the workings of the grand systems which we so painstakingly monitor for so much of our archaeological lives.

But it is not only the sensational finds which allow windows into the fine grain of temporal sequences. Indeed, it could be argued that archaeologists are better equipped at studying specific moments and daily rhythms than larger scale processes. Archaeologists can reconstruct in great detail the sequences of actions behind the knapping of a flint nodule. Knowledge of the sequences involved in making and firing a pot may be understood down to a few minutes. Seasonal activities may be constructed from teeth growth or shell middens. Medieval archaeologists may be able to reconstruct the daily routes from house to field, and the weekly passages from house to church and back again. In many ways, it is the human scale which is the stuff of archaeology; it is the larger scale which is more distanced from archaeological material.

From one point of view, archaeologists best describe and explain things (cultures, systems, evolution) which are the unintended consequences of numerous small events and actions. What we observe is a very generalized, distant abstraction from the events that filled individual lives. Much contemporary theory in archaeology, from Chaos Theory to neo-Darwinism or poststructuralism, aims to model or include this local contingency and diversity. From another point of view, archaeologists understand best the fine grained detail of daily lives. In practice, archaeologists are able to observe at both scales.

I would argue, however, that few approaches in archaeology adequately recognize that different types of account are needed at different scales. Archaeologists have developed effective techniques for dealing with the large scale and the long term. When it comes to individuals and events, there have been few successful studies. Rather than abstract mathematical modelling of diversity and contingency, attention must be paid to lived experience. Rather than accounts of 'being' which remain materialist, dichotomous and disembodied, narrative interpretations are needed of the specificity of meaningful action (Kus 1992; Gero 1991b). Grand narratives of the long term and small narratives of lived moments may not be commensurable, but both are needed in an archaeology which accepts diversity, uncertainty and relationality in human behaviour.

9 Archaeology and Globalism

The aim of this chapter is to contextualize the moves towards diversity, fluidity and reflexivity which have become the main themes of this volume. It is inadequate to see these themes as intellectual outgrowths or logical results of feminist or dialectical archaeology or of the post-processual critique of processual archaeology. The very fact that some archaeological theory has embraced 'interpretive archaeology' at much the same time as, yet apparently unconnected to, the proliferation of 'interpretive centres' in heritage and environmental conservation, suggests that a wider process is at work. I will argue that it is necessary for archaeologists to understand the broader economic, social and cultural processes within which archaeology and heritage are embedded. To understand critically these wider processes is to provide a reflexive context for archaeological reflexivity itself.

It is often argued today, in many areas of life, that something radically new is happening in the world, or at least the developed world. This new discourse of 'the new' is partly fuelled by the end of the millennium debates and retrospectives. But it began independently of these in the 1970s and 1980s. In the area of information technology, Negroponte (1996) has claimed a new world order in which there is a shift from atoms to bits. For Castells (1996, 477–8) 'it is the beginning of a new existence, and indeed the beginning of a new age, the information age'. In the area of philosophy and cultural critique, this new phase is called variously consumer society, post-industrial society, media society, or high or postmodernism (Lyotard 1984). Fukuyama (1992) too, though critical of postmodern views, heralds 'the end of history'.

In order to understand postmodernist claims for 'the new' it is necessary to identify that against which they react. The 'modern' can be defined in countless ways. I argue that it refers to a world anchored by a particular starting point which was also an endpoint, an origin and a destiny. This point from which all perspectives derived was progress, not only technological but also social (the march towards liberty and equality) and philosophical (the triumph of reason). Hobsbawm (1994) has argued that this Enlightenment view has continued to dominate western societies through most of the twentieth century. It is only at the end of that century that these modernist assumptions have been widely challenged.

In the postmodern world there is a collapse of perspective, a lack of a fixed point except that lack – and so immediately the contradictions emerge which form so much a part of the postmodern world. With a lack of a vantage point everything is simultaneously true and not true, real and virtual, universal and local. This loss of fixed points is often linked to changes in communication technologies and to the increasing importance of information in postindustrial capitalist societies. People become atomized within these new systems; the individual becomes a node in a network of communication. Production processes too become dispersed within global systems of the division of labour. As a result of these processes of fragmentation, beliefs in universal notions of progress become undermined. There is 'incredulity toward metanarratives' and 'the grand narrative has lost its credibility' (Lyotard 1984, 37).

Globalism   A central concept which lies behind many of the discussions of postmodernism is globalism. What is meant by this term and what are the globalizing processes which are emerging? Castells (1996) has described some of the changes in economics and media. For example, in the area of computers he describes the shift from mainframe computers to personal computers and computer networking and hence the rise of the centrality of software in order to meet the need for the flexible, interactive manipulation of computers. Information networking technology took a quantum leap in the early 1990s, due to the linking together of three trends: digitalization of the telecommunications network, development of broadband transmission, and a major increase in the performance of computers connected by the network.

All this has allowed the emergence of fully interactive, computer-based, flexible processes of management, production, and distribution. A global labour force has resulted to some degree (ibid., 201) and a trend towards the individualization of work and the fragmentation of societies. 'The flexibility of labour processes and labour markets induced by the network enterprise, and allowed by information technologies, affects profoundly the social relationships of production inherited from industrialism, introducing a new model of flexible work, and a new type of worker: the flex-timer' (ibid., 264).

But it is not just patterns of work that are transformed within global culture. Take, for example, the shift in the presentation of information from the printed word (linear typography) to the audio-visual world of TV. It can be argued (Castells 1996, 332) that 'while print favours systematic exposition, TV is best suited to casual conversation'. There is a shift from a medium which is linked to detachment and perhaps objectivity, to a medium which is multi-sensory, often involving little effort, and linked to play and the casual. But further down the line which we have been travelling in developed countries over recent decades, new communication media produce further effects. Walkmen emerge, as do VCRs which can be organized to allow more personalized viewing. Camcorders allow filming of events in your own home, and there is a multiplication of TV channels. The result is enormous choice and segmentation. It is no longer possible for one message to be given. There is decentralization, diversification and customization. The linking of TVs to computers and the arrival of the Internet create increased individualization, but also greater interactivity.

Another set of important changes concerns the increasing importance of consumerism and consumer culture. For Featherstone (1991) the rise of consumer culture describes a process in which people are involved in a race to spend money on commodities, but these commodities have become simply signs so that people are reproducing signs rather than producing them. The endless reduplication of signs by the market leads to the 'aestheticization' of reality and of everyday life, whereby people become 'fascinated by the endless flow of bizarre juxtapositions' (ibid., 15). There is a lack of stable sense and a depthlessness.

What are the overall effects of these changes? On the one hand, the result is clear. At least for those participating in the new networks of production, exchange and information flow there is a process of homogenization. The world shrinks and becomes a 'global village'. As Bill

Gates (1995, 263) puts it, 'the information highway is going to break down boundaries and may promote a world culture, or at least a sharing of cultural activities and values'. But at the centre of the idea of globalism there is a contradiction. For example, Featherstone (1991, 114–15) suggests that there has been a shift from marking and emulating categories of difference (nation states or class, or feudal hierarchical distinctions) to a new pattern in which everyone is both the same (for example, they all have access to the same fashions) and different (as in the emphasis on individual life-style). 'The network will draw us together, if that's what we choose, or let us scatter ourselves into a million mediated communities' (Gates 1995, 274). Within globalism, diversity, heterogeneity, ethnic conflict, and increases in disparities between rich and poor seem to go hand in hand with homogenization. New emphases on the global and the local seem inextricably linked.

On the one hand, global flows decrease the importance of national institutions and separate identities are threatened by the homogenizing tendencies. On the other hand, the European Court of Human Rights might support the individual against the state, or information technologies allow small groups (whether these be ME sufferers or goddess worshippers) to form and be empowered (Featherstone and Lash 1995).

It is possible to argue that the homogenization of cultural expression is linked to the domination of computerized network codes by a few central senders. Certainly, the price to pay for inclusion in the new information systems is that one has to adapt to its logic, to its language, to its points of entry, to its encoding and decoding. But rather than a centrally dispatched multimedia system, the overall tendency seems to be towards a multinodal, horizontal network of communication, of Internet type (see also the proliferation of local radio stations). The diversification, multimodality, and versatility of these communications systems allow different forms of expression, as well as a diversity of interests, values and social positions (Castells 1996, 374).

Thus in the developed world, globalism produces homogeneity through enhanced and extended communication networks and through processes of production and consumption which have a global scale. Everything becomes commodified in a global market. At the same time, the character of the new economies and information technologies allows diversity and fragmentation. It allows special interest groups to form and create new identities and local meanings.

Many parts of the world, especially Africa, are not well integrated into this new network society. Maps of the global diffusion of the

Internet, for example, show a gradual spreading out from a concentration in the United States and Europe in 1991 to cover much of the world except Africa and central Asia by 1994 (Castells 1996). Even within more developed regions, there is increasing social stratification among the users of the new networks. The multimedia world increasingly contains two populations: the interacting and the interacted (ibid., 371). Economic position and educational background affect whether people are able to select their multidirectional circuits of communication, or whether they are provided with a restricted number of pre-packaged choices. The ability to participate actively is linked to class, race and gender, but also to country and region. On the one hand there is emerging an interactive network of self-selected communes. On the other hand there is a customized mass media culture.

Outside the developed countries there are infra-structural limits to the extent to which people can participate in the new networks. In these areas, there is no opportunity for active engagement and empowerment via the new media. There is certainly some extension of mass consumer culture through the participation in global production and consumption processes. But these areas remain largely 'un-networked' in relation to the new information technologies. There is little relevance here for ideas about postmodernism and aestheticization.

Archaeology and global diversity   It is no accident that the label used for processual archaeology was 'new' and for its critique was 'post'. The term 'new' suggests again the progressive development of modernism. The term 'post' refers to the uncertainty and diversity of postindustrialism, postmodernism, postpositivism and so on. Of course, archaeologists look at the debates within their discipline parochially. They understand them as internal developments within the discipline. They see the rise and fall of successive theories as linked to their success in promoting archaeological work.

But a different view is that different archaeological perspectives are simply products of their time (e.g. Trigger 1984; Patterson 1995). I want to argue that the reflexive approach outlined in this volume is both a symptom of and can play an active part in something much wider – a debate, tension, contradiction within developed contemporary societies. I want to show that reflexivity in archaeology cannot only be set within wider intellectual movements but can also be related to wider changes in the nature of economies and societies.

It is not, in any simple sense, the case that the introduction of uncertainty in archaeology was associated with postprocessual archaeology and with the diversity of archaeology in the 1990s. Processual archaeology embraced science and evolution and origins. In all these ways it can be linked to modernism (as defined above) with its emphasis on fixed points and grand narratives. But in some respects, processual archaeology already introduced doubt. It undermined a self-evident relationship with the past by emphasizing hypothesis testing in order to combat bias. The resulting 'loss of innocence' (Clarke 1973) ensured that statements about the past were from now on open to critique. The self-evident nature of the archaeological record also came to be scrutinized and the role of formation processes recognized (e.g. Schiffer 1987). Simple grand narratives concerning social evolution had gradually to be tempered with notions of multi-linearity and complexity (Yoffee 1994).

These trends towards the undermining of universal schemes and grand narratives came to dominate in postprocessual archaeology (as defined in the box on p. 3). Many of the abstract claims of postprocessual archaeology were paralleled in the theoretical debates of postmodernism. The focus on context (Hodder 1982a) emphasizes the local and the diverse as against the grand narratives of cross-cultural anthropological archaeology. The focus on the individual and the agent (ibid., and Shanks and Tilley 1987) resonated with contemporary notions of fragmentation and the autonomy of the individual within networks. The overall emphasis on the interpretation of symbols and meanings recalled the growth of a wider cultural discourse on consumer culture and 'style wars' (York 1980). The postprocessual flirtation with relativism paralleled a wider willingness to accept uncertainty and a diversity of views. The commitment to social engagement seen in many postprocessual writings (e.g. Shanks and Tilley 1987) was part of a wider breaking of the separation between low and high culture.

My concern here is to focus on contextualizing the theme of diversity discussed in this book. Processual archaeology placed a great emphasis on variability. But by variability was meant systematic adaptation to environments. The variability in past systems was seen as being controllable within generalizing frameworks. But the view of diversity which has emerged in recent decades and which is described in this book is more radical. It concerns differences which are not necessarily subsumable within controlling schemes. One expression of this desire to foreground diversity has been the attempt to see the past as 'other' or 'different' (e.g. Hill 1992; J. Thomas 1990; 1993; 1996; Barrett 1994). The aim is to show that we cannot assume that the past is the same as the present. We should not impose the present on the past.

But in evaluating this emphasis on difference, it is important to remember the contradictions identified above within the globalizing trends in developed countries. Perhaps this concern with the past as 'other' does resonate with the needs of different communities within contemporary societies, however virtual those communities might be, to create a sense of identity and purpose. For example, some black communities in the United States might be strengthened by the notion that slaves in the ante-bellum South actively resisted their domination (Ferguson 1991). Also, some New Age or Ecofeminist groups may develop a sense of coherence by reference to Gimbutas' (1982) view that prehistoric 'Old Europe' saw a matrifocal society (Conkey and Tringham 1996). In these ways the past plays a role in forming diverse identities, sometimes at the small-scale. The fragmen-tation and pluralism of societies is enhanced in terms of the formation of active communities. The past as 'other' here has a positive role. Some postmodern writers have suggested that prehistoric sources can be used as hooks to construct community and to create resistance to and critique of globalization (Featherstone and Lash 1995, 23). Halton (1995, 275) argues that we should search in history and prehistory in order to find different senses of value (about self, family, community and so on).

But all too easily, 'otherness' comes to mean something very different – the past as play and pastiche, the past as wished for. I referred above (p. 150) to the fascination with the endless flow of bizarre juxtapositions which has come to be such a central part of consumer culture. The archaeological past has come to play a full part in the provision of the exotic, bizarre or nostalgic 'other'. This is the past as theme park which I will examine below (p. 163); the past as time travel. All too easily such perspectives impact on archaeology as when evidence of prehistoric female figurines comes to be used in superficial scholarship in order to bolster claims about the goddess (Meskell 1995). The past as 'other' is here involved in the play of difference, although the boundaries between 'play' and the 'passion' of identity formation may often be blurred.

The past as identity and as theme park

I think you should make a distinction between New Age or fringe archae-ologies and the archaeologies of disadvantaged minorities.

On what grounds?

A distinction should be made in terms of your separation between a past mobilized as part of the resistance of subordinate groups, and a past experienced as leisure theme park. For example, Native American rights to their past have to be considered in relation to centuries of exploitation by a dominant culture. New Age goddess groups are part of a dominant culture; these people are just involved in the past for leisure, play, nostalgia.

Well, I have tried to make a distinction and will discuss it again more fully in chapter 11. But I think the situation is much more complic-ated than you imply.

Why?

What right do you have to judge the role of archaeology for indi-viduals who believe in the goddess? I have seen them emotionally moved visiting goddess sites. Some people seem to have a profound religious experience at these sites and the visits play an important part in their sense of identity. Many of these people are women. Who are you to say that discovering the goddess does not help them to gain a stronger sense of what it means to be a woman after millennia of subjugation? What right have you to say this is just self-indulgent play manipulated by the market?

But these are not 'real' communities. They just come together on leisure tours or on the Net.

Again, what right do you have to say that these fluid or dispersed networks of people are 'virtual' and not 'real'?

I thought it was you that was making the distinction between theme park fun with the past and real identities?

I agree there is a distinction between theme park and social resist-ance. My point is rather that in any particular case it may be extremely difficult to disentangle the two strands – those uses of the past that are part of the spread of the market, play and pastiche, from those uses of the past that define the rights of disadvantaged groups. This is 'difference as play' versus 'difference as agency'. In practice, the two strands often seem to feed off each other.

So is there a point in making the dichotomy?

The extremes seem clear. A heritage play park can usually be distinguished from the rooted claims of indigenous groups. But there are many other cases in which the distinction is not clear so that careful consideration has to be given to the potential impact of a particular use of the past.

A similar point about the past 'other' as play derives from poststructuralist debate about difference and 'differance' (Yates 1990). Any interpretation of the past can be seen as just an 'other' interpretation, constructed in opposition to existing interpretations. Thus Said (1978) has shown that the Oriental 'other' constructed as the object of study within western discourse is very much an inversion of the Occident's view of itself. If the West sees itself as dynamic and democratic, the Orient must be static and despotic. In producing the past as 'other' are we just producing inverse images of ourselves? Are we simply engaged in a play of difference, of relevance only to our contemporary selves?

Thus the emphases on diversity and difference within archaeology can be related to the same emphases in globalized western culture. But also the same tensions emerge in both archaeology and society. The archaeological past helps communities to engage in a different, alternative identity. Or it undermines difference and otherness as just a play within the global market of signs. Both Engelstad (1991) and Wylie (1992) argue that postprocessual archaeology repeats androcentric assumptions and biasses. Its openness to diversity is thus illusory. Indeed, its whole tenor appears to support a dominant and closed intellectual position. To argue that 'the past can have different meanings' is easier for dominant groups (see box on p. 159). The dominated may have less resources to engage in alternative theories. More important, the notion that the past can have multiple meanings undermines claims by dominated groups concerning the concrete reality of their subjugation. From this point of view, all attempts to argue for the past as 'other' may be seen as simply the play of difference within the dominant discourse.

The point is more forcefully made if we consider the use of the past amongst those groups marginal to, or external to, the new network society. One of the most important developments in archaeology which has led to a critique of positivism and universal science has been the emergent voices of non-western and indigenous peoples. Anthropology more generally has seen an increasing awareness of the colonial origins of its discourse on the 'other' and has subjected its own concern with 'universal' (actually western) theorizing to radical critique (e.g. Marcus and Fischer 1986). Much social and cultural anthropology thus focuses now on the local rather than on grand narratives.

In archaeology too, Trigger (1984) has shown how Native Americans have been constructed as 'other' by changing generations of archaeologists. For culture historical archaeologists it was assumed that prehistoric cultures would reveal little evidence of internal change or development. Any major change observed by US archaeologists was attributed to diffusion or migration. After 1960 New Archaeologists did recognize the role of indigenous change, but there was not a serious interest in the native peoples themselves. Rather, the archaeological evidence of prehistory was used to establish universal generalizations about human behaviour. Trigger (ibid.) sees the New Archaeology as the archaeological expression of post-War American imperialism. Its emphasis on law-like generalizations trivialises the study of Native American prehistory as an end in itself. The investigation of any national or ethnic tradition is seen as only of relevance for a general (western-centred) study of humanity. 'By denying the validity of studying the prehistory of specific parts of the world, the New Archaeology asserts the unimportance of national traditions themselves and of anything that stands in the way of American economic activity and political influence' (ibid., 626–7).

The past of non-western or indigenous peoples has frequently been seen as static and lost in time. It has thus been constructed as a typical 'other' – simply an inversion of the way colonial and imperial societies see themselves. Increasingly, however, the 'others' have, in a postcolonial world, starting talking back (see below). They have confronted taken-for-granted assumptions about universal science and argued that there are other ways of doing archaeology. Reburial and repatriation claims in many parts of the world have forced greater co-operation between archaeologists and indigenous peoples, and some training of indigenous archaeologists. Of course there is a danger that this process will simply lead to the transfer of western methods and assumptions to a global archaeological community. For the moment, however, there is evidence of diversity and critique as indigenous people enter into a global debate and critique western approaches to archaeology and heritage (Swidler et al. 1997).

For example, on behalf of the Tasmanian Aboriginal Community, Langford (1983) argues that objective science does not have a natural right to study her culture and she opposes the static 'otherness' constructed by archaeologists and the dynamic lived past understood by community members. Mamani Condori (1989) shows how the past of the Aymara in Bolivia is not dead and silent as supposed by the positivist scientific attitude. There is an increasing awareness of the potential for a global diversification of theoretical debate in archaeology (Ucko 1995). Indian archaeology, for example, has long been dominated by the colonial heritage of Wheeler. But Paddaya (1995) has begun to explore alternative directions, drawing links between traditional Indian philosophies and postprocessual archaeology. In more general terms, Paranjpe (1990) argues against the universalist assumptions of western scholarship. 'Europe is not the world', but the agony for Indian intellectuals is the feeling that not being Eurocentric makes them powerless (ibid., 160). 'To generate our own counter-colonial discourses from our experience, tradition, and imagination, to not regret our powerlessness in the world given to us, but to fight from this position to one of greater self-determination and self-respect – these are the challenges for the third world intellectual. The radical response to the West is the response from a different, non-European centre' (ibid., 160–1).

Paranjpe argues that theoretical debate in the West is an endless process of dialectical substitution. Theory replaces theory in a violent and usurpatory way. This game or play of difference is essentially for power. Instead of participating in such a conflict, Indian intellectuals should find alternative positions from within their own traditions. For example, Indian theories of meaning and interpretation should be considered – Bharata, Nagarjuna, Anandavardhana, and Abhinavagupta. 'Poststructuralists like Barthes, Derrida, and Lacan talk a great deal about the indeterminacy of meaning and the eternal play of signifiers. This is akin to the Indian concept of *leela* and *maya*' (ibid., 158). Concepts such as the play of difference can be accessed through Indian ideas rather than having to be derived from Europe. The ultimate hope is for dialogue rather than confrontation. In a global network clear distinctions such as those between east and west may become less central. Rather, there is increasing dispersal and debate between different traditions.

In general and oversimplified terms we might argue that views of the past that groups hold are linked to the position of those groups in relation to the global networks. Within the networks of high-speed, interactive and multimedia information flow notions of progress or evolution have given way increasingly to a 'timeless time' (Castells 1996, 465). Here there is fragmentation of time sequences, flexitime, blurring of life-cycles, and instantaneity in information flow. Senses of grand narrative, sequence, duration are disturbed. Temporal difference is just part of the overall play of difference. It is important to recognize that even when the past is used to create identities and support communities in networked regions, these communities may be placeless or virtual. For example, when New Age communities are created and reproduced through interaction on the Web, these communities may only exist virtually in space/time. This is not to argue that they are not real, but that their reality is virtual – unlocated in place and time.

Time and the past are understood differently away from the networked centres. Here the past is used to create links and continuities into the present. Time is continuous and has duration. Time is central to the establishment of rights over land and to the formation of identities. As already noted, history and prehistory play an important role. Heritage is central to rights and identities.

From relativism to pluralism and multivocality

As noted in the box on p. 23, relativism is often understood in archaeology as the view that truth is relative so that all constructions of the past are equally valid. Thus it becomes impossible to 'expose the misuse of archaeology by fascists, extreme nationalists and cranks' (Trigger 1995, 330; see also Kohl and Fawcett 1995; Kohl 1993; Renfrew 1989).

Sophisticated discussions of relativism are provided by Fotiadis (1994), Wylie (1989, 1992, 1994), and Pinsky and Wylie (1989), and a thorough account of the different types and implications of relativism is provided by the Lampeter Archaeology Workshop (1997). Most archaeologists, however relativist, would today accept that archaeological interpretation is and should be answerable to data. They would also acknowledge that this 'guarded' (Hodder 1991) or 'mitigated' (Wylie 1992) objectivity is necessary in order to counter political misuse of the past.

But in my view it is wrong, even dangerous, to assume that some commitment to objectivity will protect archaeology from misuse.

Your view frightens me. Take the following quote from Wylie (1992, 21): 'I myself find inescapable the suspicion that strong constructivist and relativist positions embody what seems patently an ideology of the powerful. Only the most powerful, the most successful in achieving control over their world, could imagine that the world can be constructed as they choose'. Wylie is here arguing that relativism undermines the ability of those who lack power to take a stand, to argue that their subordination is grounded in the objective realities of their existence. Relativism appears to make all standpoints equal, and to destroy the universal and objective bases of claims for emancipation.

But note how one can return to Wylie's quote and substitute an objectivist for a relativist perspective and retain the meaning of the sentences: 'I myself find inescapable the suspicion that strong positivist and objectivist positions embody what seems patently an ideology of the powerful. Only the most powerful, the most successful in achieving control over their world, could imagine that the world can only be constructed in one way, objectively'. One of the great realizations for many in the West in the twentieth century has been that western notions of science have done unaccountable harm. In a postcolonial world, in the world left from the Great War, the Holocaust and Hiroshima, universalist western traditions, including positivism and objectivism, have come under scrutiny. Little (1994) discusses for archaeology the link between positivist rationality and male domination. In reburial issues throughout the world, objectivist science is used on the side of those who confront the disempowered.

So you are saying that both objectivism and relativism can be used in the interests of the dominant against the subordinate?

Yes. It is naive, wrong and dangerous to believe that an epistemology can guard us against misuse of the past. 'Truth' will not protect us from 'politics'. Neither objectivism nor relativism nor any other philosophical -ism can stand in for social and moral evaluation of political uses and abuses in archaeology. Misuse of the past can only be evaluated socially and ethically. As members of society we make ethical evaluations of the use to which epistemologies are put in the service of politics.

It is my opinion that in the present historical moment of global information capitalism and postcolonialism, a dialogue between diverse perspectives on the past is needed in a morally and politically aware archaeology. We live in a plural and multivocal world. This is not the same as saying that we live in a relativist world if by that is meant that we cannot make judgements between the claims of different groups. The difference between plurality and relativism is that the former refers to the rights and dignity of diverse groups. Multivocality is grounded in our diverse needs, morally and materially evaluated (McGuire 1992).

The Modern and the Postmodern in 'Heritage'

As argued above, a characteristic of globalization is the dual process of homogenization and fragmentation. Homogenization can be seen as the result of the market, of new information technologies, and of global environmental issues. Fragmentation can be described in two contrasting ways: (a) On the one hand, fragmentation is an essential part of the global networked economy since the latter depends on a dispersed, de-regulated and de-unionized process of labour. The global economy also depends on defining new markets and tailoring its products for special interests, hence the concept of niche marketing or the constituency or 'market of one'. The new information technologies allow the market to be extended from the mass to the individual. Fragmentation also serves the economy in a less direct way – through nostalgia and false consciousness. 'Getting in touch with yourself', or your locale or group involves small-scale solidarities and often a nostalgia for a more 'centred' way of life. This is parallel to the 'me as monument' view described in chapter 8. Fragmentation in these terms may be a way of dealing with alienation and the dispersal of power; it may alleviate the frustration at not being able to identify the source of power. Nostalgia for community may involve making the best out of the experience of fragmentation. In all these ways, fragmentation serves and is part of the economy. (b) On the other hand, fragmentation can be seen as part of empowerment. The fragmentation can be seen as a reaction against homogenizing tendencies, against the dispersal and concealment of power. It allows people to act back, to use the new technologies to resist globalization, to form not a false but a real 'centre that holds', and to argue for rights and resources.

'Heritage' is centrally involved in the dual homogenization/fragmentation process, and the growth of heritage issues has all the complexities and paradoxes just described. On the one hand, there are universal notions of a common heritage for all humankind. Such notions lie behind the specification of certain world monuments as 'World Heritage Sites'. At a different scale, within Europe, sites are identified as prime examples of 'European heritage'. They are assumed to have a common meaning for all Europeans despite the fact that Europe itself is a historical construction. So heritage is common to us all. A similar point can be made in quite a different way. The term 'heritage' conjures up a commercialized world open to the market, a 'theme-parking' of history and the past. Our changing relationship with the past has been documented by many. For example, Lowenthal (1985) has argued that we have in the West increasingly become alienated and distanced from the past which has become 'another country' which, as Fowler (1992) has shown, we are both protected from (by the state) but encouraged to visit on vacation. We sit in 'time cars' and travel to distant worlds miraculously reconstructed for us. It is no accident that Baudrillard and Eco use this changing relationship as an exemplar of the shift to the postmodern pastiche of depthlessness. The 'theme-parking' creates the past as universal commodity.

On the other hand, the term heritage is linked to inheritance and to ideas of belonging, nation and community. It refers not to depthlessness but to deep links with the past, to rights and senses of place, to ownership and roots, to origins. In many countries, national heritage is still defined by and controlled by the state. The link between archaeology and nationalism is strong if variable (Diaz-Andreu and Champion 1996; Dietler 1994). Areas of conflicting interests from the reburial of human remains in North America to the riots at the Ayodhya site in India (Rao 1994; Bernbeck and Pollock 1996) are now the subject of intense archaeological, heritage or museum involvement. In such cases, the past is connected, deep, inherited. Thus the conferring of the labels 'World Heritage Site' or 'European Heritage Site' to an archaeological site may have the result of reinforcing local identities and claims. The notion of heritage raises issues of ownership and of the relationship between local groups and global processes. Archaeologists routinely recognize this when they say that it is important to 'work with the locals'. Locality and time sequence are important in the strategies of the un-networked.

Does the contemporary world of heritage serve only the interests of the new global economy or does it also enhance and engender community empowerment and resistance?

In several ways, contemporary approaches to heritage are not empowering. For example, many interpretive centres and heritage experiences are designed primarily for fun or pleasure as in the typical historical theme park (in Britain a good example is 'The World of Robin Hood' in Sherwood Forest). The concern here is with depthless pastiche. Other uses of heritage are primarily nostalgic rather than empowering. For example, many of the men's, goddess, Ecofeminist or Gaia movements are deeply embedded in a symbolism derived from the past (Meskell 1995). In my experience, some of these groups are primarily concerned with helping their members to get in touch with themselves so that they can better deal with the world around them. Even in cases in which participants feel empowered (for example, as 'women' or 'men') within such movements, the use of the past by such groups may be largely nostalgic. It may not be the links to the past which create empowerment, and the past is often treated in superficial and stereotypical ways.

However, in other cases the past clearly does play a central role in empowerment (for the goddess groups see box on p. 155). For example, in the museum and archaeological excavation in District 6 in Cape Town, a fragmented and dispersed community is refinding its existence and reforming its identity (Hall 1998). Throughout the Americas and in Australia, the past is being used to justify claims to land, rights and resources and new alliances are being formed between indigenous peoples. In such cases, marginalized groups are undoubtedly empowered through their engagement with their heritage. In the contemporary world there is an increasing concern to open up the past to all citizens – to say 'this is your heritage'. Museums, in particular, have been undergoing a major transformation. In trying to go 'beyond the glass case' (Merriman 1991) museums are increasingly concerned with participation, interaction, multiple interpretations, gender and other social issues.

Or are they? Superficially and temporarily yes. But what of the longer term? In most cases, the debate over conflicting claims regarding heritage takes place in the terms of the dominant discourse. In other words, the terms and techniques used are those of western science. When indigenous groups learn to look after and 'do' their own archaeology, they normally adopt western archaeological concepts and are trained by and within the western academy. In Cultural Resource Management, the past comes to be seen as a quantifiable resource. Certainly there are examples in which a different view is maintained.

For example, in excavations in the Andes, foreign archaeologists are often obliged to hold rituals to ensure the success of the project or to placate the spirits or gods on the recovery of a human or llama burial. But after the rituals, the western conception of archaeological science reasserts itself. Certainly there are regional differences in the way archaeologists excavate. Japanese, British and North American archaeologists go about the task of excavation in rather different ways, using different tools and techniques. But I can think of no example in which minority groups within these societies have developed their own approaches to excavation. In the end, it could be argued that the approaches and techniques of the dominant culture will prevail. Over the long term, there is a homogenization of techniques and terms.

So in one way or another, the globalization process wins out in the end. Either heritage serves the global economy by fragmenting into pastiche and individual nostalgia, or the process of negotiating heritage rights homogenizes and makes same. Either way, the market and new forms of the dispersal or power are engendered. Power is centralized and its effects dispersed at the same time.

We construct interactive multi-media displays or hypertext narratives, or we make all our data available on the Web – and yet this 'empowerment' serves the dual process so well. Individuals can 'construct their own pasts'. In this way they are fragmented, atomized, prepared as individual units in the market. And at the same time they are all using the same systems, being homogenized in a global netscape.

Is there any way out of the Gordion knot? Not easily and perhaps not at all, but there are two points worth considering: (a) There is a sense in which, despite all the above, some empowerment is enabled, however marginally and temporarily. Despite their central production and control, the new information technologies do allow the formation of and liaison between small interest groups, the creation of identities, the greater awareness of gender issues, a greater awareness of one's own abilities to act. Subordinate groups are perhaps being drawn into a homogenized global archaeological language, but at least they can then participate in the debate. (b) The technologies also have the potential to deepen engagement with the past as well as to counteract the depthlessness so often claimed for postmodernism (Smith 1994). This is because the power and interactivity of the information systems allow access to enormous amounts of data. As Lyotard (1984, 67) has noted, computerization 'could aid groups . . . by supplying them with the information they usually lack for making knowledgeable decisions'. Archaeology has tended to see an absolute divide between 'deep' specialist information (published, if at all, in heavy data tomes) and 'shallow' popular books, films and exhibits. Modern information systems allow the two to be provided together (for example, on line or a book published together with a CD-Rom). Potentially, one can now bypass the duality of 'I have the data/techniques/specialist knowledge; you can play with the interpretation'. Public access to 'depth' can be provided, and alternative perspectives empowered.

The new technologies available within the world of heritage enhance the homogenizing and fragmenting tendencies, but also perhaps leave room for some empowerment in the face of, or via, those tendencies. The technologies homogenize and centralize and so serve the market but they also allow for indepth engagement which is both less hierarchical than in the past and less like postmodern play. And yet, as I have tried to indicate, the balance between the interests of the new global economies and empowerment is subtle, difficult and unstable. There are many fine lines to walk along and many difficulties of interpretation. In the end, there is no substitute for local and specific resolution of the various opposing tendencies. The impact of the use of the past in a particular context has to be established in terms of local issues, for different groups, and in relation to both short-and long-term considerations. 'Context' may itself be the product of global fragmentation processes, but it is within those contexts that the global issues have to be worked out and acted upon.

Global Processes Versus Local Heritage: The Example of Çatalhöyük

It may be helpful to clarify the theoretical account in relation to a particular example; recent experience at the Çatalhöyük project in central Turkey (Hodder 1998) has exposed many of the issues described above. One of the commercial sponsors of the project is an international credit card company. With its Istanbul-based PR firm, this company is genuinely interested in supporting the project while at the same time making use of its commercial potential. For example, during press visits to the site all the excavation staff wear hats with the company logo, and a replica of the Çatalhöyük 'Mother Goddess' (a figurine discovered at the site by James Mellaart in the 1960s) with the company name is handed out to clients at receptions in Istanbul. The company saw a particular link to Çatalhöyük when I, as project director, argued that obsidian could be seen as the first 'credit card'. Members of the team laughed when I told them and the obsidian specialist was embarrassed. Perhaps I was embarrassed too, but I justified my compliance by arguing that obsidian was exchanged widely (like credit cards) and that ethnographically artifacts such as obsidian can come to act as media for exchange, and exchange involves setting up debt (and thus credit) between the giver and receiver.

At one level, the credit card company and other global interests in the site are using the project to 'trade in the exotic'. The site's foreign-ness, distance in time, strange name, make it an ideal 'other'. The exoticness and otherness can be used to promote international corpor-ate relations within the company and to promote an international credit card designed for a multicultural global society. The sponsorship can be promoted in terms of 'the first payment system', and the company remains primarily interested in a commercial involvement. While individuals in the company may be interested in the archaeology which takes place at the site, the prime motive of the company is commercial.

But global commercializing processes of the type entered into with the credit card company also have an impact locally, such as in the rural areas of central Turkey where the site is situated. The company wanted to set up an exhibit in the on-site museum which showed the development of 'credit cards' from the first obsidian to the latest credit cards with microchips. One could not help but see the probable out-come of this. Turkey is seeing a massively expanding market for credit cards, but the main take-up is in the urban centres. In rural areas there has been less impact. The exhibit and the message about prehistoric credit cards might not only legitimate the modern company's claim to be concerned with Turkish culture but also might encourage local interest and take-up.

Nevertheless, the support of the company was very much needed if the project was going to be able to continue and have any long-term benefit for local identity, tourism, employment and social change through development of the site as a heritage resource.

I wanted to hold a ceremony at the site to open the dig house. I invited the Turkish Minister of Culture as well as local politicians. The Minister of Culture had recently changed to be a member of Refah, the religious fundamentalist party (later banned). I wanted our sponsors to come so that all parties could thank them. Indeed the Minister of Culture would unveil a plaque listing the support of the sponsors. This 'photo-opportunity' was rejected by the credit card company which decided it did not want to be associated in this way with the Refah party. Here commerce and Islam confronted each other and the former stood down.

In the end the Minister did not attend and sent his Director General of Monuments and Museums. The European Ambassador also came. West and east, secular and religious met, and talked at a podium decked out by the local Mayor in a Turkish flag. The speeches described the importance of the project and I presented the buildings to the Turkish state. But the currents of differing meanings, strategies and interpretations were rife.

In all the political manoeuvering, the site and the local concerns seemed to play little role. They seemed overrun by larger-scale processes and oppositions. But on the other hand, the town Mayor and other local officials made their speeches too and there was considerable coverage in the local press. Black Mercedes, flags flapping at high speed, swept in in clouds of dust. Armed guards surrounded the mound, and out got the national officials. They came and went, involved in their own strategies. Local people had to be bussed in to create a crowd at the ceremony – a true 'rent-a-crowd'. The local people seemed to understand the motives behind the show for what it was. They tolerated the event as long as it meant they could continue to work, make money, and follow their own strategies. The ceremony, and the national, fundamentalist and global strategies in which it was enmeshed, were necessary if their own lives were to continue to change in ways they, from different points of view, wanted.

Thus, in this case there is no simple opposition between global and local. In the local villages around Çatalhöyük people participate differentially and purposefully. They use the global processes to their own ends. For example, one of the site guards has applied to open a shop at the site so that his family's meagre income can be increased by the profits from sales to the increasing numbers of tourists. Women's lives also change. The images of 9000 year old naked 'goddesses' confront local Islamic attitudes in many ways, but particularly in regard to women who always have their heads covered. Initially their men-folk refused to allow them to work at the site. In the end they were allowed to work and, even though their husbands may have wanted to control their resulting wages, some women were able to use the situation to their advantage.

As another illustration of local manipulation of global processes, I wish to take the example of the strategies of the Mayor in the local town of Çumra. The recent Mayor is a member of the MHP party – Islamic but primarily nationalist. The rhetoric of the party is at times anti-Europe, anti-foreign involvement and anti-secular. At times it was difficult working with local officials who might be members of the MHP or the religious Refah party. Some would very pointedly not shake hands with female members of the team, especially on Fridays, since such contact would mean washing again in preparation for the mosque. Our English-speaking Euro-centric friends in Istanbul were always surprised that we got on so well with the Mayor. In our early years at the site he helped us with accommodation in Çumra, with equipment and materials.

He always embraced me and showed the greatest of respect. In 1995 he asked us for some photographs, especially of the naked 'Mother Goddess', to put in the foyer of the hotel in Çumra. Inside, it was full of Islamic religious references in its decor. Guests had to remove their shoes at the door. In such a context large images of the 'Mother Goddess' seemed so inappropriate, especially in a town in which all women always remained covered in public. Why did the Mayor want to do this?

The contradictions increased. In 1996 the Mayor made a formal proposal to the authorities in Ankara to set up a Çatalhöyük museum in Çumra itself. In the same year he announced to us that he wanted to call his annual agricultural festival the Çumra Çatalhöyük Festival. We were to provide a film and slide show, which we did, to a large and attentive audience. After the slide show the Mayor started handing out prizes for the best tomatoes and melons. I was embarrassed suddenly to be called on to the stage to be honoured and embraced in my turn, and presented with a plaque.

Why this public endorsement? What was the public advantage? After all, here was a foreign team digging a pre-Islamic site which confronts Islamic teaching both in its use of images and in its specific representations of women. Certainly the naked images are only acceptable because of their non-Islamic context. But the project clearly introduces commercialism and western attitudes. Why should it be so overtly embraced by an Islamic nationalist from a political party on the far right? Part of the answer is simply that our work brings money into the region, it increases employment, and it encourages tourism. It contributes to economic development and helps to gain a popular vote. It was for these reasons that the Mayor wanted to build a museum in Çumra – so that tourists would come to the town as well as to the site, 12 km away. But also, more personally, the Mayor found himself, as a result of the project, the centre of media attention and the host to political figures who visit the site from Konya and Ankara. His wider political ambitions were served.

The Mayor's rhetoric at public occasions involving the site dealt with the contradictions in subtle ways. Çatalhöyük, he said, is a site of great national significance. 'It is the source of Anatolian civilization. And yet it belongs to the world. Its knowledge is for everyone, without boundaries. We wish to give it to the world. The international scientific interest shows the importance of Anatolian civilization.'

The Mayor continued, 'Çatalhöyük is for all humanity'. When I told my Turkish friends in Istanbul about this they gasped. 'Did he really say that?' And in many ways his strategy was risky. There was all the reason in the world for him to be distrustful of us. There were many local people in the Çumra area who were suspicious of foreign contacts. The site and its imagery might be seen as confronting Islamic traditionalists. The site is certainly pre-Turkish if by Turk one means the movement of Turkish people into Anatolia in historic times. And yet, overall, the Mayor had decided, at least for the moment, that it was in his interests to support, embrace and even promote the project.

In the above instance, rather than a simple opposition between Islamic groups and religion and the international and commercial components of the project, we see subtle ways in which adjustments are made in order to achieve specific aims, such as increased employment and political status. At least in Turkey some accommodation between the global and the Islamic is clearly possible.

The local people are not simply duped into being 'globalized'. People have to be bussed to the opening ceremony. A blind eye is turned to the naked goddess in the visitor centre at the site, and to the busloads of people who turn up at the site on 'Goddess Tours'. Locally women may obtain their own wages and the Mayor follows his political ambitions. Locally men and women use the past in their own ways. They may be drawn into a global process but they reject some aspects and emphasize others. Change occurs, but in a complex and diverse way. There is a diversity of global and local experiences and responses within which Çatalhöyük is embroiled.

Cultural and Archaeological Resource Management

A similar linking of the global and the local can be engendered in the management of the archaeological resource. It has been argued in this book that the rise of contract archaeology created the need for field methods based on codification and structured management systems. The archaeological resource had to be managed quickly and efficiently. Standardized, repeatable and 'objective' methods were the result. But Adams and Brooke (1995) suggest that the methods employed in contract archaeology were not simply the result of the functional need for an efficient system of resource management. Rather, they argue that both the methods used and the management systems employed were underpinned by the same scientific objectivist paradigm. Certainly there are clear links between processual methods and contract archaeology. For example, much Cultural Resource Management is based on sampling procedures and the testing of specific research questions, both hallmarks of the processual contribution to archaeological method. But it is widely recognized that a rigid adherence to hypothesis testing in contract archaeology has negative results. This is because the cultural resource manager has to be responsible to the totality of what is in the ground. The testing of a narrow range of hypotheses is in conflict with the wider public interest.

And yet the sampling and analysis of the archaeological resource must be seen to be publically accountable and open to scrutiny. I have argued, following Grahame Clark (1934), that the rise of a scientific archaeology in the late-nineteenth century was intimately linked to the growth of a state interest in the guardianship of the archaeological heritage (Hodder 1989). It was of fundamental importance that the first Inspector of Ancient Monuments, Pitt-Rivers, was also recognized as the first scientifically meticulous field archaeologist. In line with Foucault, I argued (ibid.) that authoritative statements about the past were increasingly taken into the public domain where they had to be seen to be neutral, soundly documented and distanced from speculation. An objective and scientific method was born in this context. In recent decades similar arguments apply. The expansion of contract archaeology has led to decentralization but also to the need for regulation and repeatable methods. A positivist framework appeared to provide the necessary method, while at the same time a positivist approach to management appeared to ensure functional efficiency. 'A mechanistic view of information, or "data", derived from Newtonian science, and a passive view of the human resource which grew out of early management theory, have reinforced one another – this is hardly a coincidence' (Adams and Brooke 1995, 98).

Within the 'scientific' mode of management which came to be adopted by cultural resource managers, the emphasis is on replication, monitoring and strict functional division of tasks. The overall model involves planning and control and it is linear, reminiscent of the factory production line. The 'product' (the archaeological resource) is passed along the line. This linear process is shown, for example, in the process of archaeological project assessment in figure 9.1 (HBMC 1991). Although this scheme aims to be iterative and to incorporate some flexibility, most users in the UK have found that in practice it remains linear and structured.

An emphasis on formal rules and procedures within management has unattractive consequences which Adams and Brooke (ibid.) outline: people may feel less responsible for decision-making; they may be less able to adapt to sudden changes in conditions; their ability and motivation to produce creative solutions may be limited. Archaeological work thus becomes unfulfilling. The interactive and exploratory nature of archaeological enquiry becomes suppressed within rigid procedures and motivation decreases.

Alternatives to this type of linear approach to management focus on participative procedures in which employees are involved in decision-making. Employees are empowered by establishing systems in which interpretation and reinterpretation are encouraged at all levels. As already noted, the single context recording system used widely in contract archaeology in the UK was designed to allow greater participation in the recording and interpretation of field information. Employees now filled in their own forms and drew their own plans. More recently a fuller management system with these alternative aims in mind was introduced in a small professional field unit attached to Durham University (ibid.). The aim was specifically to design a set of recording tools compatible with other regional units but able to cope with 'fuzzy' (subjective, interpreted, fluid) data; to empower employees to implement such tools through training and gaining new skills; to pay employees at a high level to retain loyalty and motivation; to produce a high quality of output.

In most contract archaeology contexts it may be extremely difficult to introduce such changes. The limited resources and time constraints

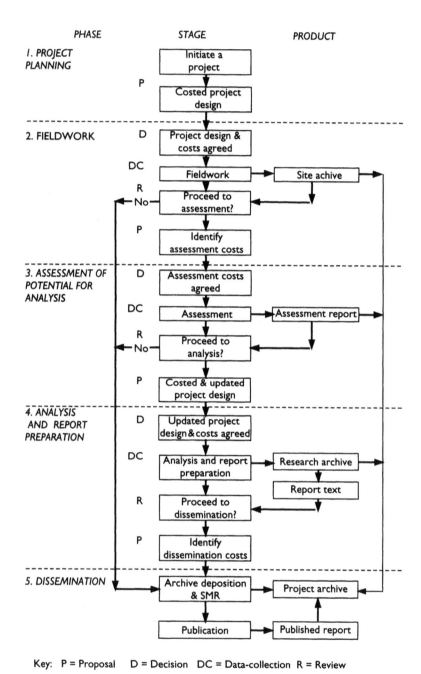

PHASE		STAGE	PRODUCT
I. PROJECT PLANNING		Initiate a project	
	P	Costed project design	
2. FIELDWORK	D	Project design & costs agreed	
	DC	Fieldwork	Site achive
	R No	Proceed to assessment?	
	P	Identify assessment costs	
3. ASSESSMENT OF POTENTIAL FOR ANALYSIS	D	Assessment costs agreed	
	DC	Assessment	Assessment report
	R No	Proceed to analysis?	
	P	Costed & updated project design	
4. ANALYSIS AND REPORT PREPARATION	D	Updated project design & costs agreed	
	DC	Analysis and report preparation	Research archive
			Report text
	R	Proceed to dissemination?	
	P	Identify dissemination costs	
5. DISSEMINATION		Archive deposition & SMR	Project archive
		Publication	Published report

Key: P = Proposal   D = Decision   DC = Data-collection   R = Review

Figure 9.1   The linear process of archaeological project assessment as suggested by English Heritage (Adams and Brooke 1995, 97).

may impede any more than the most minimal of reflexive process. But it is clear that the approaches discussed in this volume do not only have relevance in the research context. The issues of interactivity, fluidity and reflexivity are equally relevant in heritage where multiple voices are heard and where there is a wider need for participation and engagement in the construction of the archaeological resource. The same issues are central in contract archaeology, especially in multi-ethnic situations, but also they enhance the management of the archaeological resource in ways which are inclusive and rewarding for employees. The challenge in contract archaeology may be severe, but the wider movement in global societies towards participative, open, multivocal procedures has an impact in all areas of archaeology. For example, some of the attempts described in chapters 5 and 7 to embed data collection within narrative accounts may, when linked with multi-media data bases, promote wider use and foster the greater public engagement with archaeology on which a better resourced contract archaeology depends. Without greater engagement in local/global issues, and without a more relevant and public issue approach, contract archaeology is liable to remain under-resourced.

Other Implications of Diversity in Archaeology

How archaeologists write   A clear indication that archaeology is not always the same thing can be obtained by comparing the different ways archaeologists write. The same author, describing the same site, will produce very different reports, often using different data and even different conclusions, depending on the audience. Reports written for heritage managers, local administrators, academics, children, funding providers, and the popular market will vary widely.

Some of the different genres of archaeological writing are now coming under scrutiny. For example, Tilley (1989b) has explored the genre of the Cambridge Disney Professor Inaugural Lecture, and I have examined the tropes used in writing archaeological site reports from the eighteenth century to the present day (Hodder 1989). A major trend in the latter case has been towards distanced, neutral accounts in which the voice of the author is masked, and in which the contingency, uncertainty and non-linearity of the research process are hidden behind a timeless, certain and linear account. More recently, however, archaeologists have begun to experiment with writing which incorporates multiple perspectives (e.g. Tilley 1991). Especially in the gender literature there has been an increasing concern to write in ways which position people in the past and the archaeologist as author in the present (Kus 1992; Tringham 1991 and Spector 1993). In a particularly interesting example, Joyce (1994) uses a story-board technique to write a non-linear account of the life of the archaeologist Dorothy Popenoe. Such techniques can now be extended into digital media and the development of CD-Roms for interactive, multimedia engagement with archaeological sites is now increasingly found (e.g. Tringham 2000; Emele 1998).

In these ways, a supposedly singular archaeological past is defracted by different forms of writing into a kaleidoscope of forms; ultimately each 'reader' at each moment is able to construct a new version. I have already discussed some of the problems of this process. Since it is not, in my view of the information network society, a process that can be stopped, and since in my view there are benefits to archaeology in encouraging such diversity, the issue is really one of defining which types of writing, presentation or mediation are most appropriate in a given archaeological and social context. For example, I have already pointed to the idea that narrative forms of writing are more appropriate for the 'windows' we gain into the workings of past systems and large-scale structures. It is at the small-scale, in the reconstruction of individual lives, that narratives which attempt to capture the specificity of experience are most appropriate. However, some difficulties with this view will be discussed in the next section.

'Origins'   The most important and most widely referenced archaeological contributions to wider knowledge concern the search for origins – the first humans, the first culture and art, the first agriculture, the first city and state. Whether it is the first wheel or the origins of inequality that are being sought, archaeologists are looked to for an answer. By collaborating in this search for origins archaeologists become implicated in perhaps the fundamental project of modernism – the search for an origin and a destiny (progress to rationality, equality, liberty).

The political aspects of the search for origins are numerous. At one level, personal prestige may be enhanced for archaeologists who find the first hominid, or the earliest occurrence of megalithic burial. Group prestige and status may be enhanced by showing that 'our' ancestors built the first city or invented pottery. Origins research includes Childe's search for the origins of capitalism in Bronze Age Europe

(Trigger 1980). It extends to the use of archaeology to justify the territorial claims of ethnic groups.

In all these cases the claim for an origin is part of a wider narrative which ends with ourselves. Indeed, it could be said that it is the end point which has led to the focus on a particular starting point. Many narratives in archaeology mislead because they appear to concern themselves with beginnings. However, 'narratives are in fact, as so many have discussed, determined not by their beginnings but by their endings. Our stories of the past must end with the present' (Moore 1995, 51).

The whole notion of origins and the originary have been subjected to critique by postmodernist and feminist writers and there has been some discussion in archaeology (e.g. Conkey with Williams 1991). In a discipline which has evidence for the large-scale there is an obvious attraction towards grand narratives which discover origins. And yet the difficulty with writing narratives which have beginnings, middles and ends is that any such construction must be built from the present looking backwards. I do not mean to imply here that we can somehow avoid writing narratives. Neither do I argue that people do not live narratives in their lives (Hodder 1993). But in many instances the archaeological emphasis on origins tends to mislead and misrepresent.

When looked at in detail many of the major transformations in human history seem to be incremental, gradual and diverse. It is increasingly difficult to identify any point within a 4000 year period at which agriculture 'began' in the Near East, and J. Thomas (1993) has submitted the term 'Neolithic' to critical analysis. Johnson's (1996) work on the rise of capitalism provides a further example of how archaeology can contribute to an understanding of the gradual and diverse processes which lie behind what we see as major originary transformations. Contextual emphases on diversity, meaning, agency and contingency undermine any notion of 'the origin'. In a multivalent world, past and present, it becomes difficult to separate out a fixed 'thing' for which an origin can be found. Rather than focusing on the origins of major transformations, it is possible to use archaeological data to gain an understanding of the indeterminate relations between large-scale processes and individual lives. At these smaller scales, issues such as the origins of agriculture or the secondary products revolution or the rise of capitalism may have little impact or relevance. As the example of the Ice Man narrative in chapter 8 attempted to show, daily lives are always 'original'. They are part of larger processes. They are of interest and relevance whether or not they mark some boundary or origin which we define ourselves in hindsight. Archaeology provides us with windows into the lives which lie within the grand narratives. Rather than the modernist search for origins, we can focus on the diversity of individual lives and their relations to long-term processes of change.

Conclusion

In this chapter I have tried to demonstrate the dangers of an open-ended commitment to diversity and difference. The intellectual pursuit of fluidity and contextuality can too easily become blind to its social implications. In an increasingly globalized network society, the search for difference and diversity can become part of a 'play', serving the interests of the dominant. It can undermine the strategies of the less networked.

Yet, the same processes of global networking and flows can empower groups and individuals. Consideration of the wider context for the archaeological concern with diversity in this chapter has aimed to point to the often difficult ethical and social judgements that have to be made in discerning whether a particular case of difference serves the dominant processes of globalization or supports the responses against them.

The emphases on diversity, fluidity and interactivity in this volume can be used to promote a centralized global society in which information systems, commercial markets and production systems become ever more efficient at identifying individuals and catering to and exploiting their every and varied needs. In the end the result is 'difference as play' within a homogenized and centralized world.

But these same systems for the creation of networks and flows can be used to encourage difference in terms of identity and agency. They can be used so that we become increasingly aware, as members of global communities, of other concerns and perspectives grounded in historically different ways of life. And they can be used to generate new communities and new ways of life. Rather than the past as play or pastiche, archaeology can be used to generate new and grounded differences. The example from Çatalhöyük suggests that in the complex interactions of daily life, the global does not in any simple way win out over the local. There is rather a negotiated process in which the past serves a variety of interests.

Given that a wider context has been identified for an archaeology incorporating diversity, to what extent can some of the new technologies which are so much part of the global processes identified in this chapter contribute to an archaeology of diversity? Answering this question is the task of the next chapter.

10 Can the New Digital Technologies Deliver a Reflexive Archaeology?

The Spatio-Temporalization of Archaeology

In this book archaeology has been described as a diverse process, with numerous theories, methodologies, areas and scales of analysis, and applications. The diversity now seen in archaeology is part of the globalization of the developed and developing world.

An underlying theme of this book has been that archaeological statements about the past involve an interpretive moment of uncertainty as the general is related to the particular. In this uncertain creative moment the main methods that are used are accommodative, involving the search for part-whole coherence and correspondence. But any accommodation that is reached can only be provisional since the hermeneutic circle is never closed – interpretation is always doubly embedded in the changing contexts of the present and of the material past. Indeed, reflexive archaeology is the first fully processual archaeology since all categories, data, theories, methods are seen as in a continual state of flux – all archaeological 'things' are in fact processes. This emphasis on archaeology as a continual process allows the archaeological past to play a transformative role in the present. The material past is part of the present experience through which we come to understand ourselves.

Thus the 'archaeological process' of the title of this book concerns both the notion that nothing in the past was essential, fixed, systematized – everything was about transformation and change. But the title also refers to the lack of fixity in doing archaeology.

It can be argued that archaeology is in crisis in three respects: (a) The rise of archaeology as a discipline was intimately linked to nationalism (Diaz-Andreu and Champion 1996). People used to *inherit* culture, and archaeology and heritage were part of that inheritance. Now, increasingly, some people can *choose* their culture. They increasingly choose how they wish to relate to and interpret the past. The past is part of the 'performativity' of fluid identities (Butler 1990; 1993). This trend is parallel to but different from the emergence of new ethnicities in a postcolonial world, but again the diversity undermines a coherent and unified scientific approach. Thus (b) archaeology is losing its role in finding universal origins and human-ness, since the 'other' is talking back and giving different perspectives on these views. (c) Commodification and commercialization of the past have increased, partly as a result of withdrawal of the state support in some countries, but also as a result of the nostalgic fascination with exotic otherness which is so much a part of global society. How can standards be maintained within the discipline in the face of the market? And how can the past be used both to create local identities and global play?

The problem is how to find a role for archaeology after the supposed 'decline of ideology' and in the face of plurality. I have argued in this book that the appropriate response is not to police yet more rigidly the boundaries of the discipline and to define yet more narrowly the definition of archaeological science. Rather, the answer is to open up the discipline to reflexivity, contextuality, interactivity and multivocality and so to create a continual process of interpretation and re-interpretation. These opportunities in fact offer an exciting challenge.

It can be argued that these global directions are enabled by the new digital technologies. A stronger claim is that the technologies have caused the economic, social and cultural changes involved in the decentralization of work practices, the creation of virtual communities, the diversification of life styles, and the fragmentation of time. While it may be difficult to accept such determinism, I do wish to argue that the new roles for archaeology and heritage in the world are parallel to and enabled by the new information technologies. How we use these technologies will vary. Some will use them to bolster established and fixed versions of the discipline. Others, as I have tried to outline in this book, will use them to involve the past in the present in new, less fixed, ways.

Within this latter view, the aim is to shift our model of archaeology from hierarchy to that prime metaphor for a global society, the net. A net or network has multiple nodes rather than one centre. It allows information to flow horizontally but to be collated locally at nodal points. It concerns flow rather than fixity. Indeed, in the latter sense, even the metaphor of the net fails since within the networks of archaeology the nodes themselves may change. Rather than a fixed network there may be an ever changing set of flows and interactions. This is what is meant by the 'spatio-temporalization' of archaeology. Theories about the 'origins of agriculture', or systems of classification such as Stone, Bronze, Iron Ages or Band, Tribe, Chiefdom, State, can now be seen to be the product of a particular perspective on the past appropriate to a particular time and place. Within the metaphors of nets and flows, all universal claims can be contested and locally situated in a spatio-temporal moment. They are a particular pulling together of the strands of an argument. They may have general validity, but only from a specific local perspective.

In this new and more 'processual', un-fixed archaeological world, there will be much reliance on technologies. I wish to explore some of the apparent links between developments in archaeological theory and digital technology. What are the potentials offered by this convergence? But also what are the dangers? Can the new technologies really deliver the more open yet critically grounded debate that is sought? I will first give an optimistic answer before examining some of the difficulties and challenges that are posed.

Theory and Technology: A Benign View

There are many grounds for arguing for a convergence between archaeological theories based on the metaphor of the text and the new information technologies (Landow 1992). The technologies allow a shift from conceptual systems based on centres, margins, hierarchies and linearity to those based on multivocality, nodes, networks and flows. The technologies promise to deliver on the theoretical emphases on textuality, narrative and new relations between the writer and reader. Writers such as Barthes (1970; 1977) and Foucault (1977) outside the discipline and Tilley (1991) and Joyce (1994) within, are concerned with texts in terms of networks and links, as having several points of entry, and as having multiple pathways through them so that meaning is always changing and constructed by the reader (rather than solely by the writer). There are obvious parallels between the poststructuralist emphasis on such factors and the technologies which produce hypertext (blocks of text linked electronically) and hypermedia (as hypertext but including pictures, sound, animation etc.). Indeed, we can explore nine ways in which a convergence between theory and technology can be claimed.

1   *Readerly and writerly texts* Barthes (1970) makes a distinction between 'readerly' and 'writerly' texts (see Olsen 1990; Bapty and Yates 1990). It is only the 'writerly' text which forces active engagement by the reader with the text. Certainly the vast majority of archaeological texts expect a passive reading process. They do not facilitate other ways of reading or thinking about the archaeological data. In hypertext, on the other hand, the reader is forced to make choices and decisions and to become implicated in the construction of an account or interpretation of textual and visual material. So it may well be the case that the new hypertext technologies can deliver the theoretical aim of more interactive and 'writerly' texts.

2   *Intertextuality* Derrida emphasizes textual openness, intertextuality, and the breakdown of clear distinctions between inside and outside the text (Yates 1990). For Derrida 'there is nothing outside the text', no boundaries between the textual and non-textual. Whatever one thinks about the extreme form of this claim, it is undoubtedly the case that texts make references outside themselves. In the discussion on p. 198, it is argued that a global approach to Çatalhöyük involved a blurring of the boundaries between who is in and who is outside 'the team'. The 'text' produced about Çatalhöyük extends outwards indefinitely. More generally, in hypertext archaeology the reader can click and move out of a text and search for references within a global network of information. Intertextual links can be explored.

3   *De-centring* A closely related idea in poststructuralism is that there are no centres or points of reference that are not themselves constructed. It is argued that our choice of centres of investigation is conventional, as are our questions and perspectives. The critique of origins research and of the assumption of original 'starting points' in chapter 9 shows the extent to which a 'centred' approach in archaeology is coming under scrutiny. The role of

the 'home page' on the Web indicates that people still need centres from which to look out. But the network technologies allow such centres to be seen as provisional, and as one of many possible entry points.

4   *Death and re-birth of the subject* The claim is widely made in post-structuralist writing that the author as a 'self' is always already a node in other texts and codes, is always already written. Derrida and Foucault have, in different ways, decentred the subject (Bapty and Yates 1990; Tilley 1990). For Ricoeur, authorial meanings escape and are reinterpreted at a distance by the reader (Moore 1990). It is certainly the case that the new information technologies raise problems of authorship and control. Archaeological site reports have increasingly become collaborative, but the new technologies allow the radical extension of this process. Placed on the Web or in some interactive hypertext environment, a site report can become a continually commented on, multiple, contested network of information. The autonomy and fixity of the text are undermined, and the author (if such a person can be identified) has less mastery and control over the message. On the other hand, there has been much theoretical reaction against the idea of the 'death of the author' and the 'decentring of the subject'. We have seen many examples in this book of attempts to introduce experiential and phenomenological and agency-centred accounts, and of attempts to write the past as a narrative transparently constructed by the author. The new technologies again facilitate this re-birth and recentring. Virtual reality allows reconstruction of different perspectives of past monuments and environments. Codified, impersonal data bases can be linked to personalized diaries so that the construction of data by team members can be recorded (see chapter 7).

5   *Fragments* Derrida conceives of texts as made up of discrete reading units. A focus on discontinuities is widely found in recent archaeological theory (Hodder and Shanks et al. 1995). Shanks and Tilley (1987) and Tilley (1989b) discuss how the past is used as 'quotes', bracketed fragments within an assemblage of knowledge. Barrett (1994) entitles his volume on interpretations of British prehistory 'fragments from antiquity'. The new on-line journal based at the University of Sheffield is called 'Assemblage'. It is precisely the structure of fragments linked together into an assemblage that defines hypertext and hypermedia.

6 *Multivocality* Much contemporary theory in archaeology emphasizes the past as dialogue rather than being represented for 'us' by
a tyrannical, unified voice. The sources of this plurality are most
directly feminism and globalism. But indirectly these changes
derive from the wider fragmentation and diversification of societies
and the proliferation of individual pursuits and identities. The
widespread availability and low cost of digital information flows
allow small-scale groups to emerge and gain mutual support. Those
marginalized within traditional systems of knowledge dissemination
find the ability to constitute themselves as other voices. Whether
such groups are within the academy (such as micro-faunal specialists) or outside it (ley-line hunters or goddess groups) the ability to
take part in dialogue is increased.

7 *Virtuality* Archaeologists have grown accustomed to the notion that
the past is not 'real' – it is at least partly how we construct it. Such
claims can be made for data catalogues (Spector 1993) as much as
they can for site reports (Hodder 1989). Archaeologists are increasingly interested in how people in the past perceived monuments
and landscapes, and how they understood them in the movements
of their bodies (chapter 8). The new technologies produce digital
information represented on a screen. We can easily change the font,
size of letters, or lay-out. What we see is a virtual representation.
The same sense of virtuality is experienced in 'virtual archaeology'
reconstructions of past monuments and landscapes (Forte and
Siliotti 1997). Archaeologists and non-archaeologists form themselves into virtual communities on the Net in order to further
their special interests. None of this is to say that the virtual is
not real. Rather, it is to say that the opposition between real and
virtual is questioned in both theory and in the application of the
technologies.

8 *Non-linearity* Writers such as Barthes, Derrida, Bakhtin and Foucault make continual reference to links, networks, paths or weaving.
In archaeology, Shanks (1992) places an emphasis on rhizomes –
expanding networks of paths and links. Themes such as causality
and power are discussed in terms of complexity and dispersal rather
than linearity (e.g. Miller and Tilley 1984). The links to non-linear
modelling and applications of chaos theory in archaeology are
evident (Shennan 1989). The brunt of these theoretical critiques is
often narrative – a coherent structured story with a beginning,
middle and end. Lyotard (1984) defines postmodernism as

incredulity towards meta-narrative. This critique of narrative may seem at odds with attempts to introduce narrative as a way of gaining a fuller understanding of the lives of prehistoric people (e.g. Spector 1993; Tringham 1991). But the narratives that are produced may themselves seek for non-linearity, as in Tringham's (2000) hypertext account of Opovo (Chimera Web). Of course, there is linearity in hypertext. There may be a 'menu' to which the user continually returns, and there are cues like 'click here' or 'start here'. And certainly the user takes a path through the hypertext environment. And yet the path is chosen by the user; it is not controlled and constructed in a linear fashion. It is certainly possible to construct experiences of the past which are more like networks and less like paths.

9 *Reflexivity* There has been widespread theoretical discussion in archaeology of the need for critique. For example, various types of Critical Theory have been used to subject taken-for-granteds to analysis (Leone et al. 1987). The post-structuralist emphasis on deconstruction has led in a similar direction (Bapty and Yates 1990; Shanks and Tilley 1987). The world of heritage and museums has in particular been the subject of critique from marginalized and indigenous groups (e.g. Gathercole and Lowenthal 1989). The new digital technologies might be said to foster at least some forms of critique and reflexivity. For example, it is increasingly possible to read a text while at the same time calling up critiques and alternative views. Often these contrasting perspectives can be called up onto the same screen and compared directly. The ability to compare different texts, different types of data, and different media simultaneously increases the potential for critical scrutiny and reflexivity. For example, it may be possible to compare statements about stratigraphical relationships on a site against field photographs or video (see chapter 7). Reflexivity is also enhanced by the existence of multiple channels in the information network so that a plurality of voices can be heard.

It might thus be argued that the cumulative effect of the above nine points of convergence between archaeological theory and the new digital technologies will be to enhance the developments outlined in this book. But we can now turn to another point of view in which the new technologies create a global world in which a supposedly multivocal archaeology continues to serve a minority.

Theory and Technology: A Critical Response

It is often assumed that the new hypermedia are essentially democratizing, leading to a more decentralized, liberated existence. If this is so then application of digital technologies in archaeology should lead to wider involvement of the past in the lives of an increased range of people.

However, contrary to the claims for decentralization, many commentators have argued that digital communications reinforce centre–periphery divergence and domination (e.g. Gillespie and Robins 1989). An increasing centralization of power amongst the already dominant is seen in the fact that digital flows are closely tied to new transnational, global corporations and tend to be focused in major metropolitan areas. An electronic democracy is endangered by the way in which Microsoft has dominated all competition in the software market, by how telecommunications conglomerates like British Telecom-MCI or Time-Warner have invested in digital technologies, and by how digital technology enables the more efficient dispersal of surveillance systems (Palattella 1995). It is argued (e.g. Kroker and Weinstein 1994) that we may be living in the 1990s in a false dawn. As the sprawling disorder of the Net gets taken over by telematics and the information superhighway, and as we all put 'boxes' on our TVs owned by multinational telecommunications conglomerates, many of the initial claims for revolutionary changes and democratization may be disappointed.

Interactivity and the Net can be seen simply as ways of drawing a yet larger market into the new technologies. The aim is not interactivity but the control and expansion of a commercial market (Kroker and Weinstein 1994). Globally, advanced regions provide technologies to marginal areas. The processes of uneven and unequal economic development continue. Kester (1994) argues that democratization and the free flow of information are undermined by the fact that information does not flow directly to 'the public'. Rather it is mediated by those who provide the information. Only a limited group of people are connected by the new technologies. The Internet creates a 'utopian' community, overwhelmingly consisting of white professionals. Its supposed openness and democracy are made possibly by its homogeneity; diversity is not embraced (Kester 1994).

It can therefore be argued that the attempt made above to identify nine points of convergence between digital technologies and theories in the humanities and social sciences is an attempt to appropriate the new technologies within an elite culture. By linking the technologies to the authority of white western male authors (Foucault, Derrida, Barthes etc.), an attempt is made to assert the relevance of theory to society (Palattella 1995). The link justifies and legitimates. And so the dominance of the established elite continues. The new technologies are de-radicalized. They simply enable an extension of existing liberal ideas of democracy. Nothing much changes.

Following Marx, Kroker and Weinstein (1994) argue that every technology releases opposing possibilities towards emancipation and domination. While undoubtedly the above dangers of increased domination exist, the archaeological case suggests that the new technologies can be steered in the direction of having beneficial and transformative effects.

Certainly, both Engelstad (1991) and Smith (1994) from different points of view have argued that the impact of postprocessual archaeology is to continue dominant structures of male-centred elite intellectualism. With regard to the impact of the digital technologies, S. Thomas (1996) has pointed out that use of hypertext cannot simply be linked to democratization. Users have to have some knowledge of archaeology before they can navigate themselves around a hypertext environment. On the other hand, I have given several examples in this book of how the technologies can be used to enhance reflexivity, contextuality, interactivity and multivocality. As described in chapter 7, sites, monuments, excavations, data bases, and textual reports can be opened to a wider scrutiny than has traditionally been available. Certainly knowledge is needed to be able to participate in global archaeological dialogues, but I have also suggested that it is possible to use visual media in order to provide 'user-friendly' 'front-ends' to archaeological information. Potential users can be led into archaeological debate and provided with the information necessary to participate if they so wish.

While the Internet is often accused of elitism, there is a growing grass-roots participation organized, for example, by local public libraries. As the digital market extends outwards, seeking to incorporate marginal or low-status groups, so those groups become integrated into the network. They can participate and be less isolated. The widespread Internet activity dealing with Egyptian archaeology, for example, has been documented by Meskell (1998). I have noted above the intense interest in Gimbutas, the goddess and Çatalhöyük by a wide range of women's groups (see also Meskell 1995; Conkey and Tringham 1996). It is increasingly possible to contact and interact with leaders of Native American and other indigenous groups through digital networks.

Conclusion

The wider dissemination and democratization of archaeological knowledge and increased interactivity with interpreters of the past are not limited to digital information channels. Many of those working in museums or heritage centres have shown a concern to engage a wider range of people, including minorities, in an interactive manner. Those concerned with writing the past have also placed emphases on alternative voices, reflexive critique and openness (e.g. Spector 1993; Tringham 1991; Tilley 1991). Leone et al. (1995) have focused on the representation of the past in tours of Annapolis.

But all these concerns with interactivity and openness may only be of interest to those already engaged in 'high culture' (Merriman 1991). Digital technologies, for example, seem little more than niceties of elite self-interest when viewed from deprived areas throughout the world. As discussed in chapter 9, those people who are relatively un-networked may be more interested in archaeology in terms of links to place and in terms of rights to resources. In contrast to the networks and fragmentation created by dominant groups, the archaeological past may provide a prime means of creating specific identities and gaining access to rights.

Thus in chapter 9 I argued that in the case of Çatalhöyük the global processes were used in complex and sometimes contradictory ways in order to further the interests of local communities. But the assertion of community rights and identities through archaeology is not limited to groups of people anchored in space. What I have described as the 'spatio-temporalization' of archaeology is a process incorporating networks and flows rather than fixed spatial and temporal boundaries. Special interest groups such as goddess worshippers may come together initially on the Internet. They may thus form a 'virtual' community. But the distinction between 'virtual' and 'real' is increasingly difficult and invidious. Network communities may be important in creating a sense of identity, with just as much efficacy as those communities tied to place. In both the spatially bound and the spatially free communities, the global network is manipulated in order to create different pasts.

11 Conclusion: Towards Non-Dichotomous Thinking in Archaeology

At various points in this volume, I have outlined a reflexive method that is being used in the excavation of the site of Çatalhöyük in Turkey (see also Hodder 1997 and box on p. 119). I wish now briefly to recapitulate and summarize 12 steps that are being attempted in that methodology.

1 Every one or two days during the excavation, the laboratory specialists visit the excavation areas on the site (Figure 5.5). This is possible because faunal, archaeobotanical, lithic, ceramic, soil micromorphological, ground stone, human remains and other specialists are present on the site during excavation. The aim of the discussions between the laboratory and field staff is twofold. From the point of view of the laboratory staff, information is gained about context. For example, it is helpful for the ceramics specialist to know if there is some uncertainty about the stratigraphical relations and dating of a layer, hearth or other context. From the point of view of the field staff, the tours by the laboratory specialists provide them with information about what they are excavating. For example, a faunal specialist might be able to recognize in the field the animal species and skeletal parts. This might help the excavator to interpret what is being excavated and thus make appropriate decisions about sampling strategies. This takes us to the second part of the Çatalhöyük methodology.

2 We have seen that many approaches in field archaeology assume, despite provisos about 'theory-ladenness', the objective sanctity of

the archaeological data. As a result, sampling strategies are often developed which can be applied in a wide variety of different contexts. The codification and systematization of archaeological recording procedures have also been encouraged by the development of cultural resource management. Sampling strategies are adopted 'off the shelf', using pre-set formulae. In practice, archaeologists have a duty to be responsible to what they find. As a result sampling strategies are often changed as a survey or excavation progresses. But even the most codified of sampling strategies involves making interpretive decisions. For example, it may have been decided to excavate 10 per cent of all pits on a site, but 20 per cent of the hearths. It becomes necessary to interpret a feature as a pit or hearth before excavation. And what happens if a new category of feature is found, such as a ritual hearth? In order to avoid these difficulties at Çatalhöyük, we have replaced decisions about sampling with negotiations about priorities. When the laboratory staff tour the excavation areas, they discuss with the field staff which layers and features should be prioritized. Different members of the team argue for this or that layer or feature to be sampled more intensively (wet sieving as opposed to dry sieving for example). The percentages of deposits of a particular type which have been prioritized can be monitored. The priority contexts are retained in all further laboratory analysis. In this way, the sampling (prioritizing) can be related to the changing interpretation of the site and its features. It can be moulded to the particular site and adapted to the particular interpretation.

3   Another characteristic of many field approaches is that they assume the self-evident nature of 'the archaeological object'. For example, when trays of artifacts are brought into the laboratory from the field they are usually divided into pottery, metal, bone, shell, lithics and so on. These divisions determine how these objects are then studied and published. The artifacts are sent off to the pottery, metal, bone and so on specialists. This common archaeological procedure involves wrenching artifacts out of their context. Decontextualized they become difficult to interpret except in universalist terms. At Çatalhöyük we have recognized that this process does not help the understanding of the site or of individual object categories. The need for interaction and integration lies behind our emphasis on having all the different types of specialist present at the site. But we have also recognized that the categories themselves are arbitrary

and dependent on the scale at which we happen to work. At the microscope pieces of obsidian might be used as filler in pottery. They are thus not 'lithics' but 'pottery'. At the large scale, we have attempted to define 'objects' which cut across traditional categories. For example, the study of 'refuse' involves all types of materials, as do the 'objects' 'burning', 'decoration', 'food' or 'domestication'. In these ways the interactions between the different types of specialists are maximized.

4   Another aim of the tours by the laboratory staff is to get information back to the field staff as quickly as possible. The reason for this is to discourage the idea of excavation as a mechanical process of recording objective data. Rather, the aim is to encourage the idea of excavation involving interpretation at the trowel's edge. In order to interpret stratigraphy properly, it helps to know the date of the pottery in the layers. In order to identify a floor it may be helpful to know about the degree of abrasion of pottery and bone. So, as we dig, we need to know as much as possible about what we are digging. This knowledge and our interpretations will determine the sampling strategies we use. At Çatalhöyük, the laboratory staff are thus asked to 'fast-track' the material from some layers and contexts. In other words, they look at this material quickly and feed back the results to the field staff. Other potential ways of speeding up the flow of information include digital recording and planning. In this way plots and plans can be examined immediately. Histograms and comparisons can be made immediately so that excavation can take place with maximum knowledge of what is being uncovered.

5   An integrated and fluid data base is essential for any attempt to link different participants in an archaeological project. At Çatalhöyük we have attempted a computer network so that the field staff and laboratory specialists can query each other's data and make comments on the provisional interpretations of their colleagues. All the different types of data, from field records to plans and drawings to measurements of lithic and ceramic artifacts to the film and diary data to be described below are available on the same data base. The separate computers are linked by a hub to one central computer to which all have access. The high degree of circuitry that is thus produced means that interpretations can always be in a state of flux, 'data' can continually be reconsidered and transformed, and conclusions are momentary.

6   However much one might want to create a fluid and flexible data base, some degree of fixity and codification is necessary. This is in order to allow comparison and in order to handle very large amounts of data. But any data base is a construct, and it is important that the user understands it as such. The user of a data base has to be able to situate it within its own context of production. In order to do this at Çatalhöyük we have reverted to the writing of a diary. This is written into the data base and cross-referenced. Thus, if a user wants to find out about layer 321, it is possible to find all the diary entries relating to layer 321 as well as the codified lists of animal bones, ceramics etc. found within it. The diary allows the user of the data base to understand what the excavators were assuming as they excavated a particular layer. It allows understanding of why the layer was excavated and sampled in a particular way. It allows the biases and pre-understandings to be explored. But writing the diary too has a beneficial effect. Other people read the entries as they are made and so the circuitry of information is enhanced. Also, the writing of the diary makes the excavator reflect on the excavation process and evaluate that process in relation to the questions that are being asked.

7   In the same way, the video recording of the excavation process leads to a reflexive stance. At Çatalhöyük, the discussions by laboratory staff on the tours of the site (see point 1 above) are video recorded, as are summaries of their work by the field and laboratory staff. These video recordings are then digitized and edited into 1 to 2 minute clips which are placed on CD-Roms. The clips can be accessed by a keyword search system (figure 7.1). Thus, it is possible to search for layer 321 in the data base and not only find the artifact and field records and the diary entries but also the video clips. These clips may show the excavator of layer 321 describing her or his work, pointing to the layer, and explaining its interpretation. This process allows the user of the data base to understand using visual information. It also allows the user to understand the assumptions and misconceptions under which the excavation was undertaken. The 'data' thus become relativized within a particular context of production of archaeological knowledge. Again, as with the diary, the process of filming itself means that information is circulated around members of the project as recording and viewing take place. Reflexivity occurs as project members are asked to explain their work and assumptions before the camera.

8   Being reflexive and self-critical involve a considerable amount of energy and commitment to theoretical awareness. In practice, archaeologists may have little time for and inclination for 'navel gazing', despite the benefits derived. In addition, most archaeologists are not trained in the observation of living cultural behaviour. Thus, at Çatalhöyük, anthropologists work with us, dedicated to the study of the construction of knowledge at the site. They participate in our daily lives on the site, observing and conducting interviews. One studies the ways our interpretations are embedded within unrecognized assumptions and pressures. Another explores the visual conventions (Molyneaux 1997; van Reybrouck 1998) through which we see and record the site (in the form of plans, section drawings, artifact drawings, photographs and video clips). Another studies the impact of our presence on the local community. The presence of people questioning assumptions has a destabilizing effect on the excavation and research teams. But a lack of stability is necessary if a critical approach is to be taken and if the project is to remain responsive to a changing world around it.

9   In order to facilitate maximum participation in the interpretation of the site from a variety of different communities, steps are being taken to place the entire Çatalhöyük data base on the Web. The aim is to provide a data base which is accessible and multimedia. This type of openness may conflict with the interests of individuals and groups with special access to the site. For example, the career paths of younger members of the project may be threatened if others have access to, and publish, primary data. Indeed, it is conceivable that alternative Çatalhöyük Web sites be set up by competing groups. However, while the rights of individuals and groups need to be protected, such concerns cannot justify the long-term secreting of archaeological information. Immediate accessibility encourages participation and engagement in the research process itself. It enhances multivocality.

10   The linearity of most archaeological narrative restricts the complexity of the stories that can be told. It also encourages the separation of evidence and interpretation. The latter is usually presented after the evidence has been set out. Hypertext, on the other hand, allows accounts with multiple pathways and incorporating multimedia. Thus a narrative account can be given and links provided between the narrative and pictures, plans, and coded

artifact data. On the computer, the hypertext user can 'click' from narrative text to data base evidence in order to check the basis on which interpretations are made (figure 7.2).

11 Archaeologists have always made plans, drawings and models of the buildings they excavate. These and other reconstructions allow hypotheses about original construction techniques to be experimented with. They also allow wider public participation in the understanding of a site. Today, the techniques of Virtual Reality allow greater speed and flexibility in the reconstruction experiments. The construction of a virtual world on the computer allows visualization and the experimentation with alternative reconstructions. Also, the virtual world can be made interactive so that the user can ask questions about a site and explore it from a non-specialist point of view. At Çatalhöyük the aim is for a virtual reconstruction of the site to become the 'front-end' to the data base. Non-specialist users can thus 'travel' to the virtual site and then find out about the archaeological information to a required level of detail. Virtuality also allows experimentation with different ways of experiencing the site.

12 At Çatalhöyük teams from different parts of the world are encouraged to excavate their own parts of the site. Equivalent recording and data systems are used, but each team uses its own traditional techniques of excavation and analysis. The assumption here is that the different teams, using different methods, will produce different results. By looking through different windows each team will see and find different Çatalhöyüks. Rather than being decried as chaotic, this diversity is welcomed since it is preferable to a single perspective and monolithic approach. The latter would produce a coherent account but that account would be based on the taken-for-granted assumptions of a particular archaeological tradition.

A Method with Flows

There seem to be four themes which underlie the twelve practical steps to excavation described above: reflexivity, relationality or contextuality, interactivity and multivocality. These have been discussed throughout this volume but they are summarized here.

Reflexivity By this I mean the examination of the effects of archaeological assumptions and actions on the various communities involved in an archaeological process, including other archaeologists and non-archaeological communities. Examples of this type of emphasis at Çatalhöyük include the work of anthropologists who study the impact of the project on the local community as well as on national and international groups interested in or visiting the site. Reflexivity is also engendered by the diary writing and video filming, since these processes encourage those on the team to examine their own assumptions. The diaries and videos also provide contextual information about the excavation process so that others can look back and critically evaluate the claims that have been made. The results of archaeological research are reflexively related to the context in which knowledge is produced.

Relationality or contextuality The notion here is that meaning is relational. This emphasis is seen in the reflexive attempts to relate findings to a specific context of knowledge production. But the emphasis is also visible in the inter-relations of contextual and artifactual information. Thus the date of a layer depends on the artifacts found in it. But in some cases, the date of the artifacts may depend on the stratigraphical relationships of the layers. In another example, at Çatalhöyük the interpretation of a building as a house rather than a shrine depends on the artifacts within it. But the interpretation of the artifacts partly depends on whether the building is seen as a house or shrine. So, usually in archaeology, everything depends on everything else within a hermeneutic whole. Our aim at Çatalhöyük has been to facilitate this circuitry, for example by having information about artifacts available to excavators as they dig contexts in a trench. The interpretations of artifact and context depend on each other and so it is necessary to have many artifact and context specialists present together on site so that information can be mutually available, especially for the excavators themselves. The aim is to be highly integrated and inter-disciplinary. Relationality also implies flexibility in the research process. If everything depends on everything else, then as I change one variable in my analysis so there are knock-on effects on all other variables. Thus a data base should be seen as open to change and as flexible as possible; conclusions are seen as momentary and always subject to change.

Interactivity   The aim here is to provide mechanisms for people to question and criticize archaeological interpretations that are being made, as they are being made. During the excavation process, interaction between laboratory and field staff is encouraged by the tours of trenches. The prioritizing (sampling) procedures are arrived at by negotiation between staff members. Interactivity is also facilitated at Çatalhöyük by the provision of the data base on the Web and by the provision of access routes (e.g. virtual reconstructions) that are 'user friendly'. It is also facilitated by the provision of information in diary and video form that situates the data base and opens it up for critique and alternative interpretation. The aim in the on-site museum is to have a community section in which a display about the site is constructed by members of the nearby village. In the museum too an interactive CD-Rom will be provided with hypertext and Virtual Reality components so that visitors and students can find out about the site in a non-linear way.

Multivocality   A wide range of different groups often have conflicting interests in the past and wish to be engaged in the archaeological process in different ways. The same point is often made in feminist archaeology (Conkey and Gero 1997). Mechanisms need to be provided so that different discourses can take place. For example, at Çatalhöyük different teams excavate different parts of the site and present their own 'windows' into the site. While the Web site may allow interaction with international, educated and networked groups, the local rural community is best able to interact through museum displays and visits to the site itself. In the future it may be conceivable to provide a modern shrine so that religious groups such as Mother Goddess visitors can pray at the site.

In still more general terms, one can argue that there is one theme which underlies these four emphases. This theme is the breaking down of boundaries and dichotomies. Archaeologists have spent much of their time throughout their history defending their subject against antiquarians, looters, Creationists, metal detector users, reburial movements, goddess worshippers. Some of these groups have been defined as 'fringe'. Others are seen as entirely outside the discipline. But in the end, the rigid maintenance of disciplinary boundaries, while effective in some circumstances, constrains the reaching of dialogue and compromise in others. For example, at least in Britain, many archaeologists now realize they can work with metal detector users within a framework that involves education and mutual understanding. The reburial conflict in Australia and the United States has involved a good deal of give and take on both sides. Wherever indigenous archaeologies develop, at least in a postcolonial era, some negotiation is involved. Wherever the market is needed as a financial underpinning for archaeological research, the views of a diverse public need to be catered for. Increasingly it is realized by archaeology that it needs to incorporate a diversity of views and provide a diversity of mechanisms for engaging with the past.

The boundaries around the specialisms in archaeology also need breaking down. As archaeology has matured it has successfully diversified and a wide range of specialisms have burgeoned. This has been healthy and necessary, but there is now a need for integration and for research which cuts across speciality boundaries. I have described above the need for relationality and interactivity in the archaeological process. We need to identify new 'objects' to study which cross-cut specialism boundaries. Greater integration is facilitated by the new information technologies.

We need to break down the boundaries around the site. This is partly a matter of opening the site to a wider range of visitors and encouraging interactivity and multivocality. But it is also a matter of recognizing the radical effects of the new information technologies. It is of interest that in the discourse of the new global 'Web-speak' the term 'site' has been taken to mean a location or address on the World Wide Web. It is possible for new Web sites to be built which act as alternatives to 'official' sites. For example, there are numerous (Web) sites at which you can find out about the (archaeological) site at Çatalhöyük. In a way, the one place that Çatalhöyük isn't is at Çatalhöyük. By this I mean that people construct their own versions of Çatalhöyük. They may do this on a Web site or in some other medium, or even just in their minds and imaginations. When they come to the archaeological site they see the site through their own perspectives, in the same way that the different teams working at the site produce their own windows. All these various interpretations of the archaeological site derive from other 'sites' (other places, Web sites, imaginations). Archaeology has to be multi-sited. It has to be open and less bounded.

Multi-sited archaeology

Despite all your emphasis on fluidity and plurality, it still seems to me that archaeologists often gain at least some of their status and identity from being linked to a particular site. When they meet, archaeologists often say 'where are you digging now?', and lists of excavations worked on are important parts of CVs. Archaeologists become very protective and in practice are seen as 'owning' the rights to work at a particular location or region. They say 'this is my site'. Many still carefully guard and control the information from a site until it has been published.

But surely notions like 'off-site' archaeology (e.g. Foley 1981) have already dispersed the focus on sites? Even when one is talking of a site excavation, note how many of these are now published by multiple authors and project participants. Certainly competitive tendering in contract archaeology in Britain has eroded the idea of an archaeologist's 'right' to a region or site. In addition, as noted in chapter 1, many archaeologists do not excavate – they may only work in laboratories or museums or libraries.

And I suppose you would see the idea of the Web 'site' further dispersing sitedness, in that people can construct different 'sites' away from the archaeological 'site'?

Yes, that's right. In all these ways the focus is shifting from a singular site excavated by a single director towards the currents that flow through a site, dispersing it into a myriad of other sites.

But is this not bringing us dangerously near the idea you have been trying to escape from in this book? I mean the postmodern idea of dispersion through play.

My argument is parallel to that of Marcus (1995) in ethnography. But I think a particular edge is given to the critique of 'site' in archaeology because of our taken-for-granted dependence on the 'site' as the building block of archaeological knowledge and careers. In this book I have argued that the dispersal of the site can be grounded in a situated plurality. Dispersal is not always a matter of postmodern play.

Perhaps it would help if you explained that.

Well, we can see that different communities engage in the archaeological site by constructing their own 'sites' (for specific examples see chapter 9). In particular, we can explore the tensions between the 'sites' constructed by different communities (global, national, local, etc.). A grounded multi-sitedness is also seen in the way that different teams working at a site, perhaps at different times, will produce different interpretations – it will seem as if they have dug different sites. Different sites are also produced by asking different questions. Archaeologists increasingly define themes which cut across categories of evidence. Rather than 'digging a site' archaeologists have increasingly followed a thing such as a type of pottery, or a theme such as decoration, or domestication, or burning. The new perspectives and technologies which emphasize plurality simply extend the multi-sitedness, but in all the examples I have given here the different perspectives are situated within the strategies of specific interest groups. Such groups may be highly dispersed globally, but their interest in an archaeological excavation is often grounded within a strategic network.

But you are not saying the archaeological site does not exist? And what of your emphasis on contextuality? We don't just construct sites in our imaginations, and you don't want to support the search for themes which are not sensitive to the site being studied, do you?

Of course not. I think we are shifting from seeing the archaeological 'site' as an object, to seeing it as a point of mediation between past and present. It is less easy now for an archaeologist to say 'this is my site', or 'I am digging this site'. Such claims are becoming undermined by the negotiation of multiple interests and by theoretical and practical reflexivity. But there is still a need to ground our statements in evidence, meticulously uncovered, even if the evidence is immediately dispersed into other sites.

As a corollary of the last point, it is necessary to break down the boundaries around the team. As more and more people become involved in the excavation, analysis and interpretation of an archaeological site, the team working at the site becomes very diffuse, open and flexible. At Çatalhöyük I have become increasingly unclear who is and who is not a member of the team. Some team members have never visited the site (except on the Web site). Other people have visited the site and contribute but are not normally described as archaeologists. Comments offered by strangers on the Web may prove very useful and be incorporated into 'the team's' research process. All the four themes identified above, but in particular interactivity and multivocality imply a blurring of the boundaries of any distinct team.

The boundaries around the author also become blurred. As more voices are involved in the archaeological process, as interactivity is encouraged, and as critical self-reflection is embraced, so the distinctive voice of the sole author is undermined. As the status and authority of the author are opened to critical evaluation and as multiple media are introduced, so the privileged place of the written word is diminished. As hypertext is increasingly used, the linearity of written text and its distinctive rhetorical devices are replaced by multi-path, multi-nodal forms of information flow.

As these boundaries are broken down, so too are the main dichotomies which have underlain archaeology since its inception. Breaking down boundaries around the discipline and around the specialisms results in breaking the dichotomy between science and humanity. Archaeology is not a science or a humanity. It is both. The archaeological process involves a heavy reliance on the natural sciences for dating, the study of site formation processes, the analysis of environmental change, the sourcing of exchanged artifacts and so on. But such information needs to be set within humanities (e.g. historical) and social science (e.g. social and cultural anthropological) knowledge about the organization of societies and the manipulation of culture. Indeed, the term material culture, the main focus of archaeological enquiry, neatly encapsulates the duality inherent within the discipline. Archaeology depends on the scientific study of materials in order to infer cultural patterning.

The causes of variability in the archaeological record are not cultural or natural. They are both. Many archaeologists would now accept that while the environment and material forces constrain human endeavour, the specific character of human behaviour is equally informed by cultural choice and human intention. This dialectical view has been arrived at from many directions. We see it in an earlier generation in the work of Grahame Clark (1957 (1939), 219) who argued that while the environment limits or constrains social choice, the latter determines cultural behaviour. We see it in neo-Marxist discussions of the relations between the forces and social relations of production (Friedman and Rowlands 1978; McGuire 1992). We see it in contemporary applications of complex systems (Flannery and Marcus 1976; 1993; van der Leeuw and Torrence 1989) and in phenomenological approaches to monuments and landscapes (J. Thomas 1996;

Tilley 1994). In all these cases attempts are made in different ways to think about culture and nature not in either/or but in both/and terms.

But perhaps the greatest dichotomy that has dogged archaeology is the Cartesian split between subject and object (Knapp and Meskell 1997). Archaeologists have always been concerned about distinguishing objective from subjective pasts. Subjective views have to be tested against objective data. But archaeologists, including processual archaeologists, have also accepted that the archaeological data are theory-laden (Renfrew and Bahn 1991) and that theory and data are related dialectically (they depend on each other in a theory-data circuit). This view is even more clearly articulated in neo-Marxist (e.g. Friedman and Rowlands 1978, McGuire 1992) archaeology and in postprocessual archaeology (Hodder 1991). If the archaeological process is opened up to interactivity and multivocality, if the boundaries around the discipline, site, team and author are broken down, then it cannot any longer be adequate to separate an objective past defined by archaeologists and a subjective past defined by non-archaeologists. We all interpret the past from different perspectives and these different interpretations can be evaluated in relation to evidence. Different theories can be compared using a variety of mechanisms. The past is not objective or subjective. It is both. By this I mean that the archaeological evidence has an 'objective' materiality which limits and confronts what can be said about it, and which contributes to the experiences of 'subjective' observers. At the same time, the 'subjective' interpreter of the evidence constructs the 'objective' data from a particular perspective.

Global Information Flows

I have described above an archaeological process which is reflexive, relational, interactive and multivocal. The effect is to break down boundaries between inside and outside the discipline, between different specialisms, between site and non-site, between author and reader, between subject and object and so on. The breaking of these boundaries encourages us to try and think in non-dichotomous terms, that is in terms of 'both/and' rather than 'either/or'. Moving away from dichotomies we search for alternative metaphors. Rather than boundaries we describe networks and flows. Rather than rigid oppositions we discern fluidity. Rather than space and time we grapple with spatio-temporality.

I have argued in this book that the search for a more inclusive discourse in archaeology should not be set up as prescriptive agenda; rather the search is part of wider changes in society which lead towards flows and networks (Castells 1996). These wider changes are termed post- or high modernism, the information age, consumer society, post-industrial society, media society, and so on. It is important to understand the nature and direction of these changes if we are going to make sense of the impetus towards non-dichotomous thinking in archaeology.

I have argued here that the trends which lead towards the flows of a network society are best understood in the context of globalism, and that globalism has the three components mapped in figure 11.1. At the apex are the homogenizing tendencies most easily and obviously associated with the Internet and the information superhighway. Homogenization is also produced by the spread of the market, the dispersal of work practices and by common environmental concerns. The end result is a loss of cultural diversity as McDonalds and Coca-Cola emerge as parts of a homogenous market and the 'global village'. National governments become subservient to multi-national companies.

But one of the fascinations of the global process is that it produces fragmentation and diversity as much as it produces homogenization. Again, non-dichotomous thinking is needed. There are two quite different fragmentation processes mapped in figure 11.1: fragmentation caused by the processes of high capitalism, and the search for identity within and against the market.

Fragmentation is produced by the market within high or late capitalism in a number of ways. For example, transformations in patterns of work produce flexible regimes according to which people work at home or at odd individual times. Fragmentation is also produced by the new information technologies. The television etc., but then also VCRs,

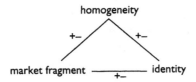

Figure 11.1 The conflicting components of globalism.

walkmen, and the multiple communication channels now available all lead to greater choice by individuals; there is decentralization and customization. It becomes possible for 'Web managers' to tailor the provision of information to individual needs. Niche marketing, and even marketing designed for individual persons, become possible.

At the same time, these same technologies can be used by individuals to create new communities and new identities. The Internet has allowed the proliferation of special interest groups. High or post-modern society has seen the emergence of small groups which may be localized or dispersed (virtual communities). These may resist 'mass culture' or they may contribute to it. They may be part of the global market or they may be antithetical to it. Equally, there are those outside the global network whose identities are linked to place and to a history on the margins. These are the less wealthy, the less educated, the less connected. Such communities receive few of the benefits of global culture; their exploitation is associated with alienation and resistance.

Mapping Global Heritage

I now want to map first heritage and then archaeology onto the scheme set out above and in figure 11.1. Heritage has become a global industry expanding at remarkable speed. It is implicated in all the contradictory processes described in figure 11.1, as indicated in figure 11.2.

The homogenization of heritage is apparent in the rise over recent decades of the concept of 'world heritage' and UNESCO designated 'world heritage sites'. The underlying concern here is to protect sites which are of global importance and which are part of a 'common humanity'. The aim is to protect 'our' common heritage, for the good of all. At a different scale, the European Commission designates sites of cultural interest for Europe as a whole rather than for individual nation states.

This homogenization process has positive and negative relations with the market. One of the effects of designation as a world or European heritage site may be commercial exploitation. The international visibility given to a site by such designation may attract tourism and the leisure industry. Travel 'to another time', whether in Disneyland time cars or as part of international travel, has become a central part of the leisure industry, an essential component of the exotic otherness to which we increasingly seem attracted. As Lowenthal (1985) has described it, the past has become 'another country' to which we wish to escape as part of our leisure travel. The result at heritage sites may be the inflow of funds and the ability of local groups or national governments to enhance the facilities available. The tourism may also increase local wealth and employment.

But there are also tensions between world heritage and the market. For example, international agencies are concerned to protect sites from commercial exploitation in the form of looting and vandalism. The commercial development of sites for tourism may benefit international companies more than local communities. Commercial development (hotels, shops, car parks) may be constrained by the heritage interests of the site.

Similarly, there are positive and negative relations between world heritage and the formation of community identities. The international attention and influx of tourism may enhance the local sense of identity. New communities may be formed through a renewed awareness of a common heritage. These communities and their common traditions may be 'invented', as in the case of a pan-Native American identity. They may also be dispersed, as in the goddess movement which involves women in the search for an original world before patriarchy. Whether local or dispersed (virtual), these communities are strengthened by being involved in global networks. The global interactions encouraged by the World Archaeological Congress support emerging identities based on heritage (Ucko 1987).

Global processes provide emancipatory mechanisms, but they also create greater possibilities for domination and exclusion. Some governments resist world heritage designation since it allows intervention by international agencies in the internal affairs of national heritage programmes. Both the world heritage status and commercial exploitation may lead to the wrenching of a site away from a local meaning and identity. Local people may find traditional understandings of sites denied or disrupted by external agencies. Local heritage identities easily become fragmented by the global process.

Groups and individuals which are not networked become separated from global information flows and have difficulty gaining access to knowledge about heritage. They may use languages which exclude them from international debate (e.g. Olsen 1991). The multivocality and openness to subaltern voices may occur primarily amongst the networked. The result may be a silencing of other voices and an ultimate incorporation into a global homogenization. Alternatively, the un-networked may form cultural and heritage identities in traditional forms, reacting against the new forms of virtual community.

There are also positive and negative relations between community heritage and the leisure industry. As already noted, tourism may foster employment and growth in local communities and it may enhance community identities through the management of heritage. Cases such as the Hopi-Tewa in the American Southwest, where commercial exploitation of traditional crafts has contributed to local production and employment, can be cited. Engagement by tourists and visitors in 'other' life-ways also has 'beneficial' effects for developed countries. The nostalgia and escapism which people discover may help them to deal with alienation and the fragmentation of modern life. The interests of high capitalism and the market are thus served.

The relationship between the market and community heritage can also be negative. Local interests can easily be overwhelmed by 'big business' and local rights over-ruled. Commercialization may turn identity into pastiche, continuity into fragment. Disney-land pasts may trivialize community claims and sensitivities. The notion of an 'Auschwitz Theme Park' dramatizes the insensitivities that may occur. How can some grieve at a heritage site while others play? Such instances and such tensions are clear cut. In other cases, the lines are harder to draw between the past as leisure play and the past as community identity. For example, the travellers who come to Avebury and Stonehenge in Britain to celebrate the summer solstice include groups such as the Druids and Wessex Anarchists. Are such groups engaged in play or in political and social action? Are all members of such groups equally committed to a social cause? Where does one draw the line between play and passion? And even if individuals are passionately committed to particular causes, is their committment simply a product of the diversity engendered by high capitalism? The answers to these questions are difficult. Once again, as in the other relationships shown in figure 11.2, the relationship between the market, including

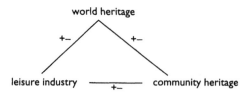

Figure 11.2 The conflicting components of global heritage.

the leisure industry, and community heritage is dialectical and non-dichotomous.

Mapping Global Archaeology

The homogenization fashioned by global processes can be compared with the search in archaeology in the later half of the twentieth century for universal laws and universal methods applicable regardless of time and place (figure 11.3). Clearly this was the clarion cry of processual archaeology. While less emphasis is placed on universals in postprocessual archaeology it is undeniable that prescriptive statements are routinely made, as in 'material culture is meaningfully constituted', 'the archaeological record is (or is not) a text', 'structure is the medium and outcome of action'. While postprocessual (and neo-Darwinian) archaeologists attempt to re-embrace history, contingency and indeterminacy, they nevertheless base their arguments for diversity and difference on general claims. All archaeologies, from whatever tradition, are then evaluated in terms of these generalizing claims.

Universalizing approaches in Anglo-American archaeology can certainly lead to an erasure of history. Trigger (1984) has emphasized that the study of Native Americans by processual archaeology led to the search for law-like generalizations and so trivialized the prehistory of specific Native American groups as an end in itself. He argued that by denying the validity of studying the prehistory of specific parts of the world, the New Archaeologist asserted the unimportance of national traditions themselves and of anything that stood in the way of American economic activity and political influence. Earlier, a colonial outlook led to the establishment of British archaeological methods in for example, India and Australia (Clark 1939). Indeed, wherever archaeology is practised today, its methods are influenced by, if not wholly dependent on, Euro-American methods and perspectives.

In some regions, especially those with recent histories of dictatorship, such as Spain or Chile, universalist claims and objective methods may provide a basis for the critique of established authority structures. They provide a common currency to expose the arbitrary assumptions of power. They promote democratization. In other regions, objective science is itself associated with the arbitrary exercise of centralized power. For example, in the conflict over the reburial of Native American remains or over Australian aboriginal land rights, archaeological objective science came to be associated with vested establishment interests against which local communities had to fight. Indeed, in a postcolonial world archaeological administration and research have increasingly been 'indigenized'. While the taking over of local pasts into local hands may promote the writing of contextualized pasts, the methods used often derive from the colonial legacy. The global debate takes place in the terms defined by the dominant centre. Much the same effect is produced by global information networks.

The widespread availability of archaeological information on the Web may undermine the identity of local communities and dilute their distinctive character. Individual career paths may be threatened – for example, researchers whose careers depend on publication of unique data from a site may not want 'their' data immediately available to all. But equally the widespread availability of information on the Web may allow communities to enhance their identities. Individuals scattered across the globe can gain access to archaeological data for their research or for their personal or political interest. For example, goddess groups can learn of the work of Marija Gimbutas (Meskell 1995). The latter process may end up in shallow scholarship close to play (ibid.), or it may simply entice local groups into the discourse of the dominant. But there is also the potential for the formulation of alternative perspectives. For example, Mamani Condori (1989) has argued for an approach to archaeology informed by indigenous perspectives concerning monuments as 'living' parts of the landscape. In India, Paranjpe (1990) has begun to explore alternative directions, arguing against the universalist assumptions of western scholarship (see also Ucko 1995). Such scholars argue that Indian theories of meaning and interpretation should be applied as a reaction against western discourse.

Archaeologists increasingly recognize that reports of their research need to be written, often in very different terms, for a wide variety of different audiences. The boundary between a universalist or contextualized account, on the one hand, and a 'popularized' version, on the other, is often difficult to draw. And it is right that, as in much of the postmodern world, the boundary between 'high' and 'low' culture should become blurred. Many of the more popular accounts have important social effects, as in writing for children or in TV presentations for a large audience. But as already noted, scholarship can easily be abused or misinterpreted. The increasing prevalence of commercial sponsorship of archaeological projects raises the possibility of bias as reports are written to 'provide what the sponsor wants'. The importance of discoveries may often be exaggerated by archaeologists in order to satisfy sponsors' needs for publicity and sensation. Commerce and play can, then, lead to the compromise of archaeological scholarship and method. On the other hand, it is undoubtedly the case that much archaeological work today, especially in the United States and Britain, is dependent on sponsorship. Relations with corporate sponsors can often be channelled and monitored so that interference is minimized and so that both sides benefit.

Perhaps the major link between commerce and archaeology occurs in those countries which have established a system of cultural resource management funded by developers. In such cases there are undoubtedly strains (Hunter and Ralston 1993). Jobs may be won by archaeological teams which compete by cutting costs to minimum levels. There may be little investment in research and publication. Employment may be short-term and insecure. There may be limited opportunities for the development of integrated research designs and regional research strategies. The growth of commercially funded archaeology has led to the setting of standards, the codification of procedures, and the monitoring of results by central agencies. It has thus created universalizing tendencies.

Cultural resource management has certainly allowed the large-scale expansion of archaeology in the countries involved. But these beneficial effects are offset by the tendencies towards codification and regulation. These latter contradict precisely the openness and multivocality of an inclusive approach to the past. They contradict directly the fluid systems, the integrated and contingent methods identified in this volume. They impede the recognition of other voices and interests. As a result, in many areas, local communities have taken over the management of their own cultural resources.

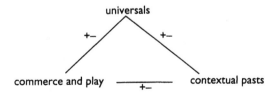

Figure 11.3 The conflicting components of global archaeology.

Conclusion: Going with the Flow

I have argued in this volume that archaeological research and fieldwork can be fluid processes of interpretation. They can be reflexive and participative, negotiated from different perspectives. In my view, this openness, which involves a breaking of dichotomies and a critiquing of assumptions, has become necessary in a world which is both increasingly homogeneous and diverse. 'Political correctness' has become a serious issue, not just because of a current trend, but because it deals with the sensitivities and rights of a diversity of groups. It is no longer possible in archaeology to police dogmatically the boundaries of the discipline. It is no longer acceptable to close off sites and teams from the wider world in which they work. It is no longer acceptable to close debate by saying 'these are the objective data', since other interests may wish to make sense of data in different ways. It is no longer acceptable to base archaeological authority on a closed discourse constructed by archaeologists themselves. In a highly networked world, authority has to argue its case.

For many in the late twentieth century, events such as the Vietnam war demonstrated the dangers of an uncritical belief in western beliefs and strategies. The decentering of authority has also been part of the widespread emergence of articulate postcolonial voices. In addition, the new processes of global information exchange have both quickened and dampened the diversification and the differentiation.

Archaeology can play an important role as these processes continue and expand into the 21st century. It is directly implicated in the homogenization and differentiation of identities. But the role it plays can be *emancipatory* or *dominating*. On the one hand, we can engage in multi-sited archaeology, facilitating the engagement of multiple interests at all levels of analysis and interpretation, from the trowel's edge to the published output. We can engender the proliferation of locations, nodes in a global network, at which the past can be reconstructed. We can create flows of the past, continua of interpretation. We can encourage the un-networked to use the past to express their rights and identities or to become networked. We can use archaeology as a flexible, open and participatory project in order to break established patterns of thought and domination. So, on the one hand, archaeology can play an emancipatory role within the global processes of postcolonialism and the information age.

On the other hand, the same technologies which liberate an open debate can be used to close off and to exclude discussion. The postmodern flow of cultural symbols (including archaeological knowledge) can easily be limited to a new, information-based elite. The un-networked become yet more disadvantaged in relation to the centres of domination in developed countries. Alternative voices become incorporated into a discourse defined and regulated at the centre. Codification and standardization become disseminated in the interests of the cultural resource market. Difference is celebrated as a necessary part of rational market identification and manipulation. So archaeology can play a role in processes of domination within the global environment.

The new technologies, and the flexibility and non-dichotomous thinking which they allow, provide not a solution but an opportunity and a challenge to archaeologists of the new millennium. They can be used to create emancipation in the sense of an open and diverse engagement with the past, a participation from multiple perspectives and interests. Or they can be used to exclude, close off, and dominate. The new technologies, postcolonial movements, and other global issues such as tourism and environmental concerns, force archaeology into a new situation to which it can either react by closing down or by opening up. It can reinforce dichotomies or it can 'go with the flow'. I hope it is clear that, in my view, the long-term future of archaeology should be in flows and networks rather than dichotomies and boundaries.

Bibliography

Adams, M. and Brooke, C. 1995 Managing the past: truth, data and the human being. *Norwegian Archaeological Review* 28, 93–104.

Anyon, R., Ferguson, T. J., Jackson, L. and Lane, L. 1996 Native American oral traditions and archaeology. *Society for American Archaeology Bulletin* 14:2, 14–16.

Arnold, B. 1990 The past as propaganda: totalitarian archaeology in Nazi Germany. *Antiquity* 64, 464–78.

Arnold, D. 1971 Ethnomineralogy of Ticul, Yucatan potters: etics and emics. *American Antiquity* 36, 20–40.

Auel, J. 1980 *The Clan of the Cave Bear*. Crown, New York.

Bailey, G. 1981 Concepts, time-scales and explanations in economic prehistory. In A. Sheridan and G. Bailey (eds) *Economic Archaeology*. British Archaeological Report S 96, 97–117.

—— 1983 Concepts of time in Quaternary prehistory. *Annual Review of Anthropology* 12, 165–92.

—— 1987 Breaking the time barrier. *Archaeological Review from Cambridge* 6, 5–20.

Baines, J. 1985 Colour terminology and colour classification – Ancient Egyptian colour terminology and polychromy. *American Anthropologist* 87, 282–97.

Bapty, I. and Yates, T. 1990 *Archaeology After Structuralism*. Routledge, London.

Barba, L. A. 1985 La quimica en el estudio de areas de actividad. In L. Manzanilla (ed.) *Unidades Habitacionales Mesoamericanas y sus areas de actividad*. UNAM, Mexico.

Barfield, L. 1994 The iceman reviewed. *Antiquity* 68, 10–26.

Barham, A. J. 1995 Methodological approaches to archaeological context recording: X-radiography as an example of a supportive recording, assessment and interpretive technique. In A. J. Barham and R. I. Macphail (eds) *Archaeological Sediments and Soils*. Institute of Archaeology, University College, London, pp. 145–82.

Barker, P. 1977 (2nd edition 1982) *Techniques of Archaeological Excavation*. Batsford, London.

Barnes, G. 1990 The 'idea of prehistory' in Japan. *Antiquity* 64, 929–40.

Barrett, J. 1994 *Fragments of Antiquity*. Blackwell, Oxford.

——, Bradley, R. and Green, M. 1991 *Landscape, Monuments and Society. The Prehistory of Cranbourne Chase*. Cambridge University Press.

Barthes, R. 1970 (Translated 1975 by R. Miller) *S/Z*. Cape, London.

—— 1977 *Image-Music-Text*. Fontana, London.

Bechtel, W. 1990 Connectionism and the philosophy of mind: an overview. In W. G. Lycan (ed.) *Mind and Cognition: A Reader*. Blackwell, Oxford.

Bell, J. A. 1994 *Reconstructing Prehistory*. Temple University Press, Philadelphia.

Bender, B., Hamilton, S. and Tilley, C. 1997 Leskernick: stone worlds; alternative narratives; nested landscapes. *Proceedings of the Prehistoric Society* 63, 147–78.

Berlin, B. and Kay, P. 1969 *Basic Colour Terms: Their Universality and Evolution*. University of California Press, Berkeley.

Bernbeck, R. and Pollock, S. 1996 Ayodhya, archaeology and identity. *Current Anthropology* 37, Supplement, 138–42.

Binford, L. R. 1962 Archaeology as anthropology. *American Antiquity* 28, 217–25.

—— 1967 Smudge pits and hide smoking; the use of analogy in archaeological reasoning. *American Antiquity* 32, 1–12.

—— 1977 *For Theory Building in Archaeology*. Academic Press, New York.

—— 1980 Willow smoke and dogs' tails: hunter-gatherer settlement systems and archaeological site formation. *American Antiquity* 45, 4–20.

—— 1981 Behavioral archaeology and the 'Pompeii premise'. *Journal of Anthropological Research* 37, 195–208.

—— 1989 *Debating Archaeology*. Academic Press, New York.

—— and Binford, S. (eds) 1968 *New Perspectives in Archaeology*. Aldine, Chicago.

—— and Sabloff, J. A. 1982 Paradigms, systematics and archaeology. *Journal of Anthropological Research* 38, 137–53.

Bintliff, J. 1991 *The Annales School and Archaeology*. Leicester University Press.

—— 1993 Why Indiana Jones is smarter than the postprocessualists. *Norwegian Archaeological Review* 26, 91–100.

Bloch, M. 1991 Language, anthropology and cognitive science. *Man* 26, 183–98.

—— 1995 Questions not to ask of Malagasy carvings. In L. Hodder, M. Shanks, et al. (eds) *Interpreting Archaeology*. Routledge, London, 212–15.

Bourdieu, P. 1977 *Outline of a Theory of Practice*. Cambridge University Press.

Bradley, R. 1990 *The Passage of Arms*. Cambridge University Press.

—— 1993 *Altering the Earth: The Origins of Monuments in Britain and Continental Europe*. Society of Antiquaries of Scotland, Edinburgh.

—— 1996 *Journal of Material Culture* 1.

Braun, D. P. 1977 *Middle Woodland – (Early) Late Woodland Social Change in the Prehistoric Central Midwestern US*. Unpublished Ph.D. dissertation, University of Michigan, Ann Arbor.

Brothwell, D. 1981 *Digging Up Bones* (3rd edition). Oxford University Press.

Brumfiel, L. 1991 Weaving and cooking: women's production in Aztec Mexico. In J. Gero and M. Conkey (eds) *Engendering Archaeology*. Blackwell, Oxford, 224–54.

Butler, J. 1990 *Gender Trouble: Feminism and the Subversion of Identity*. Routledge, New York.

—— 1993 *Bodies That Matter*. Routledge, New York.

Calgano, J. M. 1981 On the applicability of sexing material by discriminant function analysis. *Journal of Human Evolution* 10, 189–98.

Carver, M. 1989 Digging for ideas. *Antiquity*. 63, 666–74.

—— 1990 Digging for data: principles and procedures for evaluation, excavation and post-excavation in towns. *Theory and Practice of Archaeological Research* 2, 255–302 (Institute of Archaeology and Ethnology, Polish Academy of Sciences).

Castells, E. 1996 *The Rise of the Network Society*. Blackwell, Oxford.

Chadwick, A. 1998 Archaeology at the edge of chaos: further toward reflexive excavation methodologies. *Assemblage*. (online journal) 3. http://www.shef.ac.ukslashassem/3/3chad.htm.

Champion, T. C. 1991 Theoretical archaeology in Britain. In I. Hodder (ed.) *Archaeological Theory in Europe: The Last Three Decades*. Routledge, London, pp. 129–60.

Childe, V. G. 1925 *The Dawn of European Civilisation*. Kegan Paul, London.

—— 1936 *Man Makes Himself*. Collins, London.

—— 1949 *Social Worlds of Knowledge*. Oxford University Press.

Chippindale, C. 1990 *Who Owns Stonehenge?* Batsford, London.

Clark G. 1934 Archaeology and the state. *Antiquity* 8, 414–28.

—— 1939 (Revised edition 1957) *Archaeology and Society*. Methuen, London.

Clark, J. E. 1987 Politics, prismatic blades, and Mesoamerican civilisation. In J. K. Johnson and C. A. Morrow (eds) *The Organisation of Core Technology*. Westview Press, London, pp. 259–84.

Clarke, D. L. 1968 *Analytical Archaeology*. Methuen, London.

—— 1972 *Models in Archaeology*. Methuen, London.

—— 1973 Archaeology: the loss of innocence. *Antiquity*. 47, 6–18.

Clifford, J. and Marcus, G. 1986 *Writing Culture: The Poetics and Politics of Ethnography.* University of California Press, Berkeley.

Cohen, J. and Swidler, N. 1997 Painting a 'new' face on CRM: integrating traditional culture and archaeology. *Society for American Archaeology Bulletin.* 15:1, 24–5.

Coles, J. 1979 *Experimental Archaeology.* Academic Press, London.

Collingwood, R. G. 1946 *Idea of History.* Oxford University Press.

Condori, C. M. 1989 History and pre-history in Bolivia: what about the Indians? In R. Layton (ed.) *Conflicts in the Archaeology of Living Traditions.* Unwin Hyman, London, pp. 46–59.

Conkey, M. and Gero, J. 1997 Programme to practice: gender and feminism in archaeology. *Annual Review of Anthropology.* 26, 411–37

—— and Tringham, R. 1996 Archaeology and The Goddess: exploring the contours of feminist archaeology. In A. Stewart and D. Stanton (eds) *Feminisms in the Academy: Rethinking the Disciplines.* University of Michigan Press, Ann Arbor.

—— with Williams, S. H. 1991 Original narratives: the political economy of gender in archaeology. In M. di Leonardo (ed.) *Gender at the Crossroads of Knowledge.* University of California Press, Berkeley.

Conolly, J. 1996 Çatalhoyuk knapped-stone report. In I. Hodder (ed.) *On the Surface.* McDonald Institute, Cambridge.

Courbin, P. 1988 *What is Archaeology?* University of Chicago Press, Chicago.

Crown, P. and Fish, S. 1996 Gender and status in the Hohokam Pre-Classic to Classic transition. *American Anthropologist*, 93, 803–17.

Daniel, G. 1962 *The Idea of Prehistory.* Penguin, Harmondsworth.

Davis, M. B. 1983 Holocene vegetational history of the eastern United States. In H. E. Wright (ed.) *Late Quaternary Environments of the United States.* University of Minnesota Press, Minneapolis, pp. 6–81.

Dawkins, R. 1997 *Climbing Mount Improbable.* Penguin, London.

Deleuze, G. and Guattari, F. 1984 *Anti-Oedipus: Capitalism and Schizophrenia.* Athlone, London.

Denzin, N. K. 1989 *Interpretive Interactionism.* Sage, Newbury Park, CA.

—— and Lincoln, Y. S. 1994 *Handbook of Qualitative Research.* Sage, London.

Derrida, J. 1978 *Writing and Difference.* Routledge and Kegan Paul, London.

Diaz-Andreu, M. and Champion, T. 1996 *Nationalism and Archaeology in Europe.* University College London Press.

Dietler, M. 1994 'Our ancestors the Gauls': archaeology, ethnic nationalism, and the manipulation of Celtic identity in modern Europe. *American Anthropologist* 96, 584–605.

Dobres, M.-A. 1995 Gender and prehistoric technology: on the social agency of technical strategies. *World Archaeology* 27, 25–49.

Dunnell R. C. 1989 Aspects of the application of evolutionary theory in archaeology. In C. Lamberg-Karlovsky (ed.) *Archaeological Thought in America*. Cambridge University Press, pp. 35–49.

Dunnell R. C. 1992 Is a scientific archaeology possible? In L. Embree (ed.) *Metaarchaeology: Reflections by Archaeologists and Philosophers*. Kluwer Academic Publishers, Dordrecht, pp. 75–97.

Edmonds, M. 1993 Interpreting causewayed enclosures in the past and the present. In C. Tilley (ed.) *Interpretative Archaeology*. Berg, Oxford, pp. 99–142.

Egg, M., Goedecker-Ciolek, R., Groenman-Van Waateringe, W. and Spindler, K. 1993 *Die Gletschermumie von Ende der Steizeit aus den Otztaler Alpen*. Jahrbuch des Romisch-Germainischen Zentralmuseums. 39, RGZM, Mainz.

Emele, M. 1998 The assault of computer-generated worlds on the rest of time. Challenges and opportunities for documenting film-making in virtual reality. In T. Elsaesser and K. Hoffmann (eds) *Cain, Able or Cable – Film Culture in Transition*. University of Amsterdam Press.

Engelstad, E. 1991 Images of power and contradiction: feminist theory and post-processual archaeology. *Antiquity* 65, 502–14.

Erickson, C. L. 1988 Raised field agriculture in the Lake Titicaca Basin: putting ancient agriculture back to work. *Expedition* 30, 8–16.

Evans, C. 1998 Constructing houses and building context: Bersu's Manx roundhouse campaign. *Proceedings of the Prehistoric Society*.

Evershed, R., Heron, C., Charters, S. and Goad, L. 1992 The survival of food residues: new methods of analysis, interpretation and application. In A. Pollard (ed.) *New Developments in Archaeological Science*. Oxford University Press, 187–208.

Featherstone, M. 1991 *Consumer Culture and Post-Modernism*. Sage, London.

——, Lash, S. and Robertson, R. (eds) 1995 *Global Modernities*. Sage, London.

—— and —— 1995 Introduction. In M. Featherstone, S. Lash and R. Robinson (eds) *Global Modernities*. Sage, London.

Ferguson, L. 1991 Struggling with pots in colonial South Carolina. In R. McGuire and R. Paynter (eds) *The Archaeology of Inequality*. Blackwell, Oxford, pp. 28–39.

Flannery, K. and Marcus, J. 1976 Formative Oaxaca and the Zapotec Cosmos. *American Scientist* 64, 374–83.

—— and —— 1983 *Cloud People*. Academic Press, New York.

—— and —— 1993 Cognitive archaeology. *Cambridge Archaeological Journal* 3, 260–70.

Foley, R. 1981 *Off-site Archaeology and Human Adaptation in Eastern Africa*. British Archaeological Report International Series 97, Oxford.

—— 1987 *Another Unique Species*. Longman, Harlow.

Forte, M. and Siliotti, A. 1997 *Virtual Archaeology*. Thames and Hudson, London.

Fotiadis, M. 1994 What is archaeology's 'mitigated objectivism' mitigated by? Comments on Wylie. *American Antiquity* 59, 545–55.

Foucault, M. 1977 *Discipline and Punish*. Vintage, New York.

Foucault, M. 1981 *The History of Sexuality. Vol. 1: An Introduction*. Penguin, Harmondsworth.

Fowler, P. 1992 *The Past in Contemporary Society: Then, Now*. Routledge, London.

Friedman, J. and Rowlands, M. 1978 *The Evolution of Social Systems*. Duckworth, London.

Fritz, J. and Plog, F. 1970 The nature of archaeological explanation. *American Antiquity* 35, 405–12.

Frodeman, R. 1995 Geological reasonings: geology as an interpretive and historical science. *Geological Society of America Bulletin* 107, 960–8.

Fukuyama, F. 1992 *The End of History and the Last Man*. Penguin.

Gardin, J.-C. 1980 *Archaeological Constructs*. Cambridge University Press.

Garfinkle 1967 *Studies in Ethnomethodology*. Englewood Cliffs, NJ.

Garn, S., Lewis, A., Swindler, D. and Kerewsky, R. 1967 Genetic control of sexual dimorphism in tooth size. *Journal of Dental Research* 46, 963–72.

Gates, B. 1995 *The Road Ahead*. Viking Penguin, New York.

Gathercole, P. and Lowenthal, D. 1989 *The Politics of the Past*. Unwin Hyman, London.

Geertz, C. 1973 *The Interpretation of Cultures*. Basic Books, New York.

Gero, J. 1985 Socio-politics of archaeology and the women-at-home ideology. *American Antiquity* 50, 342–50.

—— 1991a Genderlithics. In M. Conkey and J. Gero (eds) *Engendering Archaeology*. Blackwell, Oxford, pp. 163–93.

—— 1991b Who experienced what in prehistory? A narrative explanation from Queyash, Peru. In R. Preucel (ed.) *Processual and Postprocessual Archaeologies*. Southern Illinois University, Carbondale, pp. 126–89.

—— 1996 Archaeological practice and gendered encounters with field data. In R. Wright (ed.) *Gender and Archaeology*. University of Pennsylvania Press, Philadelphia, pp. 251–80.

—— and Conkey, M. 1991 *Engendering Archaeology*. Blackwell, Oxford.

Gibbs, L. 1987 Identifying gender representation in the archaeological record: a contextual study. In I. Hodder (ed.) *The Archaeology of Contextual Meanings*. Cambridge University Press, pp. 79–89.

Giddens, A. 1979 *Central Problems in Social Theory*. Macmillan, London.

—— 1984 *The Constitution of Society: An Outline of the Theory of Structuration*. University of California Press, Berkeley.

Gifford-Gonzales 1991 Bones are not enough: analogues, knowledge, and interpretive strategies in zooarchaeology. *Journal of Anthropological Archaeology* 10, 215–54.

Gillespie, A. and Robins, K. 1989 Geographical inequalities: the spatial bias of the new communications technologies. *Journal of Communication* 39:3.

Gimbutas, M. 1982 *The Goddesses and Gods of Old Europe*. Thames and Hudson, London.

Goedecker-Ciolek, R. 1994 Konservierung der Beifunde einer Gletschermumie vom Ende der Steinzeit. I – Bekleidung. *Arbeitsblätter für Restauratoren* 2:94, 105–27.

Golson, J. and Gardner D. S. 1990 Agriculture and sociopolitical organisation in the New Guinea Highlands. *Annual Review of Anthropology* 19, 395–417.

Gosden, C. 1994 *Social Being and Time*. Blackwell, Oxford.

Gould, S. J. and Lewontin, R. 1979 The spandrels of San Marco and the Panglossian paradigm: a critique of the adaptationist programme. *Proceedings of the Royal Society London* B205, 581–98.

Gräslund, B. 1987 *The Birth of Prehistoric Chronology*. Cambridge University Press.

Grenville, J. 1997 *Medieval Housing*. Leicester University Press, London.

Gumerman, G. and Gell-Mann, M. 1994 *Understanding Complexity in the Prehistoric Southwest*. Santa Fe Institute Studies in the Sciences of Complexity. Proc. Vol. XVI, Reading.

Hall, M. 1998 Cape Town's District Six and the archaeology of memory. Paper presented at the World Archaeological Congress, Croatia.

Halton, E. 1995 The modern error: or, the unbearable enlightenment of being. In M. Featherstone, S. Lash and R. Robertson (eds) *Global Modernities*. Sage, London, pp. 260–77.

Hamilton, C. 1996 Faultlines: the construction of archaeological knowledge at Çatalhöyük in 1996. Paper presented at Theoretical Archaeology Group Conference, Liverpool (see http://catal.cam.arch.ac.uk/catal/catal.html).

Harris, E. C. 1989 *Principles of Archaeological Stratigraphy*. (2nd edition) Academic Press, London.

——, Brown III, M. R. and Brown, G. J. 1993 *Practices of Aarchaeological Stratigraphy*. Academic Press, London.

Hastorf, C. 1991 Gender, space, and food in prehistory. In J. Gero and M. Conkey (eds) *Engendering Archaeology*. Blackwell, Oxford, pp. 132–62.

—— and Johannessen, S. 1991 Understanding changing people/plant relationships in the prehispanic Andes. In R. Preucel (ed.) *Processual and Postprocessual Archaeologies*. Occasional Paper 10, 140–55. Southern Illinois University.

Hawkes, C. 1954 Archaeological theory and method: some suggestions from the old world. *American Anthropologist* 56, 155–68.

HBMC 1991 *The Management of Archaeological Projects*. Historic Buildings and Monuments Commission (English Heritage), London.

Heidegger, M. 1927 *Sein und Zeit*. Neomarius Verlag, Tübingen.

Hesse, M. 1995 Past realities. In I. Hodder, M. Shanks et al. (eds) *Interpreting Archaeology*. Routledge, London, pp. 45–7.

Higgs, E. 1972 *Papers in Economic Prehistory*. Cambridge University Press.

Higgs, E. and Jarman, M. 1975 Paleoeconomy. In E. Higgs (ed.) *Paleoeconomy*. Cambridge University Press, 1–8.

Hill, J. D. 1992 Can we recognise a different European past? *Journal of European Archaeology* 1, 57–75.

—— 1995 *Ritual and Rubbish in the Iron Age of Wessex*. Tempus Reparatum, Oxford.

Hill, J. and Gunn J. 1977 *The Individual in Prehistory*. Academic Press, New York.

Hobsbawm, E. 1994 *The Age of Extremes*. Michael Joseph, London.

Hodder, I. 1982a *Symbols in Action*. Cambridge University Press.

—— 1982b Theoretical archaeology: a reactionary view. In I. Hodder (ed.) *Symbolic and Structural Archaeology*. Cambridge University Press, pp. 1–16.

—— 1982c *The Present Past*. Batsford, London.

—— 1986 *Reading the Past*. Cambridge University Press.

—— 1987 *Archaeology as Long-Term History*. Cambridge University Press.

—— 1989 Writing archaeology: site reports in context. *Antiquity* 63, 268–74.

—— 1990 *The Domestication of Europe*. Blackwell, Oxford.

—— 1991 Interpretative archaeology and its role. *American Antiquity* 56, 7–18.

—— 1992 *Theory and Practice in archaeology*. Routledge, London.

—— 1993 The narrative and rhetoric of material culture sequences. *World Archaeology* 25, 268–82.

—— (ed.) 1996 *On the Surface*. British Institute of Archaeology at Ankara and McDonald Institute, Cambridge.

—— 1997 Always momentary, fluid and flexible: towards a self-reflexive excavation methodology. *Antiquity* 71, 691–700.

—— and Evans, C. 1999 *Excavations at Haddenham*. English Heritage and McDonald Institute.

—— and Shand, P. 1988 The Haddenham long barrow: an interim statement. *Antiquity* 62, 349–53.

——, Shanks, M., Alexandri, A., Buchli, V., Carman, J., Last, J. and Lucas, G. (eds) 1995 *Interpreting Archaeology*. Routledge, London.

Hole, F. and Heizer, R. F. 1973 *Prehistoric Archaeology: A Brief Introduction*. Holt, Rinehart and Winston, London.

Hudson, K. 1981 *A Social History of Archaeology: The British Experience*. MacMillan, London.

Huffman, T. 1984 Expressive space in the Zimbabwe culture. *Man.* 19, 593–612.

Hull, K. L. 1987 Identification of cultural site formation processes through microdebitage analysis. *American Antiquity* 52, 772–83.

Hunter, J. and Ralston, I. 1993 *Archaeological Resource Management in the UK: An Introduction*. Alan Sutton, Stroud.

Inizan, M. 1992 *Technology of Knapped Stone*. CNRS, Paris.

Jenkins, D. 1994 Interpretation of interglacial cave sediments from a hominid site in North Wales. In A. J. Ringrose-Voase and G. S. Humphreys (eds) *Soil*

Micromorphology: Studies in Management and Genesis. Elsevier, London, pp. 293–302.

Johnson, M. 1989 Conceptions of agency in archaeological interpretation. *Journal of Anthropological Archaeology* 8, 189–211.

—— 1996 *An Archaeology of Capitalism.* Blackwell, London.

Jones, W. 1996 *Dictionary of Industrial Archaeology.* Sutton, Stroud.

Jørgensen, L. B. 1992 *North European Textiles Until* AD *1000.* Aarhus University Press.

Joukowsky, M. 1980 *A Complete Manual of Field Archaeology.* Prentice Hall, Englewood Cliffs, NJ.

Joyce, R. 1994 Dorothy Hughes Popenoe: Eve in an archaeological garden. In C. Claassen (ed.) *Women in Archaeology.* University of Pennsylvania Press.

Kester, G. 1994 Access denied: information policy and the limits of liberalism. *Afterimage* 21:6.

Kinnes, I. 1992 *Non-Megalithic Long Barrows and Allied Structures in the British Neolithic.* British Museum Publications, London.

Knapp, A. B. 1992 *Archaeology, Annales and Ethnohistory.* Cambridge University Press.

—— and Meskell, L. 1997 Bodies of evidence in Cypriot prehistory. *Cambridge Archaeological Journal* 7:2, 183–204.

Kohl, P. 1993 Limits to a postprocessual archaeology (or, The dangers of a new scholasticism), In N. Yoffee and A. Sherratt (eds) *Archaeological Theory. Who Sets the Agenda?* Cambridge University Press, pp. 13–19.

—— and Fawcett, C. (eds) 1995 *Nationalism, Politics, and the Practice of Archaeology.* Cambridge University Press.

Kosso, P. 1991 Method in archaeology: middle range theory as hermeneutics. *American Antiquity* 56, 621–7.

Kristiansen, K. 1981 A social history of Danish archaeology (1805–1975). In G. Daniel (ed.) *Towards a History of Archaeology.* London, 20–44.

Kroker, A. and Weinstein, M. A. 1994 *Data Trash: The Theory of the Virtual Class.* St Martin's Press, New York.

Kuhn, T. S. 1962 *The Structure of Scientific Revolutions.* University of Chicago Press.

Kus, S. 1992 Toward an archaeology of body and soul. In J.-C. Gardin and C. S. Peebles (eds) *Representations in Archaeology.* Bloomington, pp. 168–77.

Lacan, J. 1977 *Ecrits: A Selection.* (edited by A. Sheridan) Methuen, London.

Lampeter Archaeology Workshop 1997 Relativism, objectivity and the politics of the past. *Archaeological Dialogues* 4, 164–98.

Landow, G. P. 1992 *Hypertext.* Johns Hopkins University Press, Baltimore.

Langford R. F. 1983 Our heritage – your playground. *Australian Archaeology.* 16, 1–6.

Laqueur, T. 1990 *Making Sex: Body and Gender from the Greeks to Freud.* Harvard University Press.

Lathrap, D. W. 1983 Recent Shipibo-Conibo ceramics and their implications for archaeological interpretation. In D. K. Washburn (ed.) *Structure and Cognition in Art*. Cambridge University Press, pp. 25–39.

Latour, B. 1988 Mixing humans and nonhumans together: the sociology of a door closer. *Social Problems* 35, 298–310.

—— and Woolgar, S. 1986 *Laboratory Life: The Construction of Scientific Facts*. Princeton University Press.

Layton, R. 1989 *Conflict in the Archaeology of Living Traditions*. Unwin Hyman, London.

Lechtmann, H. 1984 Andean value systems and the development of prehistoric metallurgy. *Technology and Culture* 25, 1–36.

Lemonnier, P. 1986 The study of material culture today: towards an anthropology of technical systems. *Journal of Anthropological Archaeology* 5, 147–86.

Lennstrom, H. A. and Hastorf, C. A. 1995 Interpretation in context: sampling and analysis in paleoethnobotany. *American Antiquity* 60, 701–21.

Leone, M. 1982 Childe's offspring. In I. Hodder (ed.) *Symbolic and Structural Archaeology*. Cambridge University Press, pp. 179–84.

—— 1984 Interpreting ideology in historical archaeology: the William Paca garden in Annapolis, Maryland. In D. Miller and C. Tilley (eds) *Ideology, Power and Prehistory*. Cambridge University Press.

——, Potter, P. and Shackel, P. 1987 Toward a critical archaeology. *Current Anthropology* 28, 283–302.

—— et al. 1995 Can an African-American historical archaeology be an alternative voice? In I. Hodder, M. Shanks, et al. (eds) *Interpreting Archaeology*. Routledge, London, pp. 110–24.

Leroi-Gourhan, A. 1964 *La Geste et la Parole*. Michel, Paris.

Lincoln, Y. S. and Guba, E. G. 1985 *Naturalistic Inquiry*. Sage, Beverly Hills, CA.

Little, B. 1994 Consider the hermaphroditic mind: comment on 'the interplay of evidential constraints and political interests: recent archaeological research on gender'. *American Antiquity* 59, 539–44.

Llobera, M. 1996 Exploring the topography of mind: GIS, social space and archaeology. *Antiquity* 70, 612–22.

Lloyd, S. 1963 *Mounds of the Near East*. Edinburgh University Press.

Lowenthal, D. 1985 *The Past is a Foreign Country*. Cambridge University Press.

Lubbock, J. 1865 *Prehistoric Times as Illustrated by Ancient Remains and the Manners and Customs of Modern Savages*. Williams and Northgate, London.

Lyotard, J.-F. 1984 *The Postmodern Condition*. University of Minnesota Press.

—— 1991 *The Inhuman*. Polity Press, Cambridge.

Marcus, G. 1995 Ethnography in/of the World Systems: the emergence of multi-sited ethnography. *Annual Review of Anthropology* 24, 95–117.

—— and Fischer, M. 1986 *Anthropology as Cultural Critique*. University of Chicago Press.

Matthews, W., French, C., Lawrence, T. and Cutler, D. 1996 Multiple surfaces: the micromorphology. In I. Hodder (ed.) *On the Surface*. McDonald Archaeological Institute and the British Institute of Archaeology at Ankara, pp. 301–42.

McGlade, J. and van der Leeuw, S. 1997 *Time, Process and Structured Transformation in Archaeology*. Routledge, London.

McGuire, R. 1992 *A Marxist Archaeology*. Academic Press, New York.

—— and Saitta, D. 1996 Although they have petty captains, they obey them badly: the dialectics of prehispanic western Pueblo social organisation. *American Antiquity* 61, 197–216.

Mellaart, J. 1967 *Catal Huyuk*. Thames and Hudson, London.

Merriman, N. 1991 *Beyond the Glass Case*. Leicester University Press.

Meskell, L. 1995 Goddesses, Gimbutas and New Age archaeology. *Antiquity* 69, 74–86.

—— 1996 The somatisation of archaeology: institutions, discourses, corporeality. *Norwegian Archaeological Review* 29, 1–16.

—— 1997 Electronic Egypt: the shape of archaeological knowledge on the net. *Antiquity* 71, 1073–6.

—— 1998 Intimate archaeologies: the case of Kha and Merit. *World Archaeology* 29, 363–79.

Metcalfe, D. and Heath, K. M. 1990 Microrefuse and site structure: the hearths and floors of the Heartbreak Hotel. *American Antiquity* 55, 781–96.

Middleton, W. and Price, T. 1997 Chemical analysis of soils from modern and archaeological house floors by Inductively Coupled Plasma-Atomic Emission Spectroscopy. *Journal of Archaeological Science*.

Miller, D. 1982 Artifacts as products of human categorisation processes. In I. Hodder (ed.) *Symbolic and Structural Archaeology*. Cambridge University Press, pp. 89–98.

—— 1985 *Artifacts as Categories*. Cambridge University Press.

—— 1997 *Material Cultures*. University College London Press.

—— and Tilley, C. 1984 *Ideology, Power and Prehistory*. Cambridge University Press.

Mithen, S. 1996 *The Prehistory of the Mind: A Search for the Origins of Art, Science and Religion*. Thames and Hudson, London.

Mithen, S. 1998 *Creativity in Human Evolution and Prehistory*. Routledge, London.

Mizoguchi, K. 1992 A historiography of a linear barrow cemetery: a structurationist's point of view. *Archaeological Review from Cambridge* 11, 39–50.

Molleson, T. 1994 Can the degree of sexual dimorphism provide an insight into the position of women in past populations? *Dossier de Documentation Archaeologique* 17, 51–67.

Molyneaux, B. 1997 *The Cultural Life of Images: Visual Representation in Archaeology*. Routledge, London.

Montelius, O. 1885 *Om tids bestämning inom bronsåldern med särskild hänsyn till Skandinavien.* Kongl. Vitterhets Historie och Antiqvitets Akademiens Handlingar, 30.

Moore, H. 1990 Paul Ricoeur: action, meaning and text. In C. Tilley (ed.) *Reading Material Culture.* Blackwell, Oxford, pp. 85–120.

——1995 The problems of origins: poststructuralism and beyond. In I. Hodder et al. (eds) *Interpreting Archaeology.* Routledge, London, pp. 51–3.

Morris, I. 1991 The archaeology of ancestors: the Saxe/Goldstein hypothesis revisited. *Cambridge Archaeological Journal* 1, 147–69.

Müller, S. O. 1884 Mindre Bidrag til den forhistoriske Archaeologis methode. *Aarboger for Nordisk Oldkyndighed of Historie*, 161–216.

Munsen, P. J. 1969 Comments on Binford's 'Smudge pits and hide smoking'. *American Antiquity* 34, 83–5.

Negroponte, N. 1996 *Being Digital.* Hodder and Stoughton, London.

Nicholas, G. P. 1997 Archaeology, education, and the Secwepemc. *Society for American Archaeology Bulletin* 15:2, 8–11.

Olsen, B. 1990 Roland Barthes: from sign to text. In C. Tilley (ed.) *Reading Material Culture.* Blackwell, Oxford, pp. 163–205.

Olsen, B. 1991 Metropolises and satellites in archaeology. In R. Preucel (ed.) *Processual and Postprocessual Archaeologies.* Southern Illinois University, Centre for Archaeological Investigations, Occasional Paper 10, 211–24.

Orme, B. 1981 *Anthropology for Archaeologists: An Introduction.* Duckworth, London.

Paddaya, K. 1995 Theoretical perspectives in Indian archaeology: an historical view. In P. Ucko (ed.) *Theory in Archaeology: A World Perspective.* Routledge, London, pp. 110–49.

Palattella, J. 1995 Formatting patrimony: the rhetoric of hypertext. *Afterimage* 23:1.

Paranjpe, M. 1990 The invasion of 'theory': an Indian response. *New Quest* 81, 151–61.

Parker Pearson, M. 1982 Mortuary practices, society and ideology: an ethnoarchaeological study. In I. Hodder (ed.) *Symbolic and Structural Archaeology.* Cambridge University Press.

——1993 The powerful dead: archaeological relationships between the living and the dead. *Cambridge Archaeological Journal* 3, 203–29.

Patrik, L. 1985 Is there an archaeological record? In M. Schiffer (ed.) *Advances in Archaeological Method and Theory* 8. Academic Press, New York.

Patterson, T. C. 1995 *Toward a Social History of Archaeology in the United States.* Harcount, Brace, Font Worth, Texns.

Petrie, F. 1904 *Methods and Aims in Archaeology.* London.

Pinsky, V. and Wylie, A. (eds) 1989 *Critical Traditions in Contemporary Archaeology.* Cambridge University Press.

Pitt-Rivers, A. H. L. F. 1887 *Excavations in Cranborne Chase* (4 vols).

Pitt-Rivers, A. H. L. F. 1894 Excavation of the South Lodge Camp, Rush-more Park: an entrenchment of the Bronze Age. *Wiltshire Archaeological and Natural History Magazine* 27, 206–22.

—— 1896 *The Evolution of Culture and other Essays*. Clarendon Press, Oxford.

Popper, K. 1992 *The Logic of Scientific Discovery*. Routledge, London.

Porter, D. 1997 *Internet Culture*. Routledge, New York.

Preucel, R. and Hodder, I. (eds) 1996 *Contemporary Archaeology in Theory*. Black-well, Oxford.

Quine, W. V. 1992 *Pursuit of Truth*. Harvard University Press, Cambridge, MA.

Ranger, T. and Hobsbawm, E. 1983 *The Invention of Tradition*. Cambridge University Press.

Rao, N. 1994 Interpreting silences: symbol and history in the case of Ram Janmabhoomi/Babri Masjid. In G. Bond and A. Gilliam (eds) *Social Construction of the Past: Representation of Power*. Routledge, London, pp. 154–64.

Rathje, W. and Murphy, C. 1992 *Rubbish! The archaeology of Garbage*. Harper Collins, New York.

—— and Thompson, B. 1981 *The Milwaukee Garbage Project*. American Paper Institute, Solid Waste Council of the Paper Industry, Washington, D. C.

Reilly, P. and Rahtz, S. 1992 *Archaeology and the Information Age. A Global Perspective*. Routledge, London.

Renfrew, A. C. and Bahn, P. 1991 (2nd edition 1996) *Archaeology*. Thames and Hudson.

Renfrew, C. 1973 *Before Civilisation*. Cape, London.

—— 1989 Comments on 'Archaeology into the 1990s'. *Norwegian Archaeological Review*. 22, 33–41.

—— and Zubrow, E. 1994 *The Ancient Mind: Elements of Cognitive Archaeology*. Cambridge University Press.

Richards, C. 1991 The late Neolithic house in Orkney. In R. Samson (ed.) *The Social Archaeology of Houses*. Edinburgh University Press.

—— 1996 Henges and water. *Journal of Material Culture*. 1, 313–36.

Ricoeur, P. 1971 The model of the text: meaningful action considered as text. *Social Research*. 38, 529–62.

Rick, J. and Hart, D. 1997 Panoramic virtual reality and archaeology. *Society for American Archaeology Bulletin* 15, 14–19.

Rosen, A. M. 1986 *Cities of Clay: The Geoarchaeology of Tells*. University of Chicago Press.

Rowlands, M. 1984 Objectivity and subjectivity in archaeology. In M. Spriggs (ed.) *Marxist Perspectives in Archaeology*. Cambridge University Press.

—— 1993 The role of memory in the transmission of culture. *World Archaeology*. 25, 141–51.

Said, E. 1978 *Orientalism*. Routledge and Kegan Paul.

Salmon, M. 1982 *Philosophy and Archaeology*. Academic Press, New York.

Schiffer, M. 1976 *Behavioural Archaeology*. Academic Press, New York.

—— 1987 *Formation Processes of the Archaeological Record*. University of New Mexico Press, Albuquerque.

—— 1988 The structure of archaeological theory. *American Antiquity* 53, 461–85.

Schlanger, N. 1990 Techniques as human action: two perspectives. *Archaeological Review from Cambridge* 9, 18–26.

Schnapp, A. 1993 *La Conquête du Passé*. Éditions Carré, Paris.

Schutkowski, H. 1993 Sex determination of infant and juvenile skeletons. *AJPA* 90, 199–205.

Scruton, R. 1982 *A Dictionary of Political Thought*. Macmillan, London.

Shankland, D. 1996 The anthropology of an archaeological presence. In I. Hodder (ed.) *On the surface*. British Institute of Archaeology at Ankara and McDonald Institute of Archaeology, Cambridge.

Shanks, M. 1992 *Experiencing the Past: On the Character of Archaeology*. Routledge, London.

—— and McGuire, R. 1996 The craft of archaeology. *American Antiquity* 61, 75–88.

—— and Tilley, C. 1987 *Reconstructing Archaeology*. Cambridge University Press.

Sharer, R. J. and Ashmore, W. 1993 *Archaeology: Discovering our Past*. Mayfield, Mountain View.

Shennan, S. 1986 Central Europe in the third millennium B C: an evolutionary trajectory for the beginning of the Bronze Age. *Journal of Anthropological Archaeology* 5, 115–46.

—— 1989 Cultural transmission and cultural change. In S. E. van der Leeuw and R. Torrence (eds) *What's New?* Unwin Hyman, London, pp. 330–46.

Sherratt, A. 1981 Plough and pastoralism. In I. Hodder, G. Isaac and N. Hammond (eds) *Pattern of the Past*. Cambridge University Press.

—— 1982 Mobile resources: settlement and exchange in early agricultural Europe. In C. Renfrew and S. Shennan (eds) *Ranking, Resource and Exchange*. Cambridge University Press.

—— 1990 The genesis of megaliths. *World Archaeology* 22, 147–67.

—— 1993 What would a Bronze Age world system look like? *Journal of European Archaeology* 1.2, 1–58.

—— 1995 Reviving the grand narrative. Archaeology and long-term change. *Journal of European Archaeology* 3, 1–32.

Smith, L. 1994 Heritage management as post-processual Archaeology. *Antiquity* 68, 300–9.

Smith, M. A. 1955 The limitations of inference in archaeology. *Archaeological Newsletter* 6, 3–7.

Sørensen, M. L. S. 1997 Material culture and typology. *Current Swedish Archaeology* 5, 179–92.

Spector, J. 1993 *What This Awl Means*. Minnesota Historical Society, St Paul.

Sperber, D. 1975 *Rethinking Symbolism*. Cambridge University Press.

Spindler, K. 1993 *The Man in the Ice*. Weidenfeld and Nicolson, London.

Stanislawski, M. B. 1978 Hopi and Hopi-Tewa ceramic tradition networks. In I. Hodder (ed.) *Spatial Organisation of Culture*. Duckworth, London.

Swidler, N., Dongoske, K. E., Anyaon, R. and Downer, A. S. (eds) 1997 *Native Americans and Archaeologists*. Altamira Press, Walnut Creek.

Tarlow, S. 1992 Each slow dusk a drawing down of blinds. *Archaeological Review from Cambridge* 11, 125–40.

Thieme, F. P. 1957 Sex in Negro skeletons. *Journal of Forensic Medicine* 4, 72–81.

Thomas, J. 1987 Relations of production and social change in the Neolithic of north-west Europe. *Man* 22, 405–30.

—— 1990 Same, other, analogue: writing the past. In F. Baker and J. Thomas (eds) *Writing the Past in the Present*. St David's University College, Lampeter, pp. 18–23.

—— 1993 Discourse, totalisation and 'The Neolithic'. In C. Tilley (ed.) *Interpretative Archaeology*. Berg, Oxford, pp. 357–94.

—— 1995 Where are we now?: archaeological theory in the 1990s. In P. Ucko (ed.) *Theory in Archaeology: A World Perspective*. Routledge, London, pp. 343–62.

—— 1996 *Time, Culture and Identity*. Routledge, London.

—— and Tilley, C. 1993 The axe and the torso: symbolic structures. In C. Tilley (ed.) *Interpretative Archaeology*. Berg, Oxford, pp. 225–324.

Thomas, S. 1996 On the use of hypertext in archaeological site interpretation. Paper presented at TAG, Liverpool, December 1996.

—— 1997 *Archaeology and Subjectivity*. Unpublished Ph.D. dissertation, University of Cambridge.

Tilley, C. 1989a Archaeology as theatre. *Antiquity* 63, 275–80.

—— 1989b Discourse and power: the genre of the Cambridge inaugural. In D. Miller, M. Rowlands and C. Tilley (eds) *Domination and Resistance*. Unwin Hyman, London, pp. 41–62.

—— 1990 *Reading Material Culture*. Blackwell, Oxford.

—— 1991 *The Art of Ambiguity: Material Culture and Text*. Routledge, London.

—— 1993 *Interpretative Archaeology*. Berg, Oxford.

—— 1994 *The Phenomenology of Landscape*. Berg, London.

Tixier, J. 1974 *Glossary for the Description of Stone tools*. Newsletter of Lithic Technology, Special Publication 1 (Translated by M. Newcomer).

Treherne, P. 1995 The warrior's beauty: the masculine body and self-identity in Bronze-Age Europe. *Journal of European Archaeology* 3, 105–44.

Trigger, B. 1980 *Gordon Childe: Revolutions in Archaeology*. Thames and Hudson, London.

—— 1984 Alternative archaeologies: nationalist, colonialist, imperialist. *Man* 19, 355–70.

—— 1989 Hyperrelativism, responsibility, and the social sciences. *Canadian Review of Sociology and Anthropology* 26, 776–97.

—— 1995 Archaeology and the integrated circus. *Critique of Anthropology* 15, 319–35.

—— 1998 Archaeology and epistemology: dialoguing across the Darwinian chasm. *American Journal of Archaeology* 102, 1–34.

Tringham, R. 1991 Households with faces: the challenge of gender in prehistoric architectural remains. In J. Gero and M. Conkey (eds) *Engendering Archaeology*. Blackwell, Oxford, pp. 93–131.

—— 1994 Engendered places in prehistory. *Gender, Place and Culture* 1:2, 169–203.

—— 2000 Expressing the feminist practice of archaeology through hypermedia opera. In M. Conkey and A. Wylie (eds) *Practicing Archaeology as a Feminist*. School of American Research Press.

Tschauner, H. 1996 Middle-range theory, behavioural archaeology, and post-empiricist philosophy of science in archaeology. *Journal of Archaeological Method and Theory* 3, 1–30.

Turner, B. S. 1994 *Orientalism, Postmodernism and Globalism* Routledge, London.

Ucko, P. 1987 *Academic Freedom and Apartheid: The Story of the World Archaeological Congress*. Duckworth, London.

—— (ed.) 1995 *Theory in Archaeology: A World Perspective*. Routledge, London.

van der Leeuw, S. 1989 Risk, perception, innovation. In van der S. Leeuw and R. Torrence (eds) *What's New?* Unwin Hyman, London, pp. 300–29.

—— and Torrence, R. (eds) 1989 *What's New?* Unwin Hyman, London.

van Reybrouck, D. 1998 Imaging and imagining the Neanderthal: the role of technical drawings in archaeology. *Antiquity* 72, 56–64.

Watson, P. J., Leblanc, S. and Redman, C. 1971 *Explanation in Archaeology* Columbia University Press, London.

—— 1986 Archaeological interpretation, 1985. In D. J. Meltzer, D. Fowler and J. A. Sabloff 1986 *American Archaeology. Past and Future*. Smithsonian Institution Press, Washington, pp. 439–58.

—— and Kennedy, M. C. 1991 The development of horticulture in the eastern woodlands of North America: women's role. In J. Gero and M. Conkey (eds) *Engendering Archaeology*. Blackwell, Oxford, pp. 255–75.

Watson, R. A. 1991 What the New Archaeology has accomplished. *Current Anthropology*. 32, 275–91.

Wheeler, M. 1956 *Archaeology from the Earth*. Oxford University Press.

White, J. P. and Thomas, D. H. 1972 What mean these stones? Ethno-taxonomic models and archaeological interpretations in the New Guinea Highlands. In D. Clarke (ed.) *Models in Archaeology*. Methuen, London, pp. 275–308.

Williamson, T. and Bellamy, L. 1983 *Ley Lines in Question*. World's Work, Kingswood.

Wolf, E. R. 1982 *Europe and the People Without History*. University of California Press, Berkeley.

Wylie, A. 1982 Epistemological issues raised by a structuralist archaeology. In I. Hodder (ed.) *Symbolic and Structural Archaeology*. Cambridge University Press, pp. 39–46.

—— 1985 The reaction against analogy. In M. Schiffer (ed.) *Advances in Archaeological Method and Theory* 8, 63–111. Academic Press, New York.

—— 1989 Archaeological cables and tacking: the implications of practice for Bernstein's 'Options beyond objectivism and relativism'. *Philosophy of the Social Sciences* 19 1–18.

—— 1992 The interplay of evidential constraints and political interests: recent archaeological research on gender. *American Antiquity* 57, 15–35.

—— 1994 On 'capturing facts alive in the past' (or present): response to Fotiadis and to Little. *American Antiquity* 59, 556–60.

Yates, T. 1989 Habitus and social space. In I. Hodder (ed.) *The Meanings of Things*. Unwin Hyman, London, pp. 249–62.

—— 1990 Jacques Derrida: 'there is nothing outside of the text'. In C. Tilley (ed.) *Reading Material Culture*. Blackwell, London, pp. 206–80.

—— 1993 Frameworks for an archaeology of the body. In C. Tilley (ed.) *Interpretative Archaeology*. Berg, Oxford, pp. 31–72.

Yoffee, N. 1994 Memorandum to Murray Gell-Mann concerning: the complications of complexity in the prehistoric southwest. In G. Gummerman and M. Gell-Mann (eds) *Understanding Complexity in the Prehistoric Southwest*. Addison Wesley, New York, pp. 341–58.

—— and Sherratt, A. (eds) 1993 *Archaeological Theory: Who Sets the Agenda*. Cambridge University Press.

York, P. 1980 *Style Wars*. Sidgwick and Jackson, London.

Index